Information Technology in Library and Information Services

Information Technology in Library and Information Services

Mohan Kumar Galhotra
M.Com., M.Lib.I.Sc., Ph. D.
Mata Sundri College for Women
(University of Delhi)
New Delhi

Ess Ess Publications
4837/24, Ansari Road, Darya Ganj,
New Delhi-110002
Tel. : 23260807, 41563444
Fax : 011-41563334
E-mail: info@essessreference.com
www.essessreference.com

Ess Ess Publications
4837/24, Ansari Road,
Darya Ganj,
New Delhi-110 002.

Tel.: 23260807, 41563444
Fax: 41563334
E-mail: info@essessreference.com
www.essessreference.com

Rs.825/-

First Published - 2008

ISBN: 81-7000-519-1 (10 Digit)
978-81-7000519-3 (13 Digit)

Published By Ess Ess Publications and printed at Salasar Imaging Systems

PRINTED IN INDIA

Dedicated

to

My Beloved Parents

Preface

Information is an important resource, a valuable input and power for societal development. The present information age is characterised by a society which is conscious of the value of information and its use. The information revolution is the third major force following social and economical revolutions that is shaping the way of living in the civilized world. Today, every country is aiming at collecting, organising and disseminating information to the users for an overall development. It is a well known fact that a country which is rich in information is rich in economic spheres too.

A number of interrelated factors such as quantitative growth of information, inadequate finance, escalating cost of documents, diversified and limitless information demand of the user community, etc. make problems to both the information users and information managers especially in the Third World countries. 'Information explosion' or 'information flood' due to exponential growth of documents are factors which put the users in a state of 'information anxiety'. The developments in information technology are scientific gifts which serve to overcome the existing problems in the information world.

The application of traditional methods in librarianship for information storage and retrieval is becoming more and more complex, time consuming, ineffective and it has no future even in developing countries. Developments in information science coupled with information technology are means to meet the ever increasing information demand of the modern changing society. Information technology is the combination of several components of technologies and systems which may be grouped under (i) Computer technology (ii) Telecommunication systems and services (iii) Micrographic and reprographic technology; and (iv) Information storage technology.

Information technology is the boon of the present century. It gives the accessibility to information at the finger tips. There have been discussions on 'information highways' and `superhighways' among professionals in high-tech libraries. All these technological developments in information transfer emphasise the fact that universal availability of information is no more an utopian concept. The promising and diversified possibilities of information technology have reduced the space and time between people, country, continent and ultimately have led to the emerging concepts of 'global society' and 'global village'.

Application of information technology in libraries in developed countries is rapid and dynamic. It has come to occupy the center stage of development, in the 21st century. There is now a broad consensus that Information Technology (IT) is shaping our world. It is becoming increasingly the key to national economic development and well being.

Today, no field is untouched by information technology especially by the computer. How can libraries remain without computerization. The computer is a great help to the library in automating its activities and services. Without computerization libraries cannot provide efficient services to their users.

These days with the use of internet facilities we can access quickly the desired information available in any corner of the world. The Internet has brought a revolution in the field of information. We can reach the latest information/ knowledge without losing much time through the Internet. Moreover, we can exchange messages via E-mail. It takes no time to reach its destination. In the present time computers are indispensable to the libraries. It also gets rid of clerical work and storage of files.

Besides saving the time of users, we can also save funds after computerization and Internet facilities. We need not purchase Abstracting and Indexing journals. Instead, CD-ROMs can be use for the same Abstracting and Indexing journals.

New technological developments have affected almost every function carried out in a library to some extent. Now libraries process, store and retrieve information by advances in electronic, computerization and telecommunications. The changes brought out by information technology have been so extensive that it is difficult to assess their total future effect. Therefore, the effective managing technologies in libraries and information centres need to be developed and put into operation in the near future by managers.

One of the most fundamental needs for the successful implementation of modernising of these library services using information technology is to develop mentally and technically the users and library staff at all levels who need a shared vision and positive attitude to fulfill the mission of the centre. To conclude, the success of libraries and information centres, depend upon how appropriately they (Manager/Librarian) conceive requirements and aspirations and develop appropriate strategies for providing relevent, timely information support, that too speedily and efficiently. However, the librarian with certain managerial skills and knowledge of management techniques should stand empowered to manage affairs of the library and information centre effectively.

It is hopeful that this book will be useful as a reference document for librarians, information professionals and students. Every effort have been made to cultivate in readers a 'Scientific Spirit' of modern librarianship and to enable them to share meanigfully the myriad ideas of information technology which they would acquire from this book that spreads over fifteen chapters.

I should honestly confess that my knowledge of the subject is limited and I am to stand on the shoulders of many of the pioneers and scholars in the field of information technology. A list of 'References' or 'Sources' used in the preparation of this book is given at the end. My sincere thanks to authors and publishers of these works. Users of this book are requested to extend their valuable suggestions for making it more useful in the future editions.

I would like to convey my gratitude to my Ph.D. Supervisor, Dr. B. K. Sharma (Retd.), Reader and Head, Dept. of Library and Information Science, Dr. B. R. Ambedkar University, Agra whose vast knowledge enriched and guided me to complete this work. I am very grateful to Late Dr. S. M. Tripathi (Retd.), Prof. and Head, SOS, Library and Information Sceince, Jiwaji University, Gwalior who was always generous to me and helped me a lot with his guidance in this work.

Words fail to reveal my deep sense of gratitude to Dr. (Mrs.) H. A. Singh, Reader, Mata Sundri College for Women, New Delhi who provided me with excellent guidance, selfless love and timely cooperation, and without whose insperiation and encouragement it would have been impossible for me to take up and complete this enterprise.

My heartfelt acknowledgements are also due for librarians of several libraries in Delhi for providing reference books and valuable time, which enabled me to work on and complete my project.

Gratitude in any words would be insufficient for the inspiration and the help that I received from Prof. J. L. Sardana (Retd.), Prof. Dept. of Library and Information Science, University of Delhi in my work. I am thankful to

Dr. Pandey, S. K. Sharma, Ex. SLIO, U.G.C., New Delhi, Dr. D.L. Sachdeva, Ex. Librarian, Moti Lal Nehru College, New Delhi.

I am thankful to my college Principal, Dr. (Mrs.) Satnam Kaur for encouragement.

Without the enthusiastic encouragement, good wishes and moral support of my beloved wife Mrs. Anju M. Galhotra and my Sons Himanshu and Karan and other family members, I could have not completed the work. They took upon themselves, all family responsibilities, ungrudgingly and patiently.

The publisher, M/s Ess Ess Publications, New Delhi also deserves my special thanks, who agreed to publish this book with crisp and attractive design within scheduled time frame inspite of their busy publication schedules.

New Delhi **Mohan Kumar Galhotra**

03 October, 2007

Contents

List of Abbreviations and Acronyms

ADINET	Ahmedabad Library Network
AGRIS	International Information System for Agricultural Science and Technology
BARC	Bhaba Atomic Research Centre
BASIC	Beginners All Purposive Symbolic Instruction Code
BLDSC	British Library Document Supply Centre
BONET	Bombay Library Network
BTISNET	Biotechnology Information System Network
CALIBNET	Calcutta Library Network
CAS	Current Awareness Service
CD ROM	Compact Disc Read Only Memory
CDS/ISIS	Computerised Documentation System/ Integrated Sets of Information System
COBOL	Common Business Oriented Language
CSIR	Council of Scientific and Industrial Research
DELNET	Developing Library Network (Formerly Delhi Library Network)
DESIDOC	Defence Scientific Information and Documentation Centre

DESINET	Defence Science Information Network
DRDO	Defence Research and Development Organisation
DRTC	Documentation Research and Training Centre
DSL	Defence Science Library
DVD	Digital Video Disc/Digital Versatile Disc
ED VAC	Electronic Discrete Variable Automatic Computer
ED SAC	Electronic Delay Storage Automatic Calculator
E-MAIL	Electronic Mail
ENIAC	Electronic Numerical Integrator and Calculation
ERNET	Education and Research Network
FORTRAN	Formula Translation FTP File Transfer Protocol
GUI	Graphical User Interface
HTML	Hyper Text Markup Language
HTTP	Hyper Text Transfer Protocol
IASLIC	Indian Association of Special Libraries and Information Centres
IATLIS	Indian Association of Teachers in Library and Information Science
ICAR	Indian Council of Agricultural Research
ICSSR	Indian Council of Social Science Research
IGNOU	Indira Gandhi National Open University
ILA	Inter Library Association
ILL	Inter Library Loan
INFLIBNET	Information and Library Network

INSDOC	Indian National Scientific and Documentation Centre (now NISCAIR)
ISDN	Integrated Service Digital Network
ISO	International Standards Organisation
IT	Information Technology
JANET	Joint Academic Network
LAN	Local Area Network
MALIBNET	Madras Library Network
MAN	Metropolitan Area Network
MARC	Machine Readable Catalogue
MEDLARS	Medical Literature Analysis and Retrieval System
MYLIBNET	Mysore Library Network
NASSDOC	National Social Science Documentation Centre
NIC	National Informatics Centre
NICNET	National Informatics Centre Network
NISCAIR	National Institute of Science Communication and Information Resources (formerly INSDOC)
NISCOM	National Institute of Science Communication
NISSAT	National Information System in Science and Technology
NSL	National Science Library
NTFIT	National Task Force for Information Technology and Software Development
NTIS	National Technical Information Service
OCLC	Online Computer Library Centre (Formerly Ohio College Library Centre)
OCR	Optical Character Recognition

OS	Operating System
PC	Personal Computer
PUNENET	Pune Library Network
SDI	Selective Dissemination of Information
SENDOC	Small Enterprises National Documentation Centre
SIRNET	Scientific and Industrial Research Network
SOUL	Software for University Libraries
TIFR	Tata Institute of Fundamental Research
UGC	University Grants Commission
UNESCO	United Nations Educational, Scientific and Cultural Organisation
URL	Uniform Resource Locator
VSNL	Videsh Sanchar Nigam Ltd.
WAN	Wide Area Network
WORM	Write Once Read Many Times
WWW	World Wide Web

1
Introduction

Library and Information Centre should comprise the tools, equipments, knowledge, systems and methods used in transforming materials and other inputs needed by libraries, into outputs as finished products or services. Technology can be subdivided into material and non-material technologies. Material technologies refer to tangible implements such as CD-ROM technology; hardware, software and peripheral devices associated with integrated library automation systems; other personal computer applications such as spreadsheets, word-processing etc., binding machines and other tools and equipment. Non-material technologies pertain to knowledge, skills, processes, education and methods.

As libraries and information centres deal mainly with information, the majority of their technical applications will be used in the collection, handling, storage and dissemination of information, or information technology. Different technologies are used in different types of libraries and different departments within libraries and information centres. This affects their management styles, organizational structures, control and communication systems and procedures.

1.1. TECHNOLOGY

Technology is an all embracing term covering the equipments, knowledge, systems and methods used in transforming inputs to outputs. Technology may be defined as the use of available knowledge and techniques to produce goods and services. In libraries, knowledge of classification and cataloguing schemes, use of integrated on-line library automation systems, access to local, national and international database, can all be considered technology. Satellites and ISDN networks provide new dimensions for information, transmission and video conferencing. The information technology industry, particularly in the field of communications, has experienced rapid technological changes in the recent years, and further breakthroughs with far-reaching effects are envisaged.

Technology is an important part of the transformation process which converts inputs such as financial, human and information resources into outputs in the form of goods and services. As such, it must be appropriate to the requirements of the library or information centre. The technology used will also affect the working environment of the library and information centre. Modern information technologies have had far-reaching effects upon working environments and work processes.

1.2. EFFECT AND TECHNOLOGY ON THE LIBRARY AND INFORMATION CENTRES

The introduction of modern technologies, particulary information technologies has had far-reaching effects upon organizations such as libraries and information centres. The rate of technolgical change is likely to increase still further in the future, so it is important that library and information centre managers are aware of the impact of technologies upon their organization. In addition, they must develop the skills to manage the opportunities and threats presented by these technologies. The management is not a specialized task for technical experts. It is a top level management task as it affects a very broad range of personnel and requires high-level decision making to ensure its effective use.

Information technology provides for the creation of new job opportunities and job enrichment for some, and retrenchment and fear for others. The introduction of integrated library automation systems and other information technologies has created shifts in demand for certain categories of skills, and shifts in the job emphasis of certain levels of staff. There is a growing demand for library staff with information technology management skills.

Information technologies create new areas of responsibility for managers. Issues such as the protection and security of data stored on systems and the safe-guarding of perosnal information pertaining to library membership details require consideration. While it is true that this type of information has always been gathered by libraries, the ability to both manipulate and extract data has been made easier and faster by information systems, thus rendering it more vulnerable to wrong use.

1.3. PLANNING FOR TECHNOLOGY

The purpose of the introduction of any new technology should be to assist the library or information centre to achieve its mission, statement and corporate goals. This may be accomplished by solving existing problems or by automating existing manual processes which lead to beneficial outcomes such as improved productivity, faster service or staff savings. Above all, the technical operations of a library or information centre should support its corporate plan.

A systematic approach to technological planning, be it information technology or any other technology, should be followed. Those involved in the planning process must have a good understanding of the corporate goals and critical success factors of the library or information centre and how technical strategies can support these. They must also have a clear understanding of the operational process and/or problems facing their library in order to seek the appropriate technical solution. The technology plan must be fully justified and approved by the top management prior to the commencement of any action which incurs either an organization commitment or an allocation of funds.

Strategies for managing effective library and information centre depend upon proper planning.

1.4. APPLICAITON OF INFORMATION TECHNOLOGY IN LIBRARIES AND INFORMATION CENTRES

Libraries and information centres can hardly function today without computers and information technology. The dream of librarianship is to serve the information needs of users timely, efficiently and economically. Libraries all over the world have realized that demands and expectations of their information consumers are rapidly increasing at a rate with which any library with limited resources can hardly cope with through conventional means. Therefore, it has become imperative on the part of libraries to revise their approach, mode of operation and means of information acquisition, organization, retrieval and dissemination to users. Thus, the goals of information technology-based librareis are to:

(i) Develop information/ knowleldge resources focused on patron's need.

(ii) Continue to develop a cooperative and user centred culture.

(iii) Organize information resources on modern lines.

(iv) Provide human and technologically moderate access to information.

(v) Continuing education and training.

IT offers tremendous opportunities to provide solutions to some of these major challenges the libraries are facing now. IT has great potential for variety of applications in libraries as it contributes to improved quality, increased productivity, more efficient operations, better resource sharing and more effective services to users. Early library automation efforts proved that libraries using IT have improved the efficiency and effectiveness in their operations and services. As a result of this, they are able to computerize library operations and information services successfully. Besides performing library operations efficiently and improving services effectivley, libraries are able to evolve effective computer networks towards optimum utilization of their resources, facilities and services.

Prime Minister's National Task Force for Information Technology and Software Development (NTFIT) desires that computer education and Internet use should be promoted at an early stage of education.

Computers are a manifestation of the scientific and technological revolution; their actual creation, utilization, and further development caused new theoretical and applied problems in psychology and in education. The impact of these changes is affecting all the aspects of library operations, information resources and services, staff's skill requirements and users expectations. Technological development has tremendously increased the ability to access, store, process, communicate and deliver information services in libraries. With the advent of multimedia era, the need for electronic imaging is growing rapidly. In additional to traditional text-based information, electronic libraries are adding up visual data.

Libraries in India are at a critical juncture due to the pressure created by technological changes, shrinking library budgets, high cost of documents and increasing information needs of the users.

Recognizing the fact that use of IT opens new avenues for better services, an increasing number of libraries and information centers have made several attempts to computerize their activities in India. However, it is only during the recent years that the library and information centers have become more earnest in their efforts to computerize their operations and services.

The National Information Centre has also been established at Delhi which is working towards developing ASIANET, with the help of Indian Communication Satellite. Besides, BARC and ICAR and also working as national input centres for INIS and AGRIS respectively, both of which are computer based international information systems.

Further, India has also developed on-line retrieval system facilities with the help of INSAT-1B under the NISSAT plan. India has made remarkable progress in this area, but the major aspect remains that unless computer literacy is made compulsory the expected results can not be attained.

2
Information : Concept and Meaning

2.1. INTRODUCTION

Today we are living in the information age. Post industrial age is called information age. We all have became information oriented consciously or unconsciously. Information is a vital national resource. If a nation has to develop, information is very important. It is the basic resource and link between a variety of intellectual and materialistic activities. Information has become an essential part of everyone's daily activities. It is vital to modern research in science and technology. It also plays a major role in the socio-economic progress of a country.

Information is a human product. It is the result of human thinking. Due to sensory experiences, information gets accumulated in the mind of an individual. Man always comes in contact of new thoughts through interaction with others. Thus, information is the knowledge gained by human beings through experiences, observations, experiments and other means. However, information may be abstract or concrete.

Man is a decision maker and information is the basis for decision making. Information is power. It is knowledge put to use. Information acts as the haemoglobin in the development of society. Information is becoming a vital raw material in our rapidly changing, highly cost-oriented society.

Everybody is familiar with the term 'information'. We refer to information. We know what information is. However, when we try to define information, we find that it is very difficult. We can apply a variety of statements to define information but we cannot say that any information is universally valid.

2.2. CONCEPT AND DEFINITION

The word information generally means a message, a signal or a stimulus. In the generic sense, informaiton may be defined as that which can be communicated, distributed or received through any medium of communication.

Various authors have defined information in different ways.

According to ***Bell***, "Information is news, facts, statististics, reports, legislation, text code, judicial decision, resolutions, and the like".

. According to ***Rowley*** and ***Turner***, "Information is the data which is transmitted between individuals and each individual can make whatever use he can of it".

Farradance defines information as, "Any physical form of representation or of a particular thought used for communications".

Vishwanathan defines information as "Knowledge put to use, which may produce good or bad results".

According to ***Ranganathan***, "Idea communication by other or obtained by personal study and investigation is information".

In United States, Information Industry Association has developed a definition that "Information is the result- ing intellectual work product when data elements are organised and communicated in a usual form to reduce uncertainty, for example, to help answer a question, to so- lve a problem, or to form a basis for action".

Information may be defined as "Data of value to decision making".

Most of the dictionaries define information as knowledge. It may be knowledge communicated or received, concerning a particular fact of a circumstance. Any knowledge gained through communication, research, investigation, study or instruction, is information.

On the basis of above definitions, it can be said that data, facts, intelligence, advice or knowledge which can be used, transferred, or communicated is information. It is derived from experience, observation, interaction and reading. It can be right or wrong, good or bad, organized or unorganized and even related or unrelated. The amount of information which affects the behaviour of the recipient and his ability to take some decision, however, varies from person to person, from time to time and from place to place.

Population pressure and social pressures are continuously accelerating the pace of research. Reserach is performed to solve social problems. Man always concentrates on a problem and with the help of experiments and analysis comes to a conclusion and releases some new information. In this way, information is evergrowing and infinite. It is turbulently dynamic and multi-dimensional. Information is the major source on which qualitative development of our society is based. Unless relevant information is available, the decision maker cannot choose the best course of action in development problems. Access to precise and reliable information at the right time can avoid wastage of resources like time, money and labour and one can make some fruitful decisions.

Present world scenerio can rightly be defined as one of 'information explosion'. Information is continuously increasing. One information is used as source for another information. Thus, there is a chain of information, the last link of which is never achieved. One information is used for further investigation, reserach and development and when it is achieved it again becomes information for further research.

2.3. CHARACTERISTICS OF INFORMATION

Information is the basic management tool for national planning. It is the basic resource for the development of science and technology and the basic raw material for the development and establishment of an industry. It has become a social necessity. Information is required in every phase and every walk of life. Information originates in an individual's cognitive framework.

Some important characteristics of information may be categorised as follows:

1. Information is a human product.
2. Information is the raw material from which knowledge is derived.
3. Information is the finished product of data.
4. Information is used as an aid in decision making.
5. Information is infinite and evergrowing.
6. Information is interdisciplinary.
7. Information is used but it cannot be consumed.
8. Information is inexhaustible as its value does not decrease after its use.
9. Information is cumulative.
10. Information increase the level of knowledge of the recipient.
11. Information helps in establishing a continuity from past to present and to the future.

12. Information is turbulently dynamic and multidimensional.
13. Information is interactive between human resources.
14. Information is self renewing.
15. Information can be extracted and summarised.
16. Information can be evaluated.
17. Information can be descriptive.
18. Information is self-explanatory.
19. Information should be brief and to the point.
20. Information is exchanged with the outer world not merely received.
21. Utility of information changes with time but in a fixed pattern.
22. Information can be recorded and translated.
23. Information is the result of observation and surveys.
24. Information helps in arriving at the right answers.
25. Time factor is very important in information dissemination. Once it becomes outdated, it becomes useless.

According to ***Ligomenides***, one of the inherent characteristics of information is that it is alive, it exists only in the human mind and, as such, it is both the input and output of human perception.

2.4. VALUE OF INFORMATION

The use and value of information depend upon a number of facts. These are generic and some are related to the particular environment or situation in which information is received.

According to ***Atherton,*** the value of information can be explained as follows:

(i) Improved capability of a country to take advantage of

existing knowledge and the 'know-how' achieved else where.

(ii) Wider knowledge base for the solution of various problems.

(iii) Improved effectiveness and efficiency of technical activities in the production and service sectors.

(iv) In the light of knowledge already available, nationalization and systematization of a country's research and development efforts.

(v) New alternatives for solving technical problems and options for minimizing the future ones.

(vi) Better forecasting and better decision making at all levels of responsibility.

2.5. NEED FOR INFORMATION

All our economic and social progress depends on the transfer of scientific and technical information.

People in different situations require information on a subject in different forms and with different emphasis and different depths of explanation. Even the same person seeks information in different ways and forms on various occasions, depending on his knwoeldge of the subject and the reasons for wanting information.

There are mainly four types of information needs:

(i) Current Information need : In this information need, the scientist wants to know what other scientists have recently done or are doing both in specific subject field in which he is doing research and in a broader area- knowledge of which is necessary to give meaning to his work. This type of information need arises because of the fact that every active worker wants to keep himself abreast of latest developments in his specific field and related areas. This need to keep update with the current progress of a scientist's field is called the current approach. The methods which are generally used to satisfy this information need include conversation with colleagues, attending the meetings and conferences, correspondence, regular reading of current journals, use of content listings, reading reviews and so on. Speed and timeliness of making information available are essential to satisfy this type of requirement.

(ii) Everyday information need: This type of need consists of certain types of information required by users in their day to day research activities. This need happens for some specific piece of information essential to a scientist's experimental work or better understanding of his work. Everyday information need is directly connected with the research work or the operational problem at hand. In this need, the scientist may require for statistical data, a method, an equation or an explanation of an observed phenomenon. Specific type of reference tools are essential to satisfy this type of information need.

(iii) Exhaustive information need: According to *Kawatra*, this is the need to find and check through all the relevant information existing on a given subject, usually the specific subject upon which the scientist is working. This need arises at the start of a work on a new investigation and becomes even more urgent when the results of investigation are ready to be reported. *Verma* says that 'this need arises at a time when the users want to obtain information of a field as exhaustive as possible i.e., all or almost all relevant literature on a field or subject'. This need comes less often but is equally important, is dependent to a greater extent than the others on printed sources of information.

(iv) Catching up or browsing up information need: This need arises when a scientist needs the recent and complete information of a subject field in which he is not much interested. In this type of information need, the scientist wants the information to be available in a short and simple form so that he can easily understand the subject. This short, simple information will help in quickly catching up with the subject.

This analysis over-simplifies a complex problem, for these approaches overlap. According to ***Kawatra,*** the exhaustive approach is much more important in the pure sciences than it is in the applied areas. In the applied fields, it is more important in Medicine and Agriculture than it is in Engineering. The engineer needs to have all the information less often than the chemist or even the physicist. He further says that, to the engineers, the everyday approach is all important to their work. The current approach is not so immediately important.

Williams says 'the ultimate purpose of any library is to meet the information needs of its users community'. The traditionally recognized role of the library in the users community to cater to the educational, informational, recreational needs has not changed, rather there has been a shift in emphasis and greatly stimulated users' requirem-ents. The needs of users and non-users must be identified instead of being presumed so that effective library service can be made possible.

2.6. KINDS OF INFORMATION

The word informaiton means the symbolic elements used for communicating scientific and technical and other types of knowledge, irrespective of their nature (numerical, textual, etc.) and form of presentation. It refers both to the substance or contents of the documents and to their physical existence and its communication. Information is the message conveyed or intended to be conveyed by a systematized body of ideas, or its accepted or acceptable substitution. On the basis of the above definition, three types of information can be classified as:

1. Scientific Information: Information arising from or

pertaining to research activities, usually in natural and social sciences.

2. Technological Information: Information pertaining to technology (i.e. engineering, managerial) and other knowledge necessary to produce goods and services needed by society.

3. Development Information: Economic, social and cultural information, for e.g. population and commercial statistics, which is neither scientific nor technological but is generated for operational purpose.

J. H. Shera has distinguished six kinds of information. He derives this classification on the basis of the classification of knowledge done by Hertz and Rubenstein. According to the type needed by operational research team, there may be following types of information.

1. Conceptual Information: It includes the ideas, theories, hypothesis about the relationship which exists among the variables in the area of the problem. When one concentrates on a problem and derives some hypothesis or idea, then it is called conceptual information.

2. Empirical Information: It includes the data collected through personal experience during research in a laboratory or during literary invention.

3. Procedural Information: It includes the procedure through which a researcher can perform his work more effectively. Procedural information relates to the means by which the data of investigation are collected, manipulated and examined. This information is systematic and methodological and is based on scientific attitude.

4. Stimulatory Information: A person must be motivated to make him perform better, and there are two sources for such motivation, the person him/herself and his/her environment. The environmental conditions make the information more effective. This information is known as stimulatory information. Stimulatory information, that is environmentally derived, is probably most effective when it is transmitted through direct communication - the contagious enthusiasm of another individual. But whether directly or indirectly communicated, it is probably the most difficult of all forms of information to systematize. It is by nature fortuitous, it submits unwillingly to direction or compulsion.

5. Policy Information: Policy information is the focus of a decision making process. Under this information, different activities are defined, aims and objectives and responsibilities are decided, works are distributed. Collective activity necessitates the codification of rights and privileges and the delineation of functions.

6. Directive Information: Without any co-ordination, group activity cannot proceed effectively, and it is through directive information that this co-ordination is achieved.

The source and the use of the information further determine the types of information. By source we mean the environment in which the information is generated. For example, we can have the following types of information:

1. Scientific Information: Under this category comes the observation data collected during an experiment. This also includes printed standard data tables or critical tables etc. The aim of scientific information is to provide information of scientific research.

2. Technical Information: Under this category comes the data pertaining to the specifications of various products or services. These normally cover engineering specifications.

3. Techno-economic Information: This includes data on availability of raw materials, semi-finished materials, the consumption and both the internal and international market surveys. The techno-economic information is to provide information for development, production and other economic activities.

4. Business Information: In this category, the data pertaining to manufacture, sales, warehouses, profit and losses is included. It also includes employment data on various labour forces, alongwith the data on capital generation and formation.

5. Industrial Information: This includes information on various types of industries, their production capacity, licensing capacity, the consumption of raw materials and power, product data, etc. It also includes information regarding the various skills employed in the production of products and services.

6. Manpower Information: In this category, information on various types of skills, employment potential is included.

7. Socio-demographic Information: In this category, information pertaining to the geographical distribution of the resources, as well as the manufacturing capabilities and manpower is included. This also includes the educational and training facilities, and other socio-economic data.

8. Management Information: It is the information which is relevant to policy framing and decision making, required by planners, administrators and all those engaged in the management or in research and development field.

Apart from the above, categorised information is amenable to grouping from the user's point of view and also from the stability considerations. These groups are (a) stable data which do not change frequently, (b) unstable data which require frequent updating and, (c) live data which change due to ongoing processes in an industrial context like process control, material or inventory control; or by the everyday use of the rolling stock, airline/railway reservation, etc. The complexity of the live data demands computer environment for collection, processing, servicing and display. Unstable data, depending on the frequency and types of update also requires sophisticated skills and equipment. However, stable data and some unstable data needing only replacement as an update operation are to some extent amenable to manual manipulation and servicing.

The above listing is not an exhaustive one. It only illustrates that the information can be classified on the basis of the sources generating the information and/or the purpose for which the information is generated.

Thus, information is very necessary in today's world of mechanisation and computerisation. It helps in establishing past, present and future apsects of human civilization. It acts as an input to activation. Information providers should disseminate only that kind of information which users really want. Time factor is very important in information dissemination.

Information centres are playing an important role in the development of a nation by generating, processing, disseminating and distributing the information for its optimum and maximum use. The availability of information when it is needed, improves the ability of an individual, a business, a government agency, and various other kinds of organisations, to make informed decisions, to conduct research etc., and thus achieve the overall good of socio-economic development of a country.

3
Information Communication

3.1. INTRODUCTION

Communication is an activity, a process of transmitting the ideas generated by the human mind, following an event or a fact. It is an essential component, as, without proper communication, information cannot reach its defined destination. Human communication has progressed through four distinct phases. Each phase is associated with a specific form of communication. The first phase began with verbal communication in which development of language took place. The second phase was the era of written communication. In the third phase, the printing era began with Gutenberg and his Bible in 1456. The fourth phase was the age of telecommunications which began with Morse's telegraph and was perpetuated by Marconi's wireless. Telecommunication was the fastest means among the forms of communication until the advent of communication.

After passing through the four phases, we are currently in the fifth phase in which there is an emphasis on interactive communication systems.

The three basic elements of communication process are the source, the message and the receiver. Fundamentally, communication involves the exchange of meanigful symbols (messages) among sources and receivers via a medium.

There must be some physical basis for the exchange of message; thus, communication requires a medium. Communication media could be anything ranging from paper to computers.

Communication need not be a one-way process. It could be interactive or transactional. Interactive or transactional communication occurs when the back and forth communication is of the same type. Thus, communi-cation is a dynamic process by which we exchange messages to satisfy our needs.

In this way, communication is closely related to information. In the present day context the crisis of information explosion and increase in research work has added to the problem. The only way to strike a balance between the two i.e., the literature explosion and the rising need for information, is the expeditious communication of information, availing the new technologies, to meet the increasing demands. Communication has become an essential part of the modern society. Today, everything depends directly on how speedily things are communicated, whether it be the new technologies or economic, political, educational issues or weather forecasts, all these affect our day-to-day life. Information communicated at a particular time has its own value, which, if not received in time may be useless or cause some mishap. Moreover, as progress of any kind is linked with the availability of right information at right time, so is its dissemination which is of equal importance. There should be free flow of information and any barriers in its free flow should be removed.

3.2. COMMUNICATION : CONCEPT, MEANING AND DEFINITION

The term communication comes from the Latin word *Communis* which means common. When we communicate with someone, we try to establish a certain degree of commonness by sharing some information, an idea or an attitude. Communication, therefore, refers to transmission or exchange of information, messages, etc. Information and communication are two interlinked terms in the sense that without information communication is not possible. ***John Dewey*** express that, communication is a process of sharing experience till it becomes a common possession. It modifies the disposition of both the parties who partake in it. That is, in this process, two or more people share their experiences which increase the knowledge of both the parties.

The Oxford English Dictionry defines communication as "the imparting, conveying or exchanging of ideas and knowledge whether by speech, writing or signs". In the **Columbia Encyclopaedia of Communication** it is defined as "the transfer of thoughts and messages, contrasted with transportation of goods and persons".

In the words of ***Fausti and Edward,*** communication may be defined as "an ongoing process. Ideas originate in an individual's cognitive framework, they are coded and sent through some channel or channels; the messages are received and decoded by another person who responds according to his own cognitive frame work."

Similarly, ***Shannon and Weaver*** explain, "The word communication can be used in a broad sense to include all the procedures by which one mind may affect another. This of course, involves not only written and oral speech, but also music, the pictorial arts, the theatre, the ballet, and in fact all human behaviour."

Eldridge tries to describe communication, as "when social interaction involves the transmission of meanings through the use of symbols, it is known as communication". In accordance with what ***Berelson and Gary*** have to say, communication is the transmission of information, ideas, emotions, skills, etc. It is the act or process of transmission that is usually called communication.

To sum up, the main essence that overflows from the above statements is that, whenever two or more people get together and share their emotions, ideas, thinking, etc. by way of speech, writing or sign, we call it communication. It is thus said to involve three basic components, they are: (a) Source, (b) Channel and (c) Recipient. In ordinary usage, the *verb* 'to communicate' means (i) to exchange thoughts, feelings, information; (2) to make known; (3) to make common; and (4) to have a sympathetic relationship. In the *noun* form 'communication' refers to (1) the exchange of symbols, common messages, information; (2) the process of exchange between individuals through a common system of symbols; (3) the art of expressing ideas; and (4) science of transmitting information.

In the popularly understood sense of the term, communication refers to anything from a face-to-face conversation between two persons, conversation over the telephone, correspondence between friends, the transmission of programmes on live television broadcast via communication satellite received by millions of persons.

Communication takes place when people send or receive messages of various kinds. It is not only human beings who communicate, the animals also transmit and receive messages largely by instinct. However, man has been described as the "Communicating Animal" with a variety of process of communication.

Human communication is a complex activity. We are usually not aware of its complexity as we talk, listen, read, write, watch television, or listen to the radio etc. The fact of the matter is that we are actually communicating with each other during most part of our walking life.

3.3. INFORMATION COMMUNICATION

Information communication in a broad sense of the

term, includes not merely transfer of information in the conventional sense, but also, the expression of feelings, wishes, commands, desires or whatever it may be. It covers both, the use of natural language as well as voluntary or involuntary feelings, emotions, gestures, etc. Thus, one can communicate one's unhappiness by telling that, he is unhappy or by sighing or groaning or simply by looking sad. One acquires the same information in either case.

One's own stock of information or knowledge is not going to diminish by communicating to the other. This is precisely the difference between communication of information and communication of commodities, energy, heat, etc. Thus, the ownership of information may multiply but not change hands like a physical commodity. Further, one can communicate that information which he does not have! For example, one's own behaviour may enable others to know him better than himself. In this case, the communication is not intentional. Even if it is, the intention may or may not be fulfilled.

Information plays an important role in the work of scientists, technologists, managers, planners etc. ***Hanson*** mentioned that an operational research team after studying the activities of 1,300 working chemists, came to the conclusion that half of their time was spent on communication of one sort or another, giving or receiving information through talking, listening, writing or reading. One-third of their time was spent specifically on scientific communication.

Communication is the key for the development of all disciplines. It was on account of lack of proper communication that the disciplines could not develop rapidly in the past. The growing interaction between scientists and among various disciplines is responsible for the growth and development of human knowledge. The need for organised communication and the scale and complexity of communication systems will continue to grow as:

(i) the number of scientists and technologists increases and hence, the output of knowledge;

(ii) science, technology and industry development is taking place in hitherto undeveloped parts of the world;

(iii) increase in specialization, while at the same time interpretation and interdependence of many branches of science is also increasing;

(iv) science, technology and industry are increasingly becoming large scale cooperative activities involving the co-ordination of work among people who neither work together nor even know each other;

(v) the store of knowledge 'the past' is becomeing continuously larger with the daily additions of 'the present' as it becomes the past.

The day-to-day work of scientists and technologists necessitates effective communication:

(i) to stimulate thought and action by the injection of, and interaction with, other people's ideas, knowledge, experience and achievements;

(ii) to promote continuous awareness of what others are doing so that an individual worker (or group) may know of developments in his own special field, in wider fields of discipline, technology and interest, and in science and technology generally;

(iii) to diminish the probability of unwitting duplication of work and to save time and effort;

(iv) to provide introductoy and background information for work in unfamiliar fields; and

(v) to provide specific information and data needed for work in hand.

3.4. COMMUNICATION : HISTORY AND DEVELOPMENT

Communication has taken many ways and many forms throughout the history of mankind. Sign languages or expressive body languages were perhaps the earliest form of communication. Such forms of commnication are still used by the deaf and dumb. With the evolutiuon of language, spoken words became the common form of communication. However, before the invention of telephone, it was necessary for two persons to be face-to-face in order to communicate with each other. To overcome this limitation, drum beats, smoke signals etc. were used to send messages at a distance, instead of people delivering them. These methods also had severe limitations in the sense that messages were affected by wind and other natural elements. It was also often not possible to verify whether the receiver had received the correct massage or not.

The invention of writing system by the ancient Egyptians and the people of the Near East (five thousand years ago), and after that the invention of the alphabet (about three thousand years ago), made tremendous im-pact on the communication process. With these inventions the entire concept of communication changed.

Written communication enables the record of the information to be stored. The earliest form of written communication was through the cave paintings, with the passage of time, it was followed by the invention of more sophisticated technology such as clay tablets, ink papyrus, movable type and the telegraph system.

Telephone enables people to communicate over a distance and mail services enable stored images to be transported. These two are among the common methods of communication today. In the last 40 years, electronic communication and news media have become common place and indispensable.

Science, Technology and Communication

Interest in communication has been stimulated by advances in science and technology. The first and most dramatic examples of the inventions in the field of communication as a result of technological ingenuity was the telegraph and telephone, followed by others like wireless, radio and telephoto devices. The development of popular newspapers and periodicals broadcasting, motion pictures and television led to institutional and cultural innovations that permitted efficient and rapid communic- ation between a few individuals as well as among large population. Innovation of such devices is responsible for the rise and social power of the new phenomenon known as mass communication.

Some forms of communication are virtually instantaneous, the only delay being the physial limitations such as the speed of sound or light. Face-to-face conversation, direct telecast on TV, or radio broadcasting are examples of instant communication.

In other forms of communication, the message is first recorded and stored for some time before the recipient gets it. Books, films, telex messages, etc., are examples of this delayed communication.

As a result of the insatiable demand for high speed communication of information and data of all kinds newer technologies are emerging at a tremendous rate. These newer technologies are creating a worldwide communica- tion infrastructure, transmitting not just voice but text, data and images as well.

3.5. TYPES OF COMMUNICATION

The various types of communication system may be categorised as follows:

1. Vocal and Non-vocal: Vocal communication refers to any form of communication that uses the human vocal chords. It can range from shouting to spoken languages.

Man's vocal apparatus as a device of communication represents an apex of physical and intellectual evolution. It has the potential to express the most basic instructional demands as well as a range of highly intellectual processes including the possible mastery of numerous complex languages, each with an enormous vocabulary.

Non-vocal communication refers to the use of signs, signals and symbols, gestures etc., in the communication process. Signals, signs and symbols are the three related components of non-vocal communication process which are found in all known cultures. Primitive signals could be in the form of smoke puffs, drum beats etc., they refer to some sort of interuption in a field of constant energy transfer. The most common signs encountered in daily life are pictures or drawings. The basic difference between signs and signals is that sign contains meaning of an intrinsic nature while a signal is merely a device by which one is able to formulate extrinsic meanings. Traffic signs are examples of sign frequently encountered in our daily life. Symbols are more difficult than signs to understand and define. Symbol has been defined as any device with which an abstraction can be made. Body gestures are also a form of non-vocal communication which have been used since antiquity by professional actors and dancers.

3.6. MODES OF COMMUNICATION

There are two main modes of communication, i.e. formal and informal. Both these modes of communication are part and parcel of the information industry.

3.6.1. Formal Communication

This type of communication usually refers to the printed or published mode of information transfer. In order to reach a wide audience, we have to depend on the formal modes. The message once generated, in whichever form, is to reach its audience. In doing so, the maximum number of people, availing that message or the quantity of use of that information, is the measure of its quality. To ensure its maximum utility, emphasis is laid on the published form of the information, as it would reach out to a large number of people.

The following forms of recorded information may be included under formal communication:

1. Periodicals.
2. Printed and other forms of reports, tapes etc.
3. Indexing and abstracting services.
4. Books.
5. Encyclopedic summaries.
6. Bibliographic reviews.
7. Annual reviews and state-of art reports.
8. Conference proceedings, card catalogues etc.
9. Audio-visual materials, etc.

These recorded forms of message/information are authentic and consistent in nature. They are able to produce any information, at any time in any part of the world. Due to this facility, it is a very popular mode of communication. Yet, a serious drawback faced by this formal channel is the time-lag in publication. Sometimes, it takes two to three months for printing an article, sent for publication in a journal. While a number of papers are rejected and never published, and thus the important information contained in them is lost. On the other hand, the delay in publication makes the contents of a paper out-of-date, and sometimes irrelevant, too.

3.6.2. Informal Communication

Another mode of communication of information is the informal channel. The informal channels can be both oral as well as written. But they are not recorded or published in a formal way. This type of information is usually helpful to the scientific community such as the research scholars working in a laboratory or small groups.

Some of the common sources of informal communications are:

1. Discussions and talks via telephone or personal letters.
2. Distribution of manuscripts among friends and scientists.
3. Direct talks with friends, colleagues etc.
4. Exchange of ideas in conferences and group discussions.
5. Work in progress.
6. Unpublished thesis and dissertations.
7. Technological gatekeepers.
8. Invisible colleges.

These various sources of information communication convey messages, not available in published form. They constitute very important source of information for the scientific community. Although, information exchanged or received is restricted to certain members, still the dissemination through these modes is quicker than the formal channels.

3.7. ELEMENTS OF COMMUNICATION PROCESS

Communication is an endless and continuous process in which the entire humanity is involved. The entire communication system comprises of the following basic elements:

(i) Information Source/Communicator,

(ii) Encoder,

(iii) Message,

(iv) Communication channel,

(v) Noise,

(vi) Decoder,

(vii) Receiver/ Destination.

(i) Information Source/ Communicator: Source is the point at which information, message or the news originates. A source could be a person or an institution. It is the starting point in the communication process. In the case of a book the author of the book is the information source. Researchers, specialists in different fields of study are the generators of information and hence could be considered as Information Source.

(ii) Encoder: The function of the encoder is to translate the thought or ideas into words, signs, signals etc., which combined together, constitute a message or an information. By giving a class number or subject-heading to a book we actually encode the thought content of the book.

(iii) Message: It is the meaningful representation of original thought of the information source. Message could be considered as the verbalisation of the ideas through language. However, messages could be non-verbal also in the form of signs, symbols, gestures etc. The information contained in a book or an article in a journal represents the message of the author or, in other words, his thought content.

In the case of long distance communication, the message must be converted into signal which represents it and which is also suitable for transmission over the given communication channel. The signals themselves are, generally speaking, electrical, electronic or electromagnetic. Signals may be classified into analogue and digital. In the conventional voice telephone system, the changes in pressure at the microphone are represented by a corresponding variation in electrical voltage. This continuous variable wave is an example of an analogue signal. In contrast, communication between computer systems involves the transmission of data represented by discrete pulses of fixed amplitude representing 0 or 1 i.e., they transmit digital signals.

(iv) Channel: The medium through which a message is sent is called the channel. In other words, channels are the transmission media through which the message travels from the source to the destination. In the case of oral communication, the channel is the air surrouding the speaker and the listener. In the case of written commu- nication, pen and paper is the transmission channel. In radio broadcasting, radio waves constitute the transmission channel. Electromagnetic transmission channels could be classified as bounded media and free space. Bounded media include twisted pair of wires, coaxial cables, optical fibres etc. Free space is utilized for transmission between anten- nas or radar sources and sensors.

In a library or an information centre, the communication process involves the use of print as well as non-print media as the channels of communication. A book or a journal are example of printed channels of communication while non-print media may range from microphones, audio-video cassettes to CD-ROM databases.

(v) Noise: Noise in the communication process refers to anything that interferes with the message or information to be communicated in any way. All communication process or systems are subject to this unwanted disturbance or interference, which is not part of the signal but can cause it to break up or otherwise degrade it.

Any redundant data could be referred to as the noise in the information to be communicated.

(vi) Decoder: The process of translation of the messages or information by the receiver is known as decoding. The function of the decoder is, therefore, to interpret the information or messages. A decoder could be anything ranging from human beings, telephone receiver to computers. In the case of electromagnetic transfer of information through various types of channels, the message is transformed into signals before being transferred. At the receiver end, the signals need to be transformed back into original form which is done by the decoder.

(vii) Receiver/ Destination: The receiver is the person or equipment who receives the message transmitted by the source. In oral communication the listener is the receiver of the message. In the case of electromagnetic communication system, the telephone, radio, teleprinter, television, computer etc., constitute the receivers of information.

In the case of oral communication, the listener is the receiver as well as the final destination in the communication process. However, in the case of electromagnetic communication process, equipments like, telephone receiver, television set, computers etc., are the receivers but the final destination is the person or group of persons for whom the message is meant. The final destination would be a single person in the case of interpersonal communication, or it could be large number of person as in the case of mass communication.

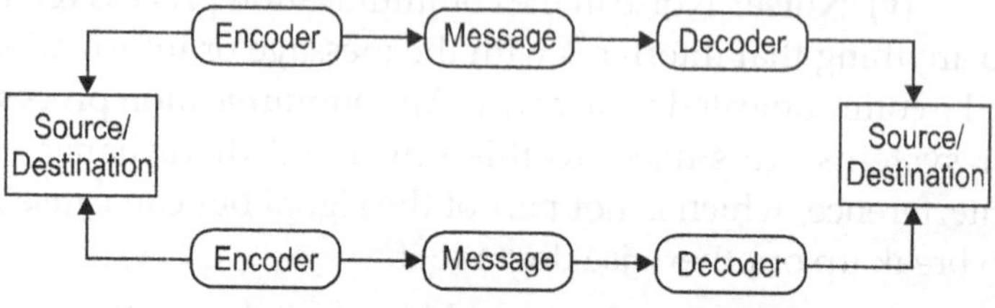

Diagram: Cycle of elements of Communication Process

3.8. LASSWELL'S COMMUNICATION MODEL

Lasswell's sociological model of communication involves five factors, namely, WHO said (source); communicated WHAT (message); to WHOM (recipient); in what WAY (channel) and what EFFECT (result or change).

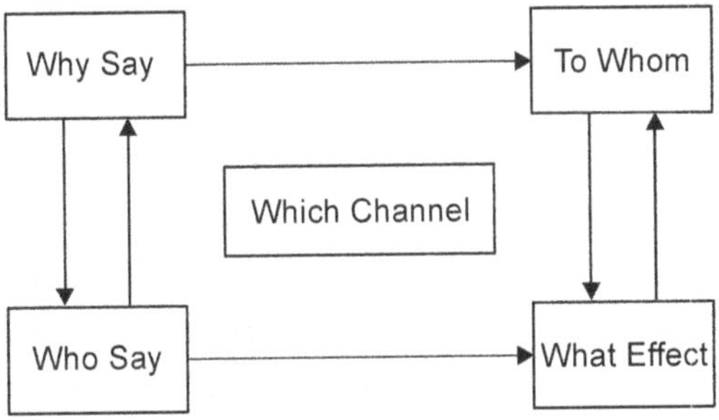

3.9. COMMUNICATION MEDIA

A media is a channel through which the messages or information are transferred to the receiver. A medium could be a spoken word or printed word or it could be in the form of electronic message.

With the advancements in science and technology, communication of information is gaining its importance. A number of communication media have been developed.

Communication media can be broadly classified into two categories:

1. Print Media
2. Electronic Media

3.9.1. Print Media

Printed words are messages prepared for specific audience. Printed media include: books, learned periodicals, conference proceedings, magazines, newspapers etc. The function of these media is to provide information, and in certain cases provide entertainment as well. The audience for these media could be specialized one in certain cases, or it could be large and diverse as in the case of newspapers, magazines etc.

(i) Newspapers have a special role of delivering information on news to the citizens. Newspapers are read by the general public. Published on a regular basis usually daily or weekly, they also interpret events behind the news, such as social trends, political developments etc. Apart from this, newspapers also provide useful information such as stock market prices, weather reports etc. They are also a popular source of reading for entertainment. Newspaper is the cheapest and most efficient mass communication media.

(ii) Magazines, like newspapers, are a popular kind of reading matter which are issued on regular basis- weekly, fortnightly, monthly, etc. Unlike most newspapers, magazines are usually printed on glossy paper with lots of colour photographs, drawings and other illustrations. A magazine is published less frequently than a newspaper. It is also published in a different format.

Since they are published less often than newspapers, magazines look into issues and situations more carefully. In magazines, there is less concern for citing the details of the day's events and more for interpreting and correlating topics in a broad context. Magazines are generally meant for mass circulation. However, some concerntrate on specialised topics e.g., Nature, Computer Today, etc. Some magazines are also meant for special target groups e.g., Femina, Women's Era, etc. (for women). Magazines, like newspapers also have dual functions, i.e., provision of information and entertainment.

(iii) Learned Periodicals are specialized journals not meant for mass circulation as is the case with magazines. They deal with specialized subjects and are the primary sources of information usually devoted to reporting of original research. Periodical articles are the main means of communication for the exchange of information in different areas of knowledge. Periodicals are, therefore, meant for specialised groups of persons and serve educational and research purposes.

(iv) Books share with other print media the functions of informing, persuading and entertaining. They differ from the other print media in that they are bound and are made to last.

Since books take a year or more to produce, the information provided in them is not recent or up-to-date. However, it explores a topic or idea in depth. Books have a smaller audience than magazines and newspapers, most books usually sell only a few thousand copies. Fiction, reference books, textbooks, research monographs are some examples of different types of books.

Apart from these four basic types of print media we have a variety of other types viz., indexing and abstracting periodicals, directories, conference proceedings, etc. Some of these print media do not communicate information directly, but they provide information about where to find information from primary sources like books, periodicals etc.

Even though faced with the challenge of electronic media, print media still remains a powerful communication media. Whether in the future, words will be printed on paper or displayed on computer terminals is not particularly important, but the survival of print media seems likely because of three features: portability, permanence and cost-effectiveness.

3.9.2. Electronic Media

Electronic media may be broadly categorised as person-to-person communication media and broadcasting media. Person-to-perosn communication media refers to such media where messages are sent by such means as telephone, telegraph, facsimile, etc. Broadcasting which is carried out by radio and television provides with news and entertainment to the general public. Now we discuss some of these communication media one by one.

(i) Telegraph: It was the earliest device for modern

telecommunication. The electric telegraph was invented by the American Samuel Morse in the 1830's. With the invention of telegraph, the speed of human communication leapt to the speed of light. Earlier it was a laborious and slow method of information transfer. It involved the manual keying of messages character by character using Morse Code. This code is built up of short and long pulses of current in the telegraph wire with the transmitter's Morse Key. A major advance was the development of the Baudot code system at the start of this century. The sender could use a sort of typewriter keyboard, each different key press would automatically generate a five bit combination (word or current pulses or pulse absence). At the receiving end, a special output unit could reproduce the message, either by punching holes in codes patterns in a paper tape or by putting readable characters directly on to a paper tape.

(ii) Telephone: The telephone differs from the telegraph mainly in that the electrical current carries the much more complex patterns of the human voice over the wire. The development of the telephone represented a solution to the technological problem of how to convert the sound patterns of voice into electrical patterns. Telephone is one of the largest established methods of electronic information transfer. Previously, telephone communication between two people could take place only through a special cable link. A major advance in telephone is the concept of multiplexing. This allows a number of different signals to pass through the same links at the same time.

(iii) Broadcasting Media: Broadcasting makes possible long-distance message transmission between sources and receivers without the need of transportation or a direct physical (wire) link. In case of broadcasting, the message is transmitted in the form of energy waves in the electromagnetic spectrum. Broadcasting includes mass communication devices like radio and television in which messages are sent out regularly by professional communicators through electronic media to a large and diverse audience.

Broadcasting as a technology means transmission of electronically generated radio waves to receiving devices. The radio and television broadcasting stations are the centres for transmission.

Recent development in the broadcasting media is the use of satellite communication systems. Space satellites now provide a worldwide television and telephone network that links nearly every country on the globe.

(iv) Electronic-Mail: It is primarily an alternative to the conventional postal mail service. Electronic-Mail is the transmission of messages or documents in an electronic form. In most Electronic-Mail systems, transmission is via a telecommunications network designed for data transmission.

Input to and output from an Electronic-Mail system can be via a video terminal, or a word processor with printer, a facsimile machine or any data terminal including computer vision and voice communication systems. The term Electronic-Mail is often assumed to refer to computer-based mail box systems but in actual practice encompasses diverse technologies such as facsimile transmission, telex and video text. The greatest advantage of Electronic-Mail as a communication media is that it overcomes the time delay associated with mailing letters. In this system mail arrives in minutes. The other advantages are that it is economical and accurate.

(v) Video text and Teletext: Both are interactive information services that allow individuals to request frames of information, but they are slightly different technologies. Teletext is delivered over the air while video text is delivered by wire. In video text, a person can request for information from a central computer for delivery over telephone or cable television lines. Teletext in contrast is a system that enables the users to view on request frames of information already being transmitted but invisible on their television screens. In video text, information is stored for transmission at the subscriber's request. In teletext, information already is there and subject to viewing on request. The terms video text and teletext are often confused. Video text is a generic term that refers to both systems. Teletext and video text are the most radical of the new communication technologies which have brought the powers of the computer to the home TV set and have transformed the entertainment medium into an information applicance.

(vi) Computer Communication: An electronic computer is the prime example of a digital communication device. Microcomputer-based communication functions usually fall into the basic categories viz., computer conferencing, database searching and electronic media.

Network are used for communication between a number of computers and between terminals and a computer.

For the sharing of information between distance users, use is made of radio, microwave, light or electric current links, through space, metal cables or optical fibres.

When computers communicate with one another over telephone lines, the message is sent in a special code. Once the message is in the other computer system, it can be decoded into a visual or printed form.

(vii) Cable TV System: A cable system is a wired communication system of high capacity that flows from a central source via a major distribution cable to neighbourhood lines and eventually to the line into the house. A cable TV system is designed to augment or substitute for over the air distribution of television signals.

Many types of communication signals can be

incorporated into a cable television network, including music channels, special information channels, and all types of text service systems with interactive capability used for home, banking or for fire, police and medical emergency services.

Electronically, humanity has progressed from the wired era of telephone and telegraph to the wireless era of broadcasting and now stands on the threshold of the era of integrated grid. Integrated grid refers to the communication infrastructure now taking shape in post-industrial societies. The term encompasses overhead satellites as well as microwave and fibre optic networks on earth.

The new technologies of communications are extensions of the traditional media. Most of these technologies are the convergence of advances in tele communications and computer systems.

3.10. ROLE OF LIBRARY IN COMMUNICATION

Libraries represent a major storehouse of human knowledge. Their value rests not merely on their facility to store information but to disseminate it in optimum quality and quantities to any information-seeking community. Libraries and information centres are the vital link between the producers and users of information. Libraries and information centres are vital components in the information communication chain, where the authors and writers are the originators of information, and publishers, editors etc., as the transmitters of information (for published documents). The primary documents e.g., books, periodicals etc., secondary documents e.g., bibliography, indexing and abstracting sources etc., and tertiary documents e.g., directories, bibliography of bibliographies etc., constitute the means of access to information that is being transmitted. These sources of information need to be channelled through some medium to reach users of information. The libraries and information centres, in this respect constitute the channels of communication. The role of libraries and information centres is now getting invigorated through the application of modern technology to all their activities. Now their role is not merely limited as communication links between the producers and users of information, but also between institutions, communities and even between countries as library networks are currently getting designed and operated. Recent developments in telecommunications, computers and networks are changing the way libraries are organized and operated and serve users. Libraries can now tap the resources of other libraries through resource sharing networks and disseminate information to a wide range of users or get access from any place irrespective of distances and locations.

4

Information Technology : Concept And Meaning

4.1. INTRODUCTION

Information Technology is that technology which is used for information management, which further involves acquisition, processing, storage, retrieval and dissemination of information. Reprography, printing and publishing are all other activities involved in information management. Hence, the corresponding technologies also become a part of information technology. In addition, information technology (IT) involves five different modern technologies –

(i) electronic technology; (ii) computer technology including hardware and software; (iii) communication technology; (iv) artificial intelligence technology; and (v) human machine interface technology. Of these five technologies, two play a dominant role at present–

(i) computers and (ii) communications. Hence, we can say that Inormation Technology these days generally means computers and communications (C & C). Thus, information technology is the study or use of processes, especially computers and telecommunications etc., for storing, retrieving and disseminating information of all kinds.

4.2. CONCEPT AND MEANING

Information on any subject(s) and the management

technique(s) used in handling information and processing it through electronic media is called Information Technology. Thus, Information Technology is electronic technologies used for collecting, storing, processing and communicating information.

The term 'Information Technology' is a recent addition to the language of the modern world, although the concept is as old as man's desire to communicate. History has recorded three great advances in human communication, and each one of these has changed the course of human civilization in a major way. The first was the invention of writing, second was invention of alphabets and third was the application of movable type of printing. Recent developments have revolutionized computer and communication technologies and have resulted in what has been called the fourth great communication invention.

Information is usually printed in books and journals, which serve as documents or records in libraries. It is also recorded in discs and magnetic tapes, which facilitate quick retrieval. Developments in computer and communication technology have brought about a new dimension to the programme of information handling. The introduction of microprocessor and mini computers has made things much easier. All these developments facilitate better and quicker services to the users.

Information Technology is the product of information science and technology. Information science comprises a set of practices and related disciplinary studies, which is concerned with the transmission, organization, storage, retrieval and use of information. Technology is the branch of knowledge that deals with industrial arts, applied science and engineering etc.

'Information Technology' connotes and ensembles the technologies. They particularly cover the computer's capability to store and process information, known as information processing and telecommunication technology, which are capable of transmitting information to distances. Basically, Information Technology is the tool and application support through which or by means of which information is transferred, recorded, edited, stored, manipulated and disseminated.

4.3. DEFINITIONS

The definition of Information Technology, as given in the report of ***H. M. Stationer,*** (1980) is, "The scientific, technological, engineering disciplines and the management techniques used in information handling and processing their application, computer and their interaction with men and machines and associated social, economic and cultural matters."

Caster defined information technology as, "the systems and devices used for receiving, storing, analysing and communicating information in all its forms, and their application to all aspects of our lives, including the office, the factory, and the home."

According to **ALA Glossary of Library and Information Science**, Information Technology is the application of computers and other technologies to the acquisition, organization, storage, retrieval and dissemination of information.

From the above definitions, we can understand that the covergence of three strands of technologies such as computers, microelectronics and communications constitutes the IT, for the purpose of a acquisition, processing, storage and dissemination of vocal, pictorial, textual and numerical information.

"Information Technology is a generic term used to denote all activities connected with computer based processing, storage and transfer of information. It involves computers, electronic media, satellites, telecommunications and reprography". To be precise, Information Technology has its origin in the technologies related to a restricted view of information i.e., the generating, processing, representation and distribution of information.

Recent revolution in the field of IT is creating not only wonders but is also posing a threat. Now a days, no librarian can say, "I don't want IT, I am not concerned with it. I will simply avoid it, nothing will happen to my library, etc.". Even if he says so to a gathering of friends, it will become a joke but will not be accepted. He is mentally exercised about IT and he gets ideas about how to proceeed towards implementation of IT in his library. This is because of the changes, developments and trends taking place in the information world, particularly during the present decade.

4.4. OBJECTIVES OF INFORMATION TECHNOLOGY

Information Technology plays an important role in storage, retrieval and dissemination of information due to developments such as reduction in computing time, economic storage capacities of files on video discs, capabilities of resource sharing, use of TV as readymade information screen, telecommunication and satellite communication facilities, etc. The objectives of IT are to provide better means of transmission of data in the form of written or printed records, electric, audio or video signals by using wires, cables and telecommunications techniques.

Following are the main objectives of IT in library and information centres–

1. Supporting information-handling system (such as information storage, retrieval, dissemination etc.).
2. Supporting the technical works of libraries such as technical processing, circulation, etc.
3. Supporting management information services for librarians, especially analyzing library statistics.

4. Supporting orientation courses for practicing librarians, supporting correspondence studies and library extension service and for continuing education programmes for teachers of Library and Information Science.

4.5. NEED FOR INFORMATION TECHNOLOGY

This is the era of information explosion in which large amount of information is being generated at every moment. The ability to collect, store, retrieve and disseminate large amounts of information needs application of new technologies. New information has become very vital tool or basis for power, possession of which reveals political, economic and social advantages over other groups. If IT is not acquired and applied, then the society becomes handicapped, because the socio-economic development of a nation depends upon the availability of adequate infrastructure to access the modern information (comprehensive, worldwide and up-to-date) which is an essential ingredient for day-to-day decision-making process. It is pertinent to be recalled here the address which was mentioned by Dr. Sarvepally Gopal in his valedictory address delivered at the one day seminar on 'Trends in and Impact of Informatics' held in Madras on August 23, 1991, that a democracy survives only on the "Oxygen of Information".

Following are the reasons, which necessitate IT in libraries:

1. Because of introduction of IT, information process becomes speedy, accurate and reliable etc. It also helps in searching quickly.
2. Some organizations like IASLIC, NISSAT, INFLIBNENT and ILA, etc., are providing excellent training facilities in IT. So libraries are showing a keen interest in utilizing these training facilities.
3. During the recent past, in any meeting, seminar or

conference, there was no task without a mention of the importance of computers.

4. After feeling the need for IT, the U.G.C. and the central as well as state governments have recognized the importance of computers in libraries. They are funding for the provision of infrastructure too in our country.

5. Many useful international databases such as MEDLARS, INIS and AGRIS etc., have been developed. For accessing their information, libraries should be necessarily automated.

6. Library users are also demanding the use of IT in the libraries for quick search results.

Chattopadhyay Committee has also stressed the importance of IT in libraries in its report on National Policy on Library and Information Services which as been recently submitted to the Government of India for its implementation.

It is noted that whereas the technologies are becoming smart, knowledge and information are also becoming highly complex simultaneously. This is resulting in a wide variety of media and has posed many challenges before us.

The dawn of information revolution is considered to be one of the marvels of twentieth century. The new technology has not only transformed the shape of modern libraries but has also given birth to many exciting possibilities and opportunities.

To attain national development we have to attain universal literacy, good education and excellence in global standards among a large proportion of the population. This explosive effort on the part of education and excellence in the professional courses raises the problem of how do we tackle so many numbers. It is here that the information technologies come into aid and promote the efforts required for spread of education and for attainment of excellence in teaching and learning upto global standards. New tools and instruments are being designed and marketed in the field of communication and mass media. Besides audio-visual aids of older generation, telecommunications, computers and information technology have profoundly changed the scenario of mass communications.

Information Technology (IT) has had tremendous impact on all the sectors of human activity. It has brought enormous changes and radical transformation in the functioning and management of modern libraries. It has profoundly changed library operations, information resources, services, and staff skill requirements and users' expectations.

5
Computer Technology

5.1. INTRODUCTION

The word 'Computer' comes from the word 'compute' which means to calculate. So a computer is normally considered to be a calculating device that can perform arithmetic operations at enormous speed.

In fact, the original objective for inventing the computer was to create a fast calculating machine. But more than 80% of the work done by computers today is of non-mathematical or non-numerical nature. Hence, to define a computer merely as calculating device is to ignore over 80% of its work.

More accurately, a computer may be defined as a device that operates upon information or data. Data can be anything like bio-data of various applicants when the computer is used for recruiting personnel, or the marks obtained by various students in various subjects when the computer is used to prepare results, or the details (name, age, sex, etc.) of various passengers when the computer is employed for making airline or railway reservations, or number of different types in case of application of computers for scientific research problems, etc.

Thus, data comes in various shapes and sizes depending upon the types of computer application. A computer can store, process and retrieve data as and when desired. The fact that computers process data is so fundamental that many people have started calling it a ***data processor***.

The name data processor is more inclusive because modern computers not only compute in the usual sense but also perform other functions with the datas that flow to and from them. For example, data processor may gather data from various incoming sources, merge (process of mixing or putting together) them all, sort (process of arranging in some sequence—ascending or descending) them in the desired order and finally print them in the desired format. None of these operations involve the arithmetic operations normally associated with a computing device but the term computer is often applied anyway.

5.2. DEFINITIONS

The following are some definitions of computer:

1. Computer is an electronic machine which can accept data, store it, manipulate it as instructed in a programme, retrieve it and convey the result to a user.

   —***Harrod's Librarians Glossary***

2. Any machine which can accept data in a prescribed form, process the data and supply the result of the processing in a specific format.

   —***Penguine Dictionary of Computers***

3. An electronic symbol manipulating system that is designed and organised to automatically accept and store input data, process them and produce output results under the direction of a detailed step-by-step stored programme of instructions.

   —***Donald H. Sanders***

In the context of computers, the information in the form of data is called the input, which is generally received in the form of report. The product or result is called output, which is also an information. The computer is an information storage device and stores the information on magnetic tapes/disks.

According to their nature and operations system, computers can be categorized into following two kinds.

1. Analog Computer: An analog computer operates by measuring rather than counting. In other words, an analog computer operates on inputs of signals, continuously variable quantities or physical magnitudes such as temperature, pressure etc. These are used for scientific and engineering purposes. A slide rule or a car speedometer are the examples of analog devices.

2. Digital Computer: A digital computer operates essentially by countings. In other words, a digital computer operates on electronic inputs that are on-off or incrementally stepped quantities represented by numerical digits. All quantities are expressed as numbers (binary) used in data or information processing activities.

5.3. CHARACTERISTICS OF COMPUTERS

1. Speed: A computer is a very fast device. It can perform in a few seconds the amount of work that a human being can do in an entire year – even if we worked day and night and did nothing else. To put it in a different manner, a computer does in one minute what would take a man his entire lifetime.

2. Accuracy: The accuracy of a computer is consistently high, and the degree of accuracy of a particular computer depends upon its design. But for a particular computer, each and every calculation is performed with the same accuracy.

Errors can occur in a computer, but these are mainly due to human rather than technological weaknesses, that is, due to imprecise thinking by the programmer (a person who writes instructions for a computer to solve a particular problem) or due to inaccurate data. Computer errors caused due to incorrect input data or unreliable programmes are often referred to as Garbage-in-Garbage-out (GIGO).

3. Diligence: Unlike human beings, a computer is free from monotony, tiredness, lack of concentration, etc. and hence, can work for hours together without creating any error and without grumbling. Due to this property, computers obviously score over human beings in doing routine type of jobs which require great accuracy. If ten million calculations have to be performed, a computer will perform the ten millionth calculation with exactly the same accuracy and speed as the first one.

4. Versatility: Versatility is one of the most wonderful things about the computer. One moment, it is preparing the results of particular examiantion, the next moment it is busy preparing electricity bills, and in between, it may be helping an office secretary to trace an important letter in a matter of seconds. All that is required to change its talent is to slip in a new programme (a sequence of instructions for the computer) into it. Briefly, a computer is capable of performing almost any task, provided that the task can be reduced to a series of logical steps.

5. Power of Remembering: As a human being acquires new knowledge, the brain subconsciously selects what it feels to be important and worth retaining in its memory, and relegates unimportant details to the back of the mind or just forgets them. With computers, this is not the case. A computer can store and recall any amount of information because of its secondary storage (a type of detachable memory) capability. Every piece of information can be retained as long as desired by the user and can be recalled as and when required. Even after several years, the information recalled will be as accurate as on the day when it was fed to the computer. A computer forgets or looses certain information only when it is asked to do so. So it is entirely upto the user to make a computer retain or forget a particular information.

6. No I.Q.: A computer is not a magical device. It can only performs tasks that a human being can. The difference is that it performs these tasks with unthinkable speed and accuracy. It possesses no intelligence of its own. Its I.Q. is zero, at least till today. It has to be told what to do and in what sequence. Hence, only the user can determine what tasks a computer will perform. A computer canot take its own decision in this regard.

7. No Feelings: Computers are devoid of emotions. They have no feelings and no instincts because they are machines. Although men have succeeded in building a memory for the computer, but no computer possesses the equivalent of a human heart and soul. Based on our feelings, taste, knowledge and experience, we often make certain judgements in our day to day life. But computers cannot make such judgements on their own. Their judgement is based on the instructions given to them in the form of programs that are written by us. They are only as good as man makes and uses them.

5.4. THE EVOLUTION OF COMPUTERS

Necessity is the mother of invention. The saying holds true for computers also because computers were invented as a result of man's search for fast and accurate calculating devices.

The earliest device that qualified as a digital computer is the "abacus" also known as "soroban". This device permits the users to represent numbers by the position of beads on a rack. Simple addition and subtraction can be carried out rapidly and efficiently by positioning the beads appropriately. Although, the abacus was invented around 600 B.C., it is interesting to note that it is still used in the Far East and its users can calculate at amazing speeds.

Another manual calculating device was John Napier's bone or cardboard multiplication calculator. It was designed in the early 17th century and its upgraded versions were in use even around 1890.

The first mechanical adding machine was invented by Blaise Pascal in 1642. Later, in the year 1671, Baron Gottfried Wilhelm Von Leibniz of Germany invented the first calculator for multiplication. Keyboard machines originated in the United States around 1880 and are extensively used even today. Around this period only, Herman Hoilerith came up with the concept of punched cards which are extensively used as input media in modern digital computers. Business machines and calculators made their appearance in Europe and America towards the end of the nineteenth century.

Charles Babbage, a nineteenth century professor at Cambridge University, is considered to be the father of modern digital computers. During this period, mathematical and statistical tables were prepared by a group of clerks. Even the utmost care and precautions could not eliminate human errors. Babbage had to spend several hours checking these tables. Soon he became dissatisfied and exasperated with this type of monotonous job. The result was that he started thinking to build a machine which could compute tables guaranteed to be error-free. In this process, Babbage designed a "Difference Engine" in the year 1822 which could produce reliable tables. In 1842, Babbage came out with his idea of an Analytical Engine that was intended to by completely automatic. It was to be capable of performing the basic arithmetic functions for any mathematical problem and it was to do so at an average speed of 50 additions per minute. Unfortunately, he was unable to produce a working model of this machine because the precision engineering required to manufacture the machine was not available during that period. However, his efforts established a number of principles which have been shown to be fundamental to the design of any digital computer.

THE MARK 1 COMPUTER (1937-44)

Also known as Automatic Sequence Controlled calculator, this was the first fully automatic calculating machine designed by Howard A. Aiken of Harvard University in collaboration with **IBM** (International Business Machines) corporation. Its design was based on the techniques already developed for punched card machinery.

Although, this machine proved to be extremely reliable, it was very complex in design and huge in size. It used over 3000 electrically actuated switches to control its operations and was approximately 50 feet long and 8 feet high. It was capable of performing five basic arithmetic operations: addition, subtraction, multiplication, division and table reference. A number as big as 23 decimal digits could be used in this machine. It took approximately 0.3 second to add two numbers and 4.5 seconds for multiplication of two numbers. Hence, the machine was very slow as compared to computers today.

It was basically an electro-mechanical device since both mechanical and electronic components were used in its design. Although its operations were not controlled electronically, Aiken's machine is often classified as computer because its constructions, which were entered by means of punched paper tape, could be altered.

THE ATANASOFF-BERRY COMPUTER (1939-42)

This electronic machine was developed by Dr. John Atanasoff to solve certain mathematical equation. It was called the Atanasoff-Berry Computer, or ABC, after its inventor's name and his assistant, Clifford Berry. It used 45 vacuum tubes for internal logic and capacitors for storage.

THE ENIAC (1943-46)

The Electronic Numerical Integrator And Calculator

(ENIAC) was the first all electronic computer. It was constructed at the Moorse School of Engineering of the University of Pennsylvania, U.S.A. by a design team led by Professors J. Presper Eckert and John Mauchly.

ENIAC was developed as a result of military need. It took up the wall space in a 20 x 40 square feet room and used 18,000 vacuum tubes. The addition of two numbers was achieved in 200 microseconds, and multiplication in 2000 microseconds.

Although much faster in speed as compared to Mark I computer, ENIAC had two major shortcomings: it could store and manipulate only a very limited amount of information, and its programs were wired on boards. These limitations made it difficult to detect errors and to change the programs. Hence, its use was limited. However, whatever be the shortcomings of ENIAC, it represented an impressive feat of electronic engineering and was used for many years to solve ballistic problems.

THE EDVAC (1946-52)

The operation of ENIAC was seriously handicapped by the wiring board. This problem was later overcome by the new concept of "stored program" developed by Dr. John Von Neutmann. The basic idea behind the stored program concept is that a sequence of instructions as well as data can be stored in the memory of the computer for the purpose of automatically directing the flow of operations. The stored program feature considerably influenced the development of modern digital computers and because of this feature we often refer to modern digital computers as stored program digital computers. The Electronic Discrete Variable Automatic computer (EDVAC) was designed on stored program concept. Von Neumann has also got a share of the credit for introducing the idea of storing both instructions and data in the binary form (a system that uses only two digits—0 & 1 to represent all characters) instead of the decimal numbers of human readable words.

THE EDSAC (1947-49)

Almost simultaneously with EDVAC of U.S.A., the Britishers developed the Electronic Delay Storage Automatic Calculator (EDSAC). The machine executed its first program in May 1949. In this machine, addition operation was accomplished in 1500 microseconds, and multiplication operation in 4000 microseconds. The machine was developed by a group of scientists headed by Professor Maurice Wilkes at the Cambridge University Mathematical Laboratory.

MANCHESTER MARK-I (1948)

This computer was a small experimental machine based on the stored program concept. It was designed at Manchester University by a group of scientists headed by Professor M. H. A. Newman. Its storage capacity was only 32 words, each of 31 binary digits. This was too limited to store data and instructions. Hence, the Manchester Mark I was hardly of any practical use.

THE UNIVAC I (1951)

The Universal Automatic Computer (UNIVAC) was the first digital computer which was not "one of a kind". Many UNIVAC machines were produced, the first of which was installed in the Census Bureau in 1951 and was used continuously for 10 years. The first business use of a computer, a UNIVAC I, was by General Electric Corporation in 1954.

In 1952, the International Business Machines (IBM) Corporation introduced the 701 commercial computers. In rapid succession, improved models of the UNIVAC I and other 700-series machines were introduced. In 1953, IBM produced the IBM-650 and sold over 1,000 of these computers.

The commercially available digital computers, that could be used for business and scientific applications, had arrived.

5.5. COMPUTER GENERATIONS

"Generation" in computer talk is a step in technology. It provides a framework for the growth of the computer industry. Originally, the term 'generation' was used to distinguish between varying hardware technologies. But nowadays, it has been extended to include both the hardware and the software which together make up an entire computer system.

The custom of referring to the computer era in terms of generations came into wide use only after 1964. There are totally five computer generations known till today. Each generation has been discussed below in detail alongwith their advantages and disadvantages. Although there is a certain amount of overlapping between the generations, the approximate dates shown against each are normally accepted.

FIRST GENERATION (1942-1955)

We have already discussed about some of the early computers—ENIAC, EDVAC, EDSAC, UNIVAC I, etc. These machines and other of their time were made possible by the invention of "vacuum tube", which was a fragile glass device that could control and amplify electronic signals. These vacuum tube computers are referred to as first generation computers.

Advantages

1. Vacuum tubes were the only electronic components available during those days.
2. Vacuum tube technology made possible the advent of electronic digital computers.

3. These computers were the fastest calculating device of their time. They could perform computations in milliseconds.

Disadvantages

1. Too bulky in size.
2. Unreliable.
3. Thousands of vacuum tubes that were used emitted large amount of heat and burnt out frequently.
4. Air-conditioning required.
5. Prone to frequent hardware failures.
6. Constant maintenance required.
7. Non-portable.
8. Manual assembly of individual components into functioning unit required.
9. Commercial production was difficult and costly.
10. Limited commercial use.

SECOND GENERATION (1955-1964)

The transistor, a smaller and more reliable successor to the vacuum tube, was invented in 1947. However, computers that used transistors were not produced in quantity until over a decade later. The second generation emerged with transistors being the brain of the computer.

With both the first and the second generation computers, the basic component was a discrete or separate entity. The many thousands of individual components had to be assembled by hand into functioning circuits. The manual assembly of individual components and the cost of labour involved at this assembly stage made the commercial production of these computers difficult and costly.

Advantages

1. Smaller in size as compared to first generation

computers.

2. More reliable.
3. Less heat generated.
4. These computers were able to reduce computational times from milliseconds to microseconds.
5. Less prone to hardware failures.
6. Better portability.
7. Wider commercial use.

Disadvantages

1. Air-conditioning required.
2. Frequent maintenance required.
3. Manual assembly of individual components into a functioning unit was required.
4. Commercial production was difficult and costly.

THIRD GENERATION (1964-1975)

Advances in electronics technology continued and the advent of "microelectronics" technology made it possible to integrate large number of circuit elements into very small (less than 5 mm square) surface of silicon known as "chips". This new technology was called "integrated circuits" (ICs). The third generation was based on IC technology and the computers that were designed with the use of integrated circuits were called third generation computers.

Advantages

1. Smaller in size as compared to previous generation computers.
2. Even more reliable than second generation computers.
3. Even lower heat generated than second generation computers.
4. These computers were able to reduce computational

times from microseconds to nanoseconds.

5. Maintenance cost is low because hardware failures are rare.
6. Easily portable.
7. Totally general purpose. Widely used for various commercial applications all over the world.
8. Less power requirement than previous generation computers.
9. Manual assembly of individual components into a functioning unit not required. So human labour and cost involved at assembly stage reduced drastically.
10. Commercial production was easier and cheaper.

Disadvantages

1. Air-conditioning required in many cases.
2. Highly sophisticated technology required for the manufacture of IC chips.

FOURTH GENERATION (1975-1989)

Initially, the integrated circuit contained only about ten to twenty components. This technology was named small scale integration (SSI). Later, with the advancement in technology for manufacturing ICs, it became possible to integrate upto a hundred components on a single chip. This technology came to be known as medium scale integration (MSI). Then came the era of large scale integration (LSI) when it was possible to integrate over 30,000 components onto a single chip. Effort is still on for further miniaturization and it is expected that more than one million components will be integrated on a single chip known as very large scale integration (VLSI).

A fourth generation computer, which is what we have now, has LSI chips as its brain. It is LSI technology which has led to the development of very small but extremely powerful computers. It was the start of a social revoltuion. A whole computer circuit was soon available on a single chip, the size of a postage stamp. Overnight, computers became incredibly compact. They became inexpensive to make and suddenly it became possible for anyone and everyone to own a computer.

Advantages

1. Smallest in size because of high component density.
2. Very reliable.
3. Heat generated is negligible.
4. No air-conditioning required in most cases.
5. Much faster in computation than previous generations.
6. Hardware failure is negligible and hence minimal maintenance is required.
7. Easily portable because of their small size.
8. Totally general purpose.
9. Minimal labour and cost involved at assembly stage.
10. Cheapest among all generation.

Disadvantage

1. Highly sophisticated technology required for the manufacture of LSI chips.

FIFTH GENERATION (1985 - Present)

Scientists are now at work on the fifth generation computers—a promise, but not yet a reality. They aim to bring us machines with genuine I.Q., the ability to reason logically, and with real knowledge of the world. Thus, unlike the last four generations which naturally followed its predecessor, the fifth generation will be totally different, totally novel, totally new.

In structure it will be parallel (the present ones are serial) and will be able to perform multiple tasks simultaneously. In functions, it will not be algorithmic (step by step, with one step at a time). In nature, it will not do just data processing (number crunching) but knowledge processing. In inference, it will not be merely deductive, but also inductive. In application, it will behave like an expert. In programming, it will interact with humans in ordinary language (unlike BASIC, COBOL, FORTRAN, etc., which present computers need). And in architecture, it will have KIPS (Knowledge Information Processing System) rather than the present DIPS/LIPS (Data/Logic Information Processing System).

The odds of coming out with a fifth generation computer are heaviest for Japan. They have already started working in this direction few years back. Japan has chosen the PROLOG (Programming in Logic) language as its operating software and plans to have the final machine talk with human beings, see and deliver pictures and hear the normal, natural language.

5.6. CLASSIFICATION OF COMPUTERS

During 1960s, computers were classified into two categories – Mini and Mainframe (including super) computers. With the arrival of Personal Computers in the market in 1975, we have the following four categories, mostly by size:

(i) Personal Computers,

(ii) Mini Computers,

(iii) Mainframe Computers,

(iv) Super Computers,

(i) Mainframe Computers

Computers are usually classified on the basis of their configuration such as word length, execution speed, number of instructions and registers, memory, number of users supported and software.

Mainframe Maxi computer is a general purpose one

and is custom built. It can be used for running hundreds of applications. It can maintain large databases. It supports a wide range of peripheral equipment and 100 or more time sharing users. It may have word length of 32 bits or more. It is very costly. Commercially available bibliogoraphical databases are very large in volume and mainframe computers have the necessary memory capacity for storage and retrieval. In a practical context, library and information systems in our country, may have to depend upon mainframe system of their host organisation or others, by having been linked through intelligent terminal(s) when they have to handle a large volume of data online. The examples of main-frame systems are IBM/370, DEC 10/20 and CYBER 7600.

Characteristics

* Custom built processor,
* Memory sizes of 1 MB to 16 MB,
* Hundreds of time-sharing users,
* Operational speeds of 1 to 10 MIPS,
* Large databases,
* Wide range of I/O Units,
* Word lengths: 32 bits and above,
* Large scale scientific, engineering, commercial applications.

(ii) Mini/ Super-Mini Computers

Mini-computer is relatively an inexpensive general purpose machine. It is dedicated to a few applications. It may have a word length ranging from 16 bits and above. It can support 20 or more time-sharing users. The examples are PDP and VAX series, HP 2000/3000 and PRIME.

Characteristics

* Custom built processor,

* Operational speeds 500 KIPS to 1 MIP,
* Multi-user/Time sharing OS,
* Hard disk, LP, Mag. Tape support,
* Memory size of 256 KB to 1MB,
* Word lengths 16 to 32 bits.

Example: HP 3000, PDP 11 series, Prime VAX 11 series (Super-Mini)

(iii) Microcomputers

Microcomputer is microprocessor (LSI chip) based. The chips have brand names, such as Intel, Zilog and Motorola, according to their manufactures. Proper specifications of the chip may be a consideration. The microcomputer may have word length of 8 bit and above. It can handle a limited number of I/O devices such as 1-2 printers, 1-8 terminals, 1-4 floppy disks and 1-4 hard disks. It is generally useful for home computing, business data processing, scientific applications and graphics. Microcomputer is having a fast technological growth that is expected to form the basis of all types of computers in future. Its modest cost, ranging from Rs. 30,000 to Rs. 5 lakhs or more depending upon the peripherals to be supported, is a strong reason for its popularity. The examples of microcomputer are IBM/PCs and local brands such as WIPRO, HCL, ZENITH, USHA and UPTRON.

Characteristics

* Inexpensive, easy to run, adaptable;
* Microprocessor based (Microprocessor is an IC chip containing the CPU);
* Word length: 8 to 16 bits (32 bit micros have been recently introduced);
* Memory size of 64 K to 1 MB.

Operating Systems

(i) Single user/single tasking

(ii) Single user/multitasking

(iii) Multiuser.

* Operation speed: 100 KIPS or above;
* Fast technological growth;
* Expected to form basis of all types of computers.

Usage Levels

Home computing (8 bits);

Single user/professional (16/32 bit);

Multiuser Micro (16/32 bit).

(iv) Super Computers

Super Computers are used for complex operations like crunching applications, weather prediction, etc.

Characteristics

* Fastest computers made to solve large scale problems involving numeric computations (Meteorological, crystallographic/molecular structural, spacecraft design).
* Word length of 64 bits and higher.
* Arithmetic speeds of 100 million floating point operations/second.
* Memory of 16 MB or higher.
* Need a mini computer as a front and processor.

(v) Personal Computers

Personal Computers (PCS) are of four kinds by the technology used in their manufacturing. These are:

1. Personal Computers (PCs),
2. Personal Computer—Extended intermediate technology (PC-XT),
3. Personal Computers—Advanced Technology (PC-AT),

4. Personal Computers—Super Advanced Technology (PC-Super AT).

5.7. BASIC COMPUTER ORGANISATION

All computer systems perform the following five basic operations:

1. Inputting: The process of entering data and instructions into the computer system.

2. Storing: Saving data and instructions so that they are available for initial or for additional processing as and when required.

3. Processing: Performing arithmetic operations or logical operations (comparisons like equal to, less than, greater than, etc.) on data in order to convert them into useful information.

4. Outputting: The processor of producing useful information or results for the user, such as a printed report or visual display.

5. Controlling: Directing the manner and sequence in which all of the above operations are performed.

The internal architectural design of computers differs from one system model to another. However, the basic organization is the same for all computer systems. Every computer system consists of a central processing unit (CPU), main memory, secondary storage, input devices and output devices. The CPU is composed of Arithmetic Logic Unit (ALU), Control unit (CU), program computer (PC), instruction register (IR) and general purpose registers (GPRs).

5.8. COMPUTER HARDWARES

Hardware is the jargon term given to the machinery itself and to the various individual pieces of equipment. It refers to the physical devices of a computer system. Thus, the input, storage, processing, control and output devices are hardware. When the hardware is linked together to form an effective working unit we have a computer installation. The general pattern of computer architecture has remained unchanged over the last four decades or so. It has a single processor, which accepts data from an input device or obtains it from backing storage, performs some operations on it, and returns the processed data to storage or to an output device. Information between the components travels by means of a high speed data channel, known as bus. The operation is serial, with a single operation being performed on a single data item.

The result is a general purpose computer, able to be used for different tasks. Over the years many improvements have been made to this sort of computer to improve its speed and power. One example is the emergence of RISC (Reduced Instruction Set Computing) machines, which give faster performance for some types of applications by using a smaller set of machine instructions.

It may be mentioned that the main change in computer architecture that is now underway is the emergence of parallel processing. In other words, parallel processing machines can perform the same operation on a number of data items at a time, or may have a number of processing units operating independently, performing different operations on different data items simultaneously. Parallelism has been first developed for super-computers. However, parallelism requires special software for its applicability. Hence, its utility is somewhat limited. It may be mentioned that parallel processor machines are now beginning to be used for database applications. Parallel processing is now becoming generally available in the form of transfer which can be attached with or added to micro computer systems to improve their performance.

Most of the professionals seeking to automate some aspects of information management will be using microcomputers. However, it is desirable to know developments in larger machines.

As mentioned before, hardware is the integration of basic elements of a computer system. They are (i) input devices, (ii) the central processing unit (CPU), (iii) the auxiliary or backing storage and (iv) the output devices. These are generally referred to as hardware.

(i) Input Devices: Each input device of a computer system reads data from a specific form and converts the data into electrical pulses. It then transmits these pulses to an input area in the CPU. There are different types of input devices such as: keyboard, pointing devices, voice input, barcodes, OCR, and image processing.

(ii) Central Processing Unit (CPU): The CPU is the physical device that controls computer operations. It is considered as the 'brain' of the computer system.

The CPU comprises three components: The control unit, the arithmetic/logic unit, and the main memory (main storage). All these are composed of microelectronic devices, virtually always based on silicon semiconductor technology. The **main memory** is the largest component of CPU, and is divided into individual *computer words,* each of which may be accessed individually by its address. All present day computers are based upon semiconductor technology, the ability to place many thousands of electronic components within a limited area of silicon, which has been doped with carefully controlled amounts of other elements. The main memory holds program instructions and data required as the programs operate.

The **arithmetic/ logic** unit contains a set of registers or accumulators, individual words of very high speed storage into which words from the main storage are copied, prior to instructions being applied to them. Attached to the registers is the circuitry which carries out the few hundreds of basic operations available to the computer. In essence, when an individual instruction needs to be carried out on some word in the main storage, that word is copied into a register, the appropriate circuitry activated, and the register's contents copied back to the main location.

The **control unit** extracts program instructions one at a time in the required sequence from their locations in the main storage, decodes them, and issues instructions to the main storage to access the required word, and to the arithmetic/logic unit to activate the required instruction circuitry.

5.9. COMPUTER STORAGE

Computer systems include two types of digital information storage: *internal storage*, within the CPU, and the *backing (back up) storage* on external devices such as disks or tapes. Different types of stroage media differ according to a number of criteria such as speed of operation, capacity, cost, reliability, the degree to which information is immediately accessible, etc.

1. Internal Storage: Internal storage is also known as main, primary, or (for historical reasons) *core storage*, or memory. It is used to hold those instructions and data required at any moment while a program is running, which must be available instantenously. Silicon semiconductor chips are now invariably used for internal storage; these are categorised as either RAM (random access memory) or ROM (read only memory) chips.

ROMs are used for data which is never altered for example, a computer's operating system instructions, while RAM is used for data which is liable to change often, and instructions used in the execution of a program.

Internal storage capacity is measured in *bits* or *bytes* and multiples thereof. The size of individual chips comprising the internal memory has rapidly increased from 4 KB (Kilobyte) chip to 16 MB (Megabyte) chips.

2. Backup Storage: Back up storage, also termed *external storage*, is used to hold programs and data which are read into internal storage when required. The most common form now, as for the last thirty years, is magnetic storage media, either tapes or disks. With both of these, data is recorded onto a plastic surface, coated with a varnish containing an oxide which can be magnetised in one or two directions; each magnetisation representing one *bit* of data. Data is written or read with the help of read/write heads, small electromagnets, close to the surface.

(i) **Magnetic tapes** are very commonly used for storing large quantum of data for which rapid access is not necessary, especially for archival data backups etc. Tapes are cheap means of storing data but access is generally slow. Small cassette tapes, of relatively low capacity are used with microcomputers.

(ii) **Magnetic Disks** are most widely used form of backing storage, suitable for holding information required rapidly, for example, data for running a program. In a disk drive in larger computer systems, data is recorded on the flat surfaces of a stack of circular disks revolving on a common spindle, with one read/write head for each disk. Access times, typically 0.01 seconds, although much faster than tape, are rather slow, in comparison to other computer operations, and disk access time is one of the main limiting factors in the speed of operation of retrieval systems with information stored on disk.

Disk capacities have increased greatly, from original values of about 10 MB (Megabytes) to present units with 1 GB (Gigabytes which is one thousand million bytes).

Smaller computer systems use **Winchester** disks, with a single hard disk in a sealed unit, floppy disks, which are compact, cheap and convenient for transfer of programs and data. They are limited in storage capacity, with relatively slow access times, and less convenient than a hard disk in day-to-day use. Floppy disks now are available in two sizes, 5.25 and 3.5 inches.

Optical disk storage is relatively new alternative to magnetic storage. Digital data is burnt into the surface of a plastic disk coated with a low wetting point metal by a laser beam. The presence or absence of a hole corresponds to *one bit* and can be read by another laser. This technology offers a high capacity storage at low cost, and in a form allowing rapid access (analogous to magnetic disks).

WORM (Write Once Read Many Times) disks are ideal for archival purposes allowing organisations to store large volumes of documentation on one disk. For instance a 12 inch disk can hold about 2.5 GB at a cost of few hundred rupees. Storage capacities of 5.0 GB is now available. But, the major problem with WORM technology is the absence of any industry standards. Now, 10 inch disks (compact version CD-WORM) is being developed.

The **CD-ROM (Compact Disk Read Only Memory)** is a 4.75" disk capable of holding 650 MB. The CD-ROM has become a means of distributing databases and documentation (including journals and patents) in electronic form.

5.10. INPUT AND OUTPUT DEVICES

The input-output (abbreviated I/O) devices provide the means of communication between the computer and the outer world. They are also known as *peripheral devices* because they surround the CPU. Input devices are used to enter data into primary storage and output devices accept results from the primary storage to supply them to the users or to store them on a secondary storage device for future processing. There are some devices which are used for both the input and the output functions. There are various types of I/O devices available for computer systems.

A wide variety of I/O devices are now available. For a particular application, one type of device may be more desirable than another. However, regardless of the nature of the I/O devices, special processors called I/O interfaces are required to convert the input data to the internal codes used by the computer and to convert internal codes to human readable form while supplying the output. These I/O interfaces are also called channels or I/O processors (IOP). It is important to note that even the fastest of the I/O devices is very slow when compared to the speed of primary storage and CPU. The main reason for this is that the speed of I/O devices in most cases depends upon mechnical movement, and the potential for improvement of such devices is limited. It has been difficult to produce I/O devices that can match the processor and storage speeds, and there is a constant demand for faster and faster I/O devices. Input/output (I/O) devices now account for more them 50% of the cost associated with microcomputer system. They also have an impact on the ease of use of computer systems, and their popularity with users. Therefore, it is necessary to think carefully about the sort of I/O hardware required. To enable appropriate choice of the equipment based on requirements of applications software which might be used, a range of available devices are discussed. Many packages, for example, require a colour screen to be fully effective, while to take advantage of the fonts and types faces available in some word processing package require a laser printer.

5.10.1. Input Devices

The data entering into the internal memory is knwon as inputting. Input devices facilitate the users to translate their data into binary-coded electronic pulses and send to the Computer Processor (CPU). Input devices can be connected/disconnected/reconnected to the computer as and when required. These devices are, therefore, known as peripherals. There are a variety of input devices like keyboard, card reader, tape drive and disc drive, optical character recognition (OCR), etc. The keyboard is the most widely used input device.

The keyboards of input terminals are designed much like that of a typewriter. The recent general purpose keyboards have 101 keys- 26 letters keys, 10 number-cum-special character keys, 17 numeric pad keys consisting of 10 numberals plus 7 characters, 13 cursor & other control keys, 12 function keys and 23 special characters. For specific applications like check-out counters in department stores the keyboards have only a few function keys arranged much like the push buttons in calculators. Many input terminals have extra fittings to control the cursor movements, in addition to the cursor control keys in the keypad. Two such gadgets are '*joystick*' and '*mouse*'. Using these gadgets is usually easier and faster than using the keyboard. Joystick is a lever much as the one used in airplanes to operate elevators and ailerons. It is capable of motion in two or more directions. Mouse is a gadget that is designed in the shape of a mouse. The physical movement of the mouse on a plain and smooth surface results in the movement of the cursor on the screen. Most of the mouse designs have three push buttons. These are known as drag, click and point buttons. The drag button, which is the middle one, is to be kept pressed while moving the mouse. This arrangement safeguards against accidental moving of the cursor due to inadvertent physical movement of the mouse. The click button which is on the left is used to select and deselect a given item. The point button on the right is used to take the mouse pointer on the screen to an item of choice.

Two other input devices that are used often are the *light pen* and the optical or magnetic *scanner*. The light pen is a hand-held (pen-like or pencil-like) device which when drawn on the screen generates input. It can be used to point to items on the screen and select them. Scanners are used to convert data encoded on documents into a form that is processable by the CPU. Scanners reduce the time required for data entry significantly and minimise human handling of data at the time of input. A problem with scanners is that if the documents are in poor condition due to causes like smudges, creases or dirt, the data is likely to be misread. Optical scanners are referred to as optical character recognition (OCR) devices when used for scanning and recognising textual data. The recognition is usually done by a software package and the scanner does not play any role in recognition. Scanners in general can be used for scanning pictures, diagrams and so on. *Magnetic scanners* are used in *bar code* applications in libraries etc.

For the last two decades, computer technology has substantially improved the storing of information in the computers. For this, there are so many input devices which are used. Input devices are those devices through which data or instructions can be fed into a computer. Some of the other important input devices are being discussed here as follows:

(i) Punched cards: Punched cards can be considered both as an input device as well as external memory or storage medium. There was a time when punched cards were the most popular input devices or storage mediums. But due to the invention of very fast and least space consuming input device spunched cards have almost become obsolete.

(ii) Magnetic disc drum: Magnetic disc drum is the most commonly used internal storage medium in a computer. The drum is like a cylinder, mounted on a shaft which rotates by a motor at a very high speed. The space of the drum is coated with metallic oxide which enables the face of the drum to be magnetised in minute discrete areas or cells. Each cell functions as a register and each has an address depending upon its position on the drum. Disc drum facilitates direct access to required data. The data speed or tabulation of data is also very fast.

(iii) Magnetic tape: Magnetic tape is an input/storage medium. The tape is made of half an inch plastic having magnetic oxide-coated surface on one side. Data is entered and retrieved with the help of read/write heads. This is very similar to the tape of a tape recorder. The access to data is sequential. It has vast storing capacity, on every centimeter of the tape about 2500 characters can be stored. In case of wrong input or old data, the same can be deleted on erased and new data can be entered on the same tape. The demerits of this device is that it gets affected by dust particles and humidity, and therefore, it neeeds to be kept under controlled environment, otherwise it may get affected.

(iv) Floppy disc: The term floppy indicates that it is flexible and thin and the term disc indicates that is round in shape. Discs are made of plastic, coated with magnetic surface, and allow random access. A flopy disc is smooth, coated with magnetic surface, and it has tracks on it. The tracks are imaginary lines. Information can be created or read here as a sequence of magnetic pulses. Information is written or can be read in floppy disc with the help of a head.

(v) Microform: The conventional books and news papers are being replaced by microfilms and microfiches. As compared to paper, microfilms and microfiches are cheaper and easier to handle and distribute. Microfilms increase the storage capacity of the stock space. 60,000 volumes of books can easily be stored in a single drawer of a filing cabinet.

(vi) Optical Storage Discs: Optical storage device make use of laser beams to both record and read backup data stored on a photo sensitive medium of a disc. It is new development in storage devices. There are three functio-nal varieties of optical media available. They are as follows:

(a) ***Read only optical Discs*:** It is the publishing and

distribution media, as the user can only read the data by placing the disc in a player. There is no facility for the user to record the data into a read only disc, for example CD-ROM.

CD-ROM stands for Compact Disc-Read Only Memory. It is a form of laser disc, 4.75 inches in diameter, that holds roughly 600,000,000 characters. The information is stored on the disc by a high powered laser. The disc is read by a CD-ROM reader that is linked to a standard micro-computer.

(b) ***Write-Once optical Discs***: The write once read many (WORM) optical disc can be used for low volume data distribution. The data can be recorded into the disc over a period of time, till the disc is full. However, any sector of the disc can be written only once and it is not possible to erase or overwrite data into the some sector, e.g. CD-PROM.

(c) ***Erasable rewritable optical discs***: In an erasable rewritable optical disc the recording process can be reversed, data deleted and new data recorded onto the same sector.

5.10.2. Output Devices

Each output unit of computer system transmits information from the CPU and converts the electrical pulses to an appropriate output form. A printer, for example, is an output device that transmits output from the CPU and converts it to a printed form. There are many other output devices that can perform the same electrical transmission and conversions to produce other output forms.

The Visual Display Unit (VDU) is the most common form of output device. Mostly, it is based on the concept of Cathode Ray Tube (CRT). But these have markedly increased in quality and decreased in price. Standards over colour monitors developed over the years include the Colour

Graphics Adaptor (CGA), Enhanced Graphics Adaptor (EGA) and Video Graphics Array (VGA). These have become widespread. Alternatives to CRT including *light emitting diodes, liquid crystals* and *gas plasma discharge panels* are coming into use, particularly for portable computers.

(1) Printers: Printers are the most commonly used output devices that can be found in almost all computer centers. They are the primary output devices used to prepare permanent documents in human readable form (hard copy). There are several types of printers that are designed for different types of applications. Depending on their speed and approach of printing, printers are classified as *character printers, line printers* and *page printers.* In addition, there is another classification according to which printers are of two types- impact and non-impact. *Impact printers* use the familiar typewriter approach of hammering a typeface against paper and linked ribbon.

Non-impact printers do not hit or impact a ribbon to print. They use thermal, electrostatic, chemical and ink-jet technologies.

(i) ***Character Printers*:** Character printers print only one charatcter at a time. A typewriter is an example of a character printer. Three of the most commonly used character printers are described below.

* ***Letter-Quality Printers*** : These printers use a printwheel font known as a daisy wheel. Each petal of the daisy wheel has a character embossed on it. A motor spins the wheel at a rapid rate. When the desired character spins to the correct position, a print hammer strikes it to produce the output. Thus, daisy wheel printers are impact printers. Their output resembles a typed output and they are noted for their print quality. The speed of these letter quality printers normally ranges from 10 to 50 characters per second.

* *Dot-Matrix Printers*: These printers print each character as a pattern of dots. The print head comprises a matrix of tiny needles, typically seven rows with nine needles in each (9 x 7 matrix), which hammers out characters in the form of patterns of tiny dots. The shape of each character, i.e., the dot pattern, is obtained from information held electronically in the printer.

 The print quality of a dot-matrix printer is inferior to that of a daisy wheel printer. But dot-matrix printers are generally faster than letter-quality printers- in the range of 40 to 250 characters/second. They are also less expensive than a daisy wheel printer and hence, if the quality of output is not an important factor then the dot-matrix printer is used with most microcomputer systems. There is an additional advantage of dot-matrix printers over letter quality printers in the sense that dot-matrix printers do not have a fixed character font. So they can print any shape of character that a programmer can describe. This allows for many special characters, different sizes of print and the ability to print graphics such as charts and graphs.

* *Ink-Jet Printers*: These are non-impact character printers based on a relatively new technology. They print characters by spraying small drops of ink onto paper. Special type of ink having a high iron content is used. Droplets of ink are electrically charged after leaving a nozzle. The droplets are then guided to the proper position on the paper by electrically charged deflection plates. Ink-jet printers produce high quality output because the characters are formed by dozens of tiny ink dots. Moreover, they are quiet (non-impact) and can form any kind of character. The document printed may contain multiple character styles and a variety of type sizes. Some models also allow for

different colours of ink for multiple colour printing. Of course, inkjet and other nonimpact printers cannot produce multiple copies of a document in a single printing which is possible with impact printers.

(ii) ***Line Printers*:** Line printers are impact printers used with most medium and large computer systems for producing high volume paper output. They are fast printers having speeds in the range of 300 to 2500 lines per minute. Their printing speeds are such that to an observer they appear to be printing a line at a time and hence the name 'line printer'. There are normally 132 to 136 print positions per line. Some line printers even have a line length of 120 characters and a few have a line length of 144 characters. Character sets vary in content and size for different line printers. The 64 set has more special characters than the 48-set and the 96-set prints in lower-case (small) letters as well as in upper-case (capitals). The output efficiency of a line printer can be increased by using multiple-part papers (pages with carbon paper inserts) when more than one copy of the output is required. Drum printer and chain printer are the two most commonly used line printers.

* ***Drum Printers*:** A drum printer consists of a solid, cylindrical drum that has raised characters in bands on its surface. There are as many bands as there are printing positions. Each band contains all the possible characters. The drum rotates at a rapid speed. For each possible print position, that is, opposite to each band of the drum, there is a print hammer located behind the paper. These hammers strike the paper, alongwith the inked ribbon, against the proper character on the drum as it passes. One revolution of the drum is required to print each line. This means that all characters on the line are not printed at exactly the same time, but the time required to print the entire line is fast enough to call them line printers. Typical speeds

of drum printers are in the range of 300 to 2000 lines per minute.

* *Chain Printers*: They use a rapidly moving chain called a *print chain*. Each link of the chain is a characters font. Instead of a chain, some models of printers use a metal band having raised print characters on it. For each possible print position, there is a print hammer located behind the paper. As the print chain or the band rotates, the properly timed print hammers strike the paper, alongwith the inked ribbon, against the proper character on the chain/band as it passes. In order to enhance the speed of the chain printers, the character set is repeated several times on the chain. Hence, it is not necessary to wait for the chain to make a complete revolution to position the desired character in the correct print position. A standard character set is of 48 characters. So, chain printers that use the 64-set or the 96-set repeat the characters fewer times than the standard set. This increases the time to position the desired character and therefore, reduces the effective print speed of the printer. Speeds of chain printers range from 400 to 2500 characters/minute.

(iii) ***Page Printers*****:** These are very high speed non-impact printers which can produce documents at speeds of over 20,000 lines per minute. Electronics, xerography, lasers, and other technologies have made these high-volume systems possible. These techniques, called *electrophotographic techniques,* have developed from the paper copier technology. Page printers can produce pages of output at a rate equal to a paper copier. Each page produced on these printers is an original one since there are no carbon copies. Because of their extremely high cost, these printers are economical only when hundreds of thousands of pages are to be printed each month.

Thus, a variety of printers is available for use with computer systems. They can be placed under two broad categories: impact printers non-impact printers. Impact printers produce hardcopy outputs by pressing print elements against paper when activated by the CPU. In the case of non-impact printer, the print elements never touch the paper. Impact printing may use either formed or dot matrix characters. An example of an impact printer is the ***daisy wheel printer (DWP)*** which uses fully formed characters These characters are on the tips of spokes of a wheel which rotates to bring the desired character in position for impact with the paper. A ***dot matrix printer (DMP)*** which also belongs to impact printer category, selects specific pins within a matrix (normally 7 x 5 size) and then presses the pins against a ribbon. Since such printers can choose pins and produce dots in any pattern, they can produce graphics as well as text. Many dots printed close together form dark shaded areas whereas dots more widely placed give lightly shaded areas. DMPs are less expensive and can print at speeds of 8-12 pages per minute.

Non-impact printers include electrostatic printers, xerographic printers, laser printers and ink-jet printers. Electrostatic printers use a dot matrix of pins through which an electrical charge is sent. The toner consists of particles that are oppositely charged. When the paper is passed in between the pins and the toner, the toner particles stick to the paper in the charged areas. No physical contact is made between the pins and the paper. Xerographic printers use a process similar to photocopying. **Ink-jet printers** produce hardcopy by controlling ink drops with an electric charge or by shooting ink from nozzles contained in the print head. Ink-jet printers have made possible colour printing by using different colour inks in their jets. Four colour ink-jet printers are available commercially at present. **Laser printer** uses a laser beam to trace characters or images into a light-sensitive drum, which attracts the toner that sticks to the paper in the form outlined by the laser.

Plotters represent another class of useful output devices. A plotter enables drawing of lines, curves, graphs, charts, engineering drawings, maps, pictures and other complex shapes. Pictures come in two varieties depending on whether they use a flat-bed or a drum for holding the paper. A carriage holding one or more pens moves across the paper to draw as required. Some plotters use ink-jets instead of pens. Multiple pens or ink-jets permit colour drawings to be made by using the plotters.

5.11. COMPUTER SOFTWARE

It is important to note that a computer cannot do anything on its own. It must be instructed to do a desired job. Hence, it is necessary to specify a sequence of instructions that a computer must perform to solve a problem. Such a sequence of instructions written in a language that can be understood by a computer is called a *computer program*. It is the program that controls the activity or processing of the computer and the computer performs precisely what the program wants it to do. The term *software* refers to the set of computer programs, procedures, and associated documents (flowcharts, manuals, etc.), that describe the programmes and how they are to be used. To be precise, software means a collection of programmes whose objective is to enhance the capabilities of the hardware machine.

Relationship Between Hardware And Software

In order for a computer to produce useful output, the hardware and software must work together. Thus, there is a special relationship between hardware and software. Both are complementary to each other. Nothing useful can be done with the computer hardware on its own and software cannot be utilised without supporting hardware.

To take an analogy, a cassette player and the cassettes purchased from market are hardware. However, the songs recorded on the cassettes are its software. To listen to a particular song, first of all that song has to be recorded on one of the cassettes which should then be mounted on the cassette player and played. Similarly, to get a particular job done by a computer, the relevant software should be loaded in the hardware before processing starts. It is immediately evident that hardware is necessary but software is vital. Another important point brought out by this analogy is that software production is difficult and expensive. Hardware is a one-time expense whereas software is a continuing expense. It may also be noted that different softwares can be loaded and run on the same hardware to perform different types of jobs just as different songs can be recorded one by one on the same cassette and played using the cassette player.

5.11.1. Types of Software

Software may conveniently be divided into two categories:

System Software: (i.e., programmes designed to control the execution of other programmes and to utilise hardware effectively), and

Applications Software (i.e., programmes which enable the computer to solve users' problems).

The methods by which software is produced have changed considerably in recent years with the emergence of the new discipline known as *'Software Engineering'*. The traditional pattern of software development used to be a systems analysis to undertake a detailed study of user's need, leading to an elaborate specification for the software, which would then be converted into a programming language. This process is considered inadequate, and leading to backlogs. It is also felt that this procedure does not meet user's need effectively and is poorly maintained.

Increased availability of packaged software and use of fourth generation languages, and flexible integrated software to produce rapidly modifed *prototypes* of programmes to meet user's need, are suggested as remedies to the software backlog problem. However, for the average user they mean that there will be an increasing array of packages to meet his requirements.

(i) System Software: Systems software is generally supplied by the hardware manufactures. It includes operating systems, assemblers, compilers, and interpreters (to convert programming languages into machine code) programmes for controlling input and output devices, copying data between storage media, etc., and utilities for sorting, merging and editing files, controlling program libraries, etc. In other words, it is an all "supporitng" software, which enables the power of the computer to be applied to user's problems.

Operating Systems

The operating system is the software that mediates between the applications programs and a level of instructions nearer to the machine's operations. In other words, it is a "software that controls the execution of a computer program, and that may provide scheduling, debugging, input/output control, accounting, compilation, storage assignment, data management and related services".

Operating system software is written specifically for the type of function the computer is going to be used for. Generally, the more complex the function is, the more complicated the operating system will be. There are many types of operating systems available: some are made to work on a variety of different types of hardware, and some are designed for only one specific type of machine. Mainframe and minicomputers generally have their own proprietory operating systems. In the early days of personal computing, all operating systems were single user. Apple, Amiga, Commodore and IBM are all computer hardware manufacturers with machines that run different single-user operating systems. The most commonly used operating system in the world today runs on the **IBM PC**. This is the Microsoft disk operating system **(MS-DOS)**. Since 1980s, **DOS** has been improved and refined many times.

A second type of operating system, described as *multi-tasking*, is still only capable of having one user but *more than one task*, operating at a time. The main task that requires the user's attention (for example a word processing programme) remains on the computer monitor, while the other task is working away in the background. The background process could be a complex statistical analysis program that takes a long time to complete, and the user could spend the waiting time for some other work. A multitasking successor to **DOS** is called Operating System 2 (OS 2).

Microsoft has gone on to develop its ***Windows*** environment, an operating system with multi-tasking and other advanced capabilities. Multi-tasking operating system must divide the CPU resources between the different tasks. In addition, multi-tasking itself is a more sophisticated operating system than the single user type, and can *take more CPU resources just to run.*

The third type of operating system is multi-user. By definition, multi-user systems are also multi processing, since each user who is working on the machine accounts for a separate process. Depending on the power of the CPU and the size of the computer, the number of users that can be working at one time might go into hundreds. The most common examples of multi-user systems are in the large mainframe environments. Systems like VMS from DEC and MVSA from IBM are examples of operating systems with the potential for large number of users.

UNIX is a multi-user operating system that has gained high popularity. Developed originally at AT&T Bell Labs,

UNIX was designed to be used by engineers and scientists. Because of its efficient design and built-in security features, and its reasonable price, application software companies have considered **UNIX** as an attractive development platform. Probably the most attractive feature of **UNIX** is that *it is an open system and multi-platform*. This means that the operating system will work on a range of hardware configurations from micro-computers to mainframes. A new competitor to **UNIX** on personal computers, workstations and networks is the ***Windows NT*** operating system, a new operating system from Microsoft Corporation. Multi-platform open operating systems are very attractive because applications that are developed for one platform can be run on another with minimum conversion problems. A **UNIX** word processing software package on a *Sun Workstation* could also be used on a **UNIX** P.C. The application is said to be 'ported' (portable) from one machine to another. From user's point of view, much of this may not be important. Factors which must be considered are the *ease of use* of the operating system, and any *restrictions it places upon the choice of software*. The latter point is particularly important, since any application program or package is restricted to specific operating systems. For example, something designed for the Macintosh will not run under an **IBM** operating system and vice-versa.

(ii) Application Software: Application software is the program that allows the user to get the required work done. In other words, application software comprises the procedurers and instructions which enable computer systems to do what the user requires. The software design essentially involves three *abstract concepts : algorithms* (i.e., procedures, or recipes, for computation- may be numerical or non-numerical, e.g., sorting, text searching); *Data structures* which indicate the way in which information is organised in the computer's memory. In other words, the structure indicates whether, it is organised in *array* or *tree* pattern. *File structures* represent the way in which large amounts of information is stored on the storage media for example, whether it is organised sequentially, or in direct access, inverted file.

Even though users do not need any in-depth knowlege relating to the above mentioned three concepts, it is desirable to have some understanding of the terminology, since it is commonly used in software supplier's literature.

Once a software procedure is expressed in such terms. It can be coded into a form which the computer can use, by means of programming language. There are a number of programming languages in use. It must be emphasised that a computer can only operate *on instructions in machine code* (binary), and early computers were indeed programmed in this way. *Assembly language,* a more convenient mnemonic form of machine code, is still used today for specialised applications.

High level languages (converted to machine code by compiler or equivalent) are much easier to programme, as well as understand. Several high level languages are in use today. Best known are the **FORTRAN** (Scientific), **COBOL** (business) and **BASIC** (interactive) languages. Most recently introduced general purpose languages include **PASCAL**, ADA and C. Most recent programming languages are called the 'fourth generation' or 'very high level' languages, generally as part of integrated programming systems, such as DBMS, which facilitate users to programme their own applications very easily.

It is not necessary for users of a program or package to have any knowledge of the language in which the package is written, or indeed to know what that language is.

5.12. SOFTWARE PACKAGES

Computer software has evolved from an item of minor economic concern with first generation digital computers to one of major concern in today's computing systems. In the early days of computers, more than 80% of the total computer cost was devoted to hardware, but today more than 80% of the cost is for software. At one time, application and system softwares were included in the purchase price of the computer. Today, however, software is usually not included in the purchase price of the computer. For most computer manufacturers the purchase price of a computer includes only the hardware alongwith a minimum of systems software. The customer normally has to pay extra charges for additional systems software and application software that he may wish to purchase.

Basically, there are two ways of obtaining software. One can either buy an existing package, or he can develop his own package. There are many financial options if one decides to buy a software package. It can be purchased, leased or rented, or obtained through lease-purchase agreement. Software can be purchased from the computer manufacturers, from a software company or software house that specializes in developing and selling softwares. Software can also be obtained from user groups, which are groups of people or organizations that use the same computer and share software. On placement of advance order, many computer manufacturers also supply specialized application packages that are developed only for a particular user for his specific need. These packages are normally supplied along with the computer system, which is normally referred to as a *turnkey system*. If the software is to be developed in-house, that is, if the user decides to develop his own package, then some computer professionals are required to plan, develop, test, implement, and maintain the computer programs. However, development and maintenance of software is not an easy task. It is a very costly and time consuming affair. Hence, thorough analysis should be done and considerable thought should be given before one arrives at a decision of either buying or developing a software package.

Firmware: Computer software in conventional systems is supplied on storage media like floppies, tapes, disks, etc. However, with the advancement in technology and the reduction in hardware cost, today software is also being made available by many computer manufacturers on read-only memory (ROM) chips. These ROM chips can be easily plugged into the computer system and they form a part of the hardware. Such programmes (software) made available on hardware are known as *firmware.* Firmware often refers to a sequence of instructions (software) that is substituted for hardware. For example, in an instance where cost is more important than performance speed, the computer system architect might decide not to use special electronic circuits (hardware) to multiply two numbers, but instead write instructions (software) to cause the machine to accomplish the same function by repeated use of circuits already designed to perform addition. This software will be stored in a ROM chip of the computer system and will be executed (used) whenever the computer has to multiply two numbers. Hence, this software will be known as firmware. To be precise, firmware is software substituted for hardware and stored in read-only memory.

Initially, only system software was supplied in the form of firmware. But today, even application programs are being supplied in firmware form. Dedicated applications are also programmed in this fashion and available in firmware. Because of the rapid improvements in memory technolgoy, firmware is frequently a cost-effective alternative to wired electronic circuits, and its use in computer design will increase. It is expected that in the near future, firmware will make possible the cost-effective production of smart machines of all types.

5.12.1. Nature and Types of Software Packages

Software packages are commercially supplied products which typically provide solutions to a particular range of software development or applications problems. Since, they are developed for commercial sale in a competitive market for use by a variety of customers, a great amount of skill and effort is put into their development. Therefore, they are reliable, easy to use and in many instances, well documented. Readymade 'Packaged' software is now becoming available for an increasing range of applications such as Office Automation Systems and Library Automation and Information Retrieval Operations.

Library and Information personnel are primarily concerned with software packages for text or information retrieval. In addition to special purpose retrieval packages, there are also a number of general purpose packages which offer some information retrieval functions. The different types of softwares can be identified as: (i) basic software, (ii) word processing software, (iii) database management systems (DBMS), (iv) text-retrieval packages, (v) software associated with online systems, and (vi) inhouse library keeping.

A brief description of each of the different types of softwares is given below:

(i) Basic Software: The basic software is also referred to as utilities. Basic software packages are available for performing operations such as data entry and validation, sorting and merging files and editing data. A data entry and validation software typically allows the user to define a format to be displayed on a screen (VDU) and by using other prompts enables data to be entered in the specific format defined by the user. Some simple checks on the data entered are also possible with this software, for instance, ensuring that there are no alphabetic characters in a numerical data field, etc. File sorting and file merging facilities are provided in such packages. Some sophisticated packages offer editing capabilities of certain specific lines in the text or even full screen editing facilities as well as automatic input and output.

(ii) Word Processing Software: Word processing is one of the most wide spread application software types in use today. Developed as a successor to primitive text-editors that were only possible on mainframe computers, word processing programme allows interactive editing of documents, enabling easy re-drafting and merging of chunks of existing documents, without the need for extensive re-typing. Most of the popular programmes contain features such as spell-checks, outlining, choice of fonts, line drawing and page layout facilities. Word processing software permits the user to manipulate the text. This is a very handy feature when laying out tables or columns for the text.

(iii) Database Management Systems (DBMS): These are essentially programming frameworks, and can offer good storage and retrieval systems. They are mainly intended for programmers to interact with and need a programmer in order to make them usable to libraries. This is specially applicable in case of network and hierarchical models. **DBMS** in general terms, have many attractions for the librarian wishing to implement automation on micro-computers.

There are three types of **DBMS** available to a micro-computer. They are file or data management systems, relational **DBMS** and network and hierarchical **DBMS**. Of these, the first two types are easy to comprehend and do not call for intense knowledge in programming for developing library applications using them.

(iv) Text Retrieval Packages: Text retrieval comprises storage and subsequent retrieval of records, essentially textual rather than numerical, tabular or graphical. Although, each of the earlier mentioned software can be used for text retrieval purposes to some extent, there are special purpose packages which are written specially for the type of retrieval functions related to libraries and information centres. The characteristics features of such software packages are: (i) the software is normally self-contained and can be set up with the minimum involvement of a computer specialist staff; (ii) the records in this software are independent, of variable length and are composed mostly of natural language texts; (iii) access to data is by content rather than by structural position; (iv) primary access is through inverted file of text terms drawn from the records as they are placed on the database. Thus, an important feature of the package is user interface, which allows a non-programmer to understand and use them directly. Search and indexing facilities are the most important features of this type of software.

(v) Software for Searching Online Retrieval Systems: Each of the major online systems has its own software which supports its activities on a host computer. Many of these hosts have begun to offer private facilities with the help of which end-users can exploit the sophisticated software developed by supporting large databases with many searches. If the user is familiar with the command language of the host, then a private file on that system avoids the need for familiarisation with a further software package. Private file facilities are expensive since a telecommunication charge is incurred each time the host computer is used. The second type of software generated in association with online searching of external databases, enables more economical access to host systems. There are a number of packages, mainly for use on micros, which support online interaction with an external database and permit the development and editing of search profiles and search outputs locally.

The availability of databases on **CD-ROM** media has influenced the online searching activity to a considerable extent, and obviated the expenditure associated with communications.

(vi) Library Housekeeping Software: The market is flooded with a variety of packages specially designed to support library housekeeping operations such as acquisitions, cataloguing, circulation control, serials control, etc. Some of these are integrated packages covering many functions, while others concentrate on individual rountines like cataloguing, etc.

5.13. COMPUTER LANGUAGES

A language is a system of communication. With our natural language such as English, we communicate to one another our ideas and emotions. Similarly, a computer language is a means of communication used to communicate between people and the computer. With the help of a computer language, a programmer tells a computer what he wants it to do. All natural languages (English, French, Gernman, etc.) use a standard set of symbols for the purpose of communication. These symbols are understood by everyone using that language. We normally call this set of symbols the vocabulary of that particular language. For example, the words we use in English are the symbols of English language that make up its vocabularly. Each word has a definite meaning which can be looked up in a dictionary. In a similar manner, all computer languages have a vocabulary of their own. Each symbol of the vocabulary has definite unambiguous meaning which can be looked up in the manual meant for that language. Hence, each symbol of a computer language is used to tell the computer to do a particular job. The main difference between a natural language and a computer language is that natural languages have a large vocabulary but most computer languages use a very limited or restricted vocabulary. This is mainly because a programming language by its very nature and purpose does not need to say too much. Each and every problem to be solved by a computer has to be broken down into discrete (simple and separate), logical steps which basically comprise of four fundamental operations—input and output operations, arithmetic operations, movement of information within the CPU, and logical or comparison operations.

Each natural languages has a systematic method of using symbols of that language. In English, this method is given by the rules of grammar. These rules tell us which words to use and how to use them. Similarly, the symbols of a particular computer language must also be used as per set rules which are known as the syntax rules of the language. In case of natural language, people can use poor or incorrect vocabulary and grammar and still make themselves understood. However, computers being a machine, are receptive only to exact vocabulary used correctly as per syntax rules of the language being used. Thus, in case of a computer language, we must stick by the exact rules of the language if we want to be understood by the computer. As yet, no computer is capable of correcting and deducing meaning from incorrect instructions. Computer languages are smaller and simpler than natural languages but they have to be used with great precision.

Unless a programmer adheres exactly to the syntax rules of a programming language, even down to the correct punctuation marks, his commands will not be understood by the computer.

Programming languages have improved throughout the years, just as computer hardware has improved. They have progressed from machine-oriented languages that use strings of binary 1s and 0s to problem-oriented languages that use common mathematical and/or English terms. However, all computer languages can be classified in the following three broad categories:

(a) Machine Language,

(b) Assembly Language,

(c) High-level Language.

We shall now examine the evolution and nature of each type of language.

(a) Machine Language

Although computers can be programmed to understand many different computer languages, there is only one language understood by the computer without using a translation program. This language is called the *machine language* or the *machine code* of the computer. Machine code is the fundamental language of a computer and is normally written as strings of binary 1s and 0s. The circuit of a computer is wired in such a way that it immediately recognizes the machine language and converts it into the electrical signals needed to run the computer.

An instruction prepared in any machine language has a two-part format, as shown in figure 5.1. The first part is the command or operation, and it tells the computer what function to perform. Every computer has an *operation code* or *opcode* for each of its functions. The second part of the instruction is the operand, and it tells the computer where to find or store the data or other instructions that are to be manipulated. Thus, each instruction tells the control unit of the CPU what to do and the length and location of the data fields that are involved in the operation. Typical operations involve reading, adding, subtracting, writing, and so on.

OPCODE (operation code)	OPERAND (Address/Location)

Fig. 5.13 : Instruction Format

We already know that all computers use binary digits

(0s and 1s) for performing internal operations. Hence, most computers' machine language consists of strings of binary numbers and is the only one the CPU directly understands. When stored inside the computer, the symbols which make up the machine language programme are made up of 1s and 0s. For example, a typical programme instruction to print out a number on the printer might be:

101100111111010011101100

The program to add two numbers in memory and print the result might look something like the following:

001000000000001100111001

001100000000010000100001

011000000000011100101110

101000111111011100101110

000000000000000000000000

This is obviously not a very easy language to learn, partly because it is difficult to read and understand and partly because it is written in a number system with which we are not familiar. But it will be surprising to note that some of the first programmers, who worked with the first few computers, actually wrote their programmes in binary from as above.

Since human programmers are more familiar with the decimial number system, most of them preferred to write the computer instructions in decimal, and leave the input device to convert these to binary. In fact, without too much effort, a computer can be wired so that instead of using long strings of 1s and 0s we can use the more familiar decimal numbers. With this change, the preceding programme appears as follows:

10001471

14002041

30003456

50773456

00000000

The set of instruction codes, whether in binary or decimal, which can be directly understood by the CPU of a computer without the help of translating program, is called a machine code or machine language. Thus, a machine language program need not necessarily be coded as strings of binary digits (1s and 0s). It can also be written using decimal digits if the circuit of the computer being used permits this.

Advantages and Limitations of Machine Language: Programmes written in machine language can be executed very fast by the computer. This is mainly because machine instructions are directly understood by the CPU and no translation of the programme is required. However, writing a programme in machine language has several disadv-antages which are discussed below.

1. Machine dependent: Because the internal design of every type of computer is different from every other type of computer and needs different electrical signals to operate, the machine language also is different from computer to computer. It is determined by the actual design or construction of the ALU, the control unit, and the size as well as the word length of the memory unit. Hence, suppose after becoming proficient in the machine code of a particular computer, a company decides to change to another computer, the programmer may be required to learn a new machine language and would have to rewrite all the existing programs.

2. Difficult to programme: Although easily used by the computer, machine language is difficult to program. It is necessary for the programmer either to memorize the dozens of code numbers for the commands in the machine's instruction set or to constantly refer to a reference card. A programmer is also forced to keep track of the storage location of data and instructions. Moreover, a machine language programmer must be an expert who knows about the hardware structure of the computer.

3. Error prone: For writing programmes in machine language, since a programmer has to remember the opcodes and he must also keep track of the storage location of data and instructions, it becomes very difficult for him to concentrate fully on the logic of the problem. This frequently results in program errors. Hence, it is easy to make errors while using machine code.

4. Difficult to modify: It is difficult to correct or modify machine language programmes. Checking machine instructions to locate errors is about as tedious as writing them initially. Similarly, modifying a machine language programme at a later date is so difficult that many programmers would prefer to code the new logic afresh instead of incorporating the necessary modifications in the old programme.

In short, writing a programme in machine language is so difficult and time consuming that it is rarely used today.

(b) Assembly Language

One of the first steps in improving the programme preparation process was to substitute letter symbols mnemonics for the numeric operation codes of machine language. A *mnemonic* (or memory aid) is any kind of mental trick we use to help us remember. Mnemonics come in various shapes and sizes, all of them useful in their own way. For example, a computer may be designed to interpret the machine code of 1111 (binary) or 15 (decimal) as the operation 'subtract', but it is easier for a human being to remember it as SUB.

Use of Symbols Instead of Numeric OpCodes

All computers have the power of handling letters as well as numbers. Hence, a computer can be taught to recognise certain combination of letters or numbers. It can be taught (by means of a programme) to add the number 14 every time it sees the symbol ADD, subtract the number 15 every time it sees the symbol SUB, and so forth. In this way, the computer can be trained to translate a program written with symbols instead of numbers into the computer's own machine language. Then we can write program for the computer using symbols instead of numbers, and have the computer do its own translating. This makes it easier for the programmer, because he can use letters, symbols and mnemonics instead of numbers for writing his programmes. For examples, the preceding programme that was written in machine language for adding two numbers and printing out the result could be written in the following way:

```
CLA     A
ADD     B
STA     C
TYP     C
HLT
```

Which would mean "take A, add B, store the result in C, type C, and halt". The computer, by means of a translating programme, would translate each line of this programme into the corresponding machine language programme.

(c) High Level Language

High-level languages are basically symbolic languages that use English words and/or mathematical symbols rather than mnemonic codes. In other words, a high-level language is a symbolic language with nothing but macro instructions. Every instruction which the programmer writes in a high-level language is translated into many machine language instructions. This is one-to-many translation and not one-to-one as in the case of assembly language. It is due to this reason that high-level languages are so called.

High level languages are also known as *problem oriented languages* because the macro instructions are especially picked to be useful for solving particular types of problems. Each such language is then best to solve a particular class of problems and may be completely useless for solving other types of problems. For example, if a high-level language is capable of handling business-type applications that consist of high input volume, relatively little processing, and a high output volume, then the language is a *business-oriented language*. On the other hand, languages excellent at performing sophisticated computations but not adept at handling large data files are *mathematically-oriented languages*. Thus, a problem-oriented language is designed in such a way that its instructions may be written more like the language of the problem. For example, a scientist using a science-oriented language can use scientific formulas, and a business man with a business-oriented language can use business terms. Hence, high-level languages are generally easier to learn and write.

Some High-Level Languages

The credit for the development of the first high-level language is usually given to Dr. Grace Hopper who described the idea of a compiler and its language as early as 1952. Two languages were developed under Dr. Hopper's directions: FLOWMATIC was a commercial and business language which could easily be put together from the contents of a flowchart, whereas MATHEMATIC was a mathematical language. These two languages were an early example of the development of high-level languages in different directions- business and commercial, and science and mathematics. Since then, many other high-level languages have been produced. Today there are over 200 high-level languages. However, most of these are for very special purposes or are designed to solve problems in a very specific applications area. Some of the most common high-level languages have been briefly described below. The primary objective is to provide some insight into these languages rather than to provide detailed knowledge required to write programs.

(i) FORTRAN

One of the oldest and the most popular high-level language is **FORTRAN** which stands for ***FOR*mula *TRAN*slation.** Originally developed by **IBM** (International Business Machine Corporation) for its 704 computer in 1957, **FORTRAN** has undergone several revisions so that the language has been evolving into a wider and more useful language with time. The original **FORTRAN** was soon followed by **FORTRAN II**. The next popular and advanced version was **FORTRAN IV**. In order to allow a program that was written for one computer system to be run on another computer system, this version was standardized by the American National Standards Institute **(ANSI)** in the year 1966. **FORTRAN** thus has the distinction of being the first standardized language. In 1977 an updated version of **FORTRAN IV,** known as **FORTRAN 77,** was announced and standardized by ANSI. It contains several additional features which are not a part of **FORTRAN IV,** e.g. character and file handling, constructs related to a more structural approach to programming.

FORTRAN was designed to solve scientific and engineering problems and is currently the most popular language among scientists and engineers. The language is oriented towards solving problems of mathematical nature and has been designed as an algebra-based programming language. Any formula, or those mathematical relationship that can be expressed algebrically can easily be expressed as a **FORTRAN** instruction, e.g. A = B + C - D. To illustrate the nature of **FORTRAN** programs, a simple **FORTRAN**

program to compute and print the sum of 10 numbers is given below.

```
C       FORTRAN PROGRAMME TO COMPUTE
C       THE SUM OF 10 NUMBERS
        SUM = 0
        DO 50 I = 1, 10
        READ (5, 10) N
10      FORMAT (F6 . 2)
        SUM = SUM + N
50      CONTINUE
        WRITE (6, 20) SUM
20      FORMAT (1X, 'THE SUM OF GIVEN
        NUMBERS =', F10 . 2)
        STOP
        END
```

From the above example you can see that a **FORTRAN** program consists of a series of statements. These statements supply input/output, calculation, logic/comparison, and other basic instructions to the computer. The words READ, WRITE, DO and STOP in the statements mean exactly what you would expect. A **FORTRAN** programme requires that certain parts of every statement be placed in certain columns. Statements numbers, which are optional in **FORTRAN**, are placed in columns 1-5 (10, 50 and 20 in this example). A comment statement starts with a C in the first column (the first statement of this example). Comment statements are used in programmes for the purpose of documentation or explanation, designed to assist anyone reading the source programme listing. Comments do not form a part of the program logic and are ignored by the computer. The actual **FORTRAN** statement is placed in columns 7-72.

A character in column 6 means that the statement in the previous line is being continued in this line. Columns 73-80 are ignored by the computers. The programmer may use these columns for any purpose, such as numbering each statement or writing a programme code name.

In the example above, the value of SUM is first initialized to 0. The next statement tells the computer to do a loop that starts at the DO statement and ends in line having label 50, which is a CONTINUE statement. Inside the loop, values of N are read and added to SUM one by one. After the computer loops 10 times, reading and accumulating the sum of 10 numbers, the computer goes out of the loop and drops down to the next statement. This is the WRITE statement which prints the message: 'THE SUM OF GIVEN NUMBERS =' followed by the computed value of SUM. The next statement, which is a STOP statement tells the computer to stop the execution of the programme. Finally, the END statement tells the computer that there are no more instructions or statements in the programme. The data for this programme is contained in a separate file and is not shown in the program.

(ii) COBOL

COBOL is an *acronym* for Common Business Oriented Language. As its name implies, this languge was designed specifically for business data processing and today it is the most widely used business-orinted programming languages. Unlike **FORTRAN**, which gradually developed into a full-fledged language, the vocabulary and grammar of **COBOL** were worked out in 1959-1960 by a committee of the Conference on Data Systems Languages **(CODASYL)** as a joint effort of computer users, manufacturers, and the United States government. After the vocabulary and grammar were defined by this committee, the various manufacturers wrote the compilers for their computers. Since 1960, the language has been revised, but revisions by manufacturers have been rare, because other **CODASYL** committees have continued to maintain, revise, and extend the initial specifications. An **ANSI COBOL** standard was first published in 1968, and a later version was approved in 1974. As long as these standards are followed, a **COBOL** programme can be run on any computer system with an **ANSI COBOL** compiler.

COBOL was designed to have the appearance and structure of a business report written in English. Thus, a **COBOL** programme is constructed from sentences, paragraphs, sections, and divisions. All **COBOL** programmes must have four divisions, namely, the identification division, the environment division, the data division, and the procedure divison. The nature of **COBOL** programme is illustrated below with the help of a simple **COBOL** programme to compute and print the sum of given numbers.

```
IDENTIFICATION DIVISION.
PROGRAMME-ID. SUM UP.
AUTHOR. B. K SHARMA.
* THIS PROGRAMME COMPUTES AND PRINTS
* THE SUM OF GIVEN NUMBERS.
ENVIRONMENT DIVISION.
CONFIGURATION SECTION.
SOURCE-COMPUTER. BURROUGHS-6700.
OBJECT-COMPUTER. BURROUGHS-6700.
INPUT-OUTPUT SECTION.
FILE-CONTROL.
        SELECT DATA-FILE ASSIGN TO DISK
        SELECTOUTPUT - FILE ASSIGN TO
        PRINTER.
DATA DIVISION
```

```
FILE SECTION
FD DATA-FILE
        RECORD CONTAINS 80 CHARACTERS
        LABEL RECORD IS OMITTTED
        DATA RECORD IS INPUT-DATA RECORD
01      INPUT-DATA-RECORD
        05 N PICTURE 9 (6) V99.
        05 FILLER PICTURE X (72).
FD      OUTPUT-FILE
        RECORD CONTAINS 132 CHARACTERS
        LABEL RECORD IS OMITTED>
        DATA RECORD IS OUTPUT-RECORD
01      OUTPUT-RECORD.
        05 FILLER PICTURE X.
        05 TITLE PICTURE X(25).
        05 SUM PICTURE 9(10)V99.
        05 FILLER PICTURE X(94).
WORKING-STORAGE SECTION.
77      MESSAGE PICTURE X(25) VALUES IS
          "THE SUM OF GIVEN NUMBERS =".
PROCEDURE DIVISION
OPEN-FILES.
        OPEN INPUT DATA FILE.
        OPEN OUTPUT OUTPUT-FILE.
INITIALIZATION.
        MOVE SPACES TO OUTPUT-RECORD.
        MOVE ZERO TO SUM.
PROCESS-LOOP.
        READ DATA-FILE AT END GO TO
```

```
        PRINT-PARA.
        ADD N TO SUM.
        GO TO PROCESS-LOOP.
    PRINT-PARA.
        MOVE MESSAGE TO TITLE.
        WRITE OUTPUT RECORD.
    END-OF-JOB.
        CLOSE DATA-FILE.
        CLOSE OUTPUT-FILE.
        STOP RUN.
```

It can be easily seen from this example that **COBOL** is a self-documenting language. Self-documenting languages are those that do not require much explanation in order to be understood by some one reading the program instructions.

The self-documenting aspect of **COBOL** is made possible by its English like sentence and paragraph structure and the very generous maximum symbolic field name length of 30 characters. With a field-name length of up to 30 characters, the name can clearly identify the field and its purpose. **COBOL** programmers should ensure that the field name that are used are meaningful, so that the self-documenting features of the languge are not lost.

Like **FORTRAN**, most **COBOL** compilers require that certain parts of every statement be placed in certain columns. There are 80 columns in a line out of which columns 1-3 are used for page number and columns 4-6 identify line numbers. The use of sequence numbers is optional and can be omitted. And asterisk (*) in column 7 indicates a comment line and the entry is not compiled to produce object code. Comment lines are actually some notes revealing the intentions of the programmer and are used for programme documentation. The actual **COBOL** statements are placed in columns 8-72.

Notice that there are two margins: A and B. The A margin that starts at column 8 is used to start a new division, section, or paragraph. The B margin that starts at column 12 is used to start any sentence. Finally, columns 73-80, which the computer ignores, can be used to write some identification.

(iii) BASIC

BASIC (Beginners All-purpose Symbolic Instruction Code) was developed by Professors John Kemeny and Thomas Kurtz in the year 1964 at Darmouth College in the United States. Their purpose was to develop a language which would be very easy to learn and thus, can be used by the undergraduate students in all fields of study. The language has few grammatical rules and can be learnt in a few hours of concentrated study. In order to understand and write program in **BASIC**, it is not necessary to learn complex programming techniques. A person with little or no knowledge of computers or programming can learn to write **BASIC** programmes in a short period of time. Because of its simplicity and bias towards the user, **BASIC** is ever being used by school students. It is a language well suited for use in education and has become extremely popular with micro-computer users.

Unlike **FORTRAN** or **COBOL**, **BASIC** is an interpreter based language. Instead of compilers, interpreters are generally used in micro-computer systems to translate **BASIC** instructions into machine-language code. Thus, as a **BASIC** programme is being entered, its statements are checked for syntax errors which can be immediately corrected. This feature of **BASIC** makes it one of the most popular computer languages used in micro-computer systems. It is available in almost all micro-computers and even in some pocket calculators. Though simple and easy to learn, **BASIC** is quite flexible and reasonably powerful. It can be used for both business and scientific applications. Probably the greatest drawback of this language is that it has not yet been standardized. The language varies significantly from one computer system to another. Thus, a **BASIC** programme written on one computer may not work on another unless modified.

A **BASIC** programme to compute and print the sum of 10 numbers is given below:

```
5     REM PROGRAM TO COMPUTE
6     REM THE SUM OF 10 NUMBERS
10    LET S = 0
20    FOR I = 1 TO 10
30    READ N
40    LET S = S + N
50    NEXT I
60    PRINT "THE SUM OF GIVEN
      NUMBERS ="; S
70    DATA 4, 20, 15, 32, 48
80    DATA 12, 3, 9, 14, 44
90    END
```

It can be observed from this example that a **BASIC** programme is made up of a series of statements. Each statement starts with a statement number and a key word, followed in most cases by some type of action. For example, in the statement, "40 LET S = S + N", 40 is the statement number, LET is the key word, and S = S + N is the action. The first statement of the programme which is a REM statement is a remark being made for the purpose of explaning or documenting a programme stop. It has no effect on the programme logic. The instruction must have a line number, the key word REM, and any remark that the programmer wishes to make. In our example, the remark statement was used to name the programme. The two DATA statements in the program are used to furnish the input data.

The FOR and NEXT statements control the loop that is meant for adding the 10 numbers one by one. The END statement stops the programme execution.

(iv) PASCAL

Named after the famous French mathematicisn Blaise Pascal, this language was first introduced in the year 1971 by Professor Niklaus Wirth of the Federal Institute of Technology in Zurich, Switzerland. His aim was to develop a languge after the concepts associated with structured programming. Thus, **PASCAL** was the first language to fully embody in an organised way the concepts of structured programming. The language is relatively easy to learn, and it allows the programmer to structure the programming problem. This means that the programme must be written in logical modules which are in turn called by a main controlling module. In other words, **PASCAL** is designed to force us to look at a problem in a logical way and to lay out a solution before we begin writing the programme. It is based on the theory that the use of too many GO TO statements in programme makes the program clumsy and unstructured. The logic of such programmes becomes complex and these programmes are difficult to understand and maintain because they lack any recognizable structure or flow of control. Hence, as a good programming practice, a programmer should avoid the use of GO TO statements in his programme as far as practicable. The features of **PASCAL** help us in overcoming this problem. The language is designed in such a way that complete **PASCAL** programmes can be written without the use of GO TO statements. The process of looping or repeating a sequence is handled automatically by special loop control statements. **PASCAL** is thus widely recognised as a language that instills good programming habits in a programmer. Owing to this reason, this language is also extensively used to teach programming to beginners. The features of **PASCAL** allow it to be used for both scientific and business applications. Hence, it is a very powerful language and has been implemented on several different computers including mini-computers and micro-computers. A **PASCAL** version of a summing programme similar to those presented earlier in other languages is shown below.

```
PROGRAMME SUMNUMS (INPUT, OUTPUT);
(* PROGRAMME TO COMPUTE THE SUM OF 10
NUMBERS *)
(* DECLARATION OF VARIABLES *)
VAR SUM, N : REAL;
VAR I : INTEGER;
BEGIN
SUM : = 0
FOR I : = 1 TO 10 DO

BEGIN
        READ (N);
        SUM : = SUM + N;
END;
WRITELN (THE SUM OF GIVEN NUMBERS =;
        SUM);
END.
```

The first line of the programme contains the name of the programme which is SUMNUMS. This is followed by two comment lines which are used for documentation purpose. Any comment can be placed within the symbols (* and *) to document a **PASCAL** programme. Then, all the variables are declared. The variables SUM and N are declared as real and hence they can be assigned any real number.

Similarly, the variable I, that has been declared to be an integer variable, can be assigned any integer value. The heart of the programme starts with the word BEGIN and ends with the word END. First, the variable SUM is initialied to zero. The next statement starts a DO loop that reads and computes the sum of the 10 numbers. Finally, the statement having WRITTEN prints the result of the programme. It may be observed that **PASCAL** programmes are composed of blocks starting with BEGIN and terming of the programme and programme statements proceed in a logical flow from start to finish.

(v) **PL/I**

PL/I stands for programming language One. It was designed in the mid-1960s by IBM as a general purpose language having features similar to **COBOL** for business applications and features similar to **FORTRAN** for scientific applications in addition to other features such as string manipulation and list processing. The intention was to create a universal language which would be adequate for programming any kind of application. A PL/I standard was produced by an **ANSI** committee in the year 1976. A subset of this fully standard, known as PL/I-G is also available for use with small computers.

Although PL/I is one of the most versatile and the most powerful of the programming languages, it is not the most commonly used. The main reason behind this is that since PL/I has features found in both **FORTRAN** and **COBOL**, it is a sophisticated language. It is enormous by any standard and is not easy to learn in its totality. Furthermore, the complexity of the language makes a compiler and support packages for the full language quite large. Because of its size and heritage, the language so far has been available primarily on IBM equipment and is not very widely used or accepted.

A PL/I programme for the summing problem is given below to illustrate the nature of the language.

```
SUMMUMS : PROCEDURE OPTIONS (MAIN);
/* PROGRAM TO COMPUTE THE SUM OF 10
NUMBERS */
DECLARE (SUM, N) FIXED ;
DECLARE I FIXED;
SUM = 0;
DO I = 1 TO 10;
        GET (N);
        SUM = SUM + N;
END;
PUT EDIT (THE SUM OF GIVEN NUMBERS =', SUM)
(A, F5);
END;
```

It can be seen from this example, that the basic element of a PL/I programme is a statement. Each statement is termited by a semicolon (;) and several statements may be comined to form a procedure. A procedure may represent an entire small programme (as in this example) or a block or module of a more complex programme. Because of its modular structure, a beginner needs to learn only a small part of the language in order to write programs for a particular type of application. Moreover, modular proceduce blocks and other features of the language allow the use of the various concepts of structured programming.

OTHER HIGH-LEVEL LANGUAGES

The high-level programming languages that were discussed above are not necessarily the most important or most popular languages. These languages were presented in some detail to give you a better understanding of computer programming and nature of high-level languages in general. There are several other programming languages which are equally important and popular. Some of these languages are briefly discussed in this section.

(i) RPG: Report Programme Generator **(RPG)** is a business-oriented, general purpose programming language. As the name implies, the language is designed to generate the output reports resulting from the processing of common business applications. The language was developed by **IBM** as a result of their customer requests for an easy and economic mechanism for producing reports and was launched in the year 1961 for use on the **IBM** 1401 computer. The lattter version of **RPG**, called **RPG II**, greatly improved the language and gave it additional capabilities.

RPG is considerably different from other programing language. Instead of writing instructions or statements, the programmer uses very detailed coding sheets to write his specifications about input, calculations, and output. These sheets specify exactly what is to be done, and then the computer uses them to generate the necessary instructions to perform the desired aplication. Thus, **RPG** is easier to learn and use as compared to **COBOL**. Moreover, **RPG** can duplicate any **COBOL** programme. Owing to these reasons, **RPG** is commonly used on many small computers and in small businesses. It is well suited for applications where large files are read, few calculations are performed, and output reports are created. However, **RPG** has restricted mathematical capability and cannot be used for scientific applications.

(ii) ALGOL: Like **FORTRAN**, **ALGOL** (*ALGO*rit-hmic *L*anguage) is also one of the earliest and the most influential high-level languages that were designed for scientific applications. It was designed by an international group of mathematicians, and developed by groups in

Europe and the United States. The language was first introduced in 1958, resulting in **ALGOL58**. Later on, it was revised in 1960 and this revised version, known as **ALGOL60**, was the most widely used version of the language. The most recent, and the most powerful, version is **ALGOL68**. Like **PASCAL** and PL/I, **ALGOL** is a block-structured or modular language that is well suited for use in a structured programming setting. One area in which **ALGOL**, as originally defined, is quite deficient is that of input/output. The language was primarily designed as a way of expressing algorithms, and I/O statements were not made a part of the official language. **ALGOL** has not proven to be as popular in the United States as in Europe for practical work, although it is widely used in universities, especially in computer science departments because of its elogance and power. The lack of I/O facilities, plus the fact that the largest computer manufacturer, IBM, did not favour **ALGOL** early in its existence, has contributed to its lack of widespread usage.

(iii) APL: APL (A Programming Language) was developed by Kenneth in 1962. It is a very powerful programming language that is well suited for specifying complex algorithms. Much of its power is vested in the rich set of mathematical operators available, enabling easy manipulation of matrices and arrays of highest rank. This language is a real-time language developed primarily for scientific applications. It is usually used in an interpretive and interactive manner an environment which greatly enhances its power. Since APL uses a rather large and unusual character set, a special keyboard and terminal is necessary for its implementation. Until recently, only certain IBM equipment supported APL. However, the advent of low cost terminals capable of handling many different type of fonts and the growing number of APL users have brought it into wider, but still limited, usage.

(iv) ADA: ADA is a new general purpose programming language. it was developed in the year 1980 at the request of the U.S. Department of Defence (DOD) for use in military applications. The language was developed at Honewell Computer Company by a group of scientists headed by Ichbah. It is named in honour of Lord Byron's daughter Ada Augustha Lovelace. Ada was a close friend of Charles Babbage, who had made significant contributions in some of the earlier developments of computer systems. Ada used to work with Babbage. She is considered by many to be the first "programmer" because she wrote the first computer programme for the mechanical computer (Analytical Engine) developed by Charles Babbage.

ADA is an extremely complicated language with large number of features. In addition to the normal types of statements and commands, ADA also allows the use of package. ADA package allows for a collection of related computational procedure and resources. Packages are specified or written into the declarative part of the programme, which is typically at the top of an ADA programme. Then various procedural statements in the programme can access the package and use it. Another important feature of ADA is the use of tasks. Tasks are used to allow concurrent programming which is very useful for military applications. Like packages, tasks have a specification part. Once specified, tasks can be used within the body of the program as and when needed. It is expected that most future programmes written for the Department of Defense, U.S.A. will have to be in this language. As a result, this new language may become very popular in the field of defense.

(v) LISP: LISP stands for List Processing. This language was designed by McCarthy and is suitable for non-numeric applications. It is a powerful language for handling logical operations. Because of this feature, the language is extensively used in the areas of pattern recognition, artificial intelligence, and for simulation of game.

(vi) SNOBOL : SNOBOL (StriNg Oriented SymBOlic Language) is another language used for non-numeric applications. As the name implies, the language was basically designed to manipulate strings of characters. SNOBOL has powerful string manipulation features that facilitate various types of operations on strings of characters such as string comparison, splitting of a string, combining two strings, etc. Thus, this language has been widely accepted for applications in the area of text processing.

(vii) C: C is a relatively, new language which is becoming very popular day-by-day. It was designed at Beel Telephone Laboratories, U.S.A. Like **PASCAL** and **ALGOL**, C is a block structured language and has several features that allow the use of the various concepts of structured programming. Moreover, a special features of this language, that is normally absent in other high-level languages, is that it allows the manipulation of internal processor registers of the computer. Thus, the language also enjoys the advantage of having some of the powers of assembly language. Because of this feature, C language is now being extensively used for systems programming like design of compilers and operating systems. Most computer vendors of today, supply this language alongwith their computer systems.

(viii) PROLOG : PROLOG stands for PROgramming in **LOG**ic. It is a very new programming language designed for handling complex logical operations. The language is being used to design intelligent computer systems and is expected to gain popularity in the near future.

CHARACTERISTICS OF A GOOD LANGUAGE

In the previous section, we have seen that there are some high-level languages which are very popular and there are others which are used only by a small group of programmers. Why do programmers prefer one language over another ? One obvious reason is the area of application. However, another equally important reason is the characteristics of the language. Several properties believed to be important with respect to making a language good and usable by human beings are briefly outlined below.

1. Simplicity: Programming languages that are simple

and easy to learn and use are liked by many programmers. For examples, **BASIC** is used by many programmers only because of its simplicity. Thus, a language should provide a programmer with a clear, simple, and unified set of concepts which can be easily grasped. There should be a minimum number of different concepts, with the rules for their combination being as simple and regular as possible. However, the power needed for the language should not be sacrificed for simplicity.

2. Naturalness: A language should be natural for the application area it has been designed. In other words, it should be problem-oriented. It should provide appropriate operators, data structures, control structures, and a natural syntax in order to facilitate the users to code their problem easily and efficiently. Often if a major amount of programming in a particular area is required, it is extremely useful to develop a programming language just for that class of applications. **FORTRAN** and **COBOL** are good examples of scientific and business languages respectively that possess high degree of naturalness.

3. Efficiency: Efficiency is certainly a major element in the evaluation of any programming language. Thus, while designing a compiler or an interpreter for a particular language, system programmers must give due consideration to space and time efficiency. A programming language should be such that its programs are efficiently translated into machine code, are efficiently translated into machine code, are efficiently executed, and acquire as little space in the memory as possible.

4. Structuredness: Structuredness means that the language should have necessary features to allow its users to write their programmes based on the concepts of structured programming. The main reason behind this is that, this property of a language greatly affects the ease with which a programme may be written, tested, and maintained. Moreover, it forces a programmer to look at his problem in a logical way and hence reducing his errors while writing a programme for his problem. **PASCAL**, PL/I, and **ALGOL** are some of the language having this property.

5. Compactness: Users of a high-level, problem-oriented language should be able to express intended operations cocncisely, since this is one of the fundamental reasons for having it. A verbose language can tax the programmer's sheer writing stamina and thus, reduce its usefulness. COBOL is generally not liked by many programmers because it is verbose in nature and lacks compactness.

6. Locality: A programming language should be such that while writing a programme a programmer need not jump around visually as the text of the program is prepared. **COBOL** lacks locality because data definitions are separated from processing statements, perhaps by many pages of code. On the other hand, APL is very local since it requires no declarations, thus permitting the programmer to concentrate almost solely on the part of the programme around the statement currently being worked with.

7. Extensibility: A good programming language should also allow extension through simple, natural and elegant mechanisms. Almost all languages provide subprogramme definition mechanisms for this purpose, but there are some languages that are rather weak in this aspect.

8. Suitability to Environment: Depending upon the type of application for which a programming language has been designed, the language must also be made suitable to its environment. For example, a language designed for real time applications must be interactive in nature. On the other hand, languages used for data processing jobs like pay-roll, stores accounting, etc., may be designed to be operative in batch mode. A language designed for interaction, say APL, is not as usable in batch mode. Likewise, a language designed for batch usage may prove quite frustrating if used interactively from a terminal.

5.14. INFORMATION STORAGE AND RETRIEVAL SOFTWARES

IBM (International Business Machines Corporation) was one of the earliest to invest money to develop software packages intended for Information Storage and retrieval.

The well known package STAIRS (an acronym for Storage and Information Retrieval System) was developed to be used on IBM machines, that too mainframe series. STAIRS was a machine dependent program which was commercially made available for any one who could afford its cost. This package has been used by some organisations to manage bibliographic databases. It was a powerful text-retrieval system which enabled string searching from any part of the record. Following the introduction of STAIRS, similar programmes soon became available on mainframes as well as mini-computers. Packages like ISIS, MINISIS came into existence. But most of these packages were hardware dependent and, therefore, could not be used on a wider scale due to lack of portability. Hence, need was felt to develop software packages which could be used for library and information storage and retrieval operations on a wider range of computers, especially micro-computer systems. Several attempts were made in this direction by commercial firms and international organisations like UNESCO, resulting in the proliferation of a number of micro-computer oriented software packages. Many of such packages are being commercially marketed, while a few packages like CDS/ISIS are supplied almost free of cost to educational and non-profit making institutions, particularly in India. Today, there are a number of micro-computer oriented software packages intended for automating library routines and information retrieval operations.

Some of the significant software packages are discussed below :

(1) CDS/ISIS Software (Micro Version): Micro CDS/ ISIS is an advanced non-numerical inforamtion storage and retrieval software package. It was developed by UNESCO in 1985 to meet the requirements of many institutions, specially in developing countries. It is meant to facilitate streamlining of the information processing activities in developing countries with the help of relatively inexpensive modern technologies. This software was originally based on the mainframe version of CDS/ISIS started in the late '60s.

Main Features

The main features of CDS/ISIS software are as follows:

(i) The handling of variable length records, fields and sub-fields, thus saving disk space and making it possible to store greater amounts of bibliographic information.

(ii) It comprises a database definition component which allows the user to define the data to be processed for a specific application.

(iii) It has a data entry component which facilitates entering and modifying data through user-created database specific worksheets.

(iv) Possesses an information retrieval component with a powerful search language providing for field level and proximity search operators, in addition to Boolean search techniques along with facilities for free-text searching.

(v) It has a powerful report generator facility allowing the user to create desired printed products such as catalogues, indexes, etc., according to required formats of the users.

(vi) It has a data interchange facility based on the ISO 2709, which is used as standard format by leading database producers.

(vii) It has an integrated application programming language (CDS/ISIS Pascal) which allows the user to tailor the software to specific needs.

(viii) It functions helping the user to build pseudo-relational databases.

(ix) The package also contains an interface between the micro

CDS/ISIS and the IDAMS software for statistical analysis.

Since the beginning CDS/ISIS has been created as a multi-lingual software, providing integrated facilities for the development of different linguistic versions. UNESCO supplies the package in English, French and Spanish versions.

Historic Background

UNESCO developed version 1.0 of the software package in 1985. It was designed to run on IBM PC/XT with 256 MB RAM and hard disk capacity. Six different programmes were required to execute the various functions. Version 1.0 was limited to databases containing 32,000 records.

In the year 1989, version 2.0 of CDS/ISIS was developed by UNESCO with integration of all programmes into one and the additional advantage of extending the capacity of the database to 16,000,000 records. The special feature of this version is the introduction of the CDS/ISIS Pascal programming language interface. The CD-ROM version of the CDS/ISIS also came out in 1989.

In 1993, version 3.0 which supports Local Area Network (**LAN**) was developed. Also, in 1993 the development of **UNIX** version of CDS/ISIS became available.

In 1997, version 1.0 of CDS/ISIS for Windows was developed.

It may be stated that at present UNESCO maintains three fully compatible versions of the software for different hardware/software platforms, which have been developed by UNESCO in response to user needs and/or to the technological developments which have taken place during recent years.

The three versions are:

1. the **MS-DOS** version, which supports the local area networks as version 3.0,
2. the **UNIX** version, initially developed to provide multi-user remote access especially through the Internet and,

3. the Windows version.

Hardware and Software Requirements

The present versions of CDS/ISIS require the following minimum hardware and software:

(i) MS-DOS Version: An IBM PC or compatible micro-computer with a minimum of 640 K RAM, 2 MB hard disk and a 3 and a 1/2 inch high density (HD) diskette unit.

(ii) UNIX Version: An Intel 386/486 processor, a 31/2 HD dxiskette unit, UNIX operating System V, release 3 or higher (or SCO), VT 100 or compatible terminals and peripherals like printer,

(iii) Windows Version: An Intel Pentium processor, at 16 MB RAM, 10 MB hard disk space and a 3 and a 1/2 inch HD diskette unit, Windows 3X or Windows 95 operating system.

As a result of a strategic development policy enunciated by UNESCO, it was decided to completely rewrite the CDS/ISIS software in C++ in order to provide a common standardised language for all its versions. This effort resulted in reducing maintenance costs of different versions of CDS/ISIS. Also, this helps in the adoption of a multi-platform software development system in order to increase the level of portability to different hardware as well as operating systems. In other words, the present change results in the portability level being increased to cover a range of hardware from stand alone PC's to powerful mini-computers. This obviously leads to the implementation of a Client Server architecture using market standard interfaces.

2. INMAGIC PLUS

INMAGIC Plus is a micro-computer-based software package designed to build, maintain and use textual databases including bibliographic databases. As a generalised text retrieval package with customers such as libraries, etc. INMAGIC Plus offers a great flexibility to the user in setting up and maintaining textual databases. It is an upgraded programme for the older INMAGIC (release 7.2).

It may be mentioned that INMAGIC Plus is not a typical automated library system. It has been designed as a general tool for text management with additional capabilities built into it for a library.

Using INMAGIC, a customer can establish multiple databases using a database design tool to create data structure. The data structure establishes what fields are found in each record within. In addition, the library can control access to the different databases using passwords. The data is stored in a separate file. Records can be imported into the database or they can be manually entered one by one. The software allows a library to build in consistency and validity checking to ensure that a high quality database is created and maintained.

INMAGIC is a screen based system. Screens are designed such that the bottom of every screen presents the *menu options*.

The menu options are: Open database, define, utilities, help and quit.

The user can move to any option by pressing the first letter of the word or by using the arrow keys. Messages on the bottom line reveal what action will result when the highlighted option is selected.

Hardware Requirements: INMAGIC Plus software package requires the following computer configuration:

(i) **Micro:** IBM PC or compatible with a minimum 640 K RAM.

(ii) **Operating System:** PC/MS-DOS 3.0

(iii) **Language:** C, FORTRAN

(iv) **LANs Supported:** Novell and other DOS-based LANs

Data Storage: INMAGIC Plus does not limit the size of a field or record. Records may be repeated. The library can define as to what fields are to be used to create what indexes and how many indexes are necessary for each record. Thus, the library has flexibility to decide how and what data is to be stored.

MARC records can be imported into INMAGIC Plus for libraries. It may however be noted that these records can neither be stored nor can they be outputted. Thus, fixed fields, indicators and sub-field information are not preserved within INMAGIC Plus.

Search Facilities: In INMAGIC Plus, the search screen is simple to use. It has five search options presented to the user. They are subject, data, title, abstract, and names. The cursor is placed immediately to the right of the first prompt. After the search request is entered, the system identifies the number of records found. The user must then request the display of these records on the screen. If in case too many records are retireved, the search can be modified. If no record format is specified by the user, INMAGIC Plus displays the complete record with the different elements labeled.

The search argument is highlighed in the display of the record. The user can specify Boolean AND, OR, and NOT, search terms, but must enter the character for the Boolean AND, OR and NOT, respectively. Truncation and proximity searching are available when a search is entered or later modified. Searches can be modified by datas including a range. Left to right or character by character phrase and key word searching is possible in this system. Also, search results can be stored, saved, and recalled for a later use. A command option is also available in INMAGIC, which allows the user to search without employing prompts. The command syntax used for this purpose is very simple. Using INMAGIC Plus, it is also possible to browse through a list of index entries in case a precise search statement is not known. It also provides a number of pre-defined reports. These include book catalogues, research reports, bibliographies, etc. One of the strengths of INMAGIC Plus is its flexible Report Writer, which allows the user to specify the reports to be created and printed.

Overall Assessment: INMAGIC Plus for libraries is an easy to use generalised text management package. It has additional features provided to make it appealing to libraries. The strength of the package lies in its flexible nature enabling the users of the package to avoid a number of repetitive activities.

The package is provided with an excellent documentation which makes it user friendly. However, some libraries may find it lacking some of the automatic features generally associated with such software packages such as *recalls, reserves,* and other *loan management facilities.* A number of users are using this software package around the world.

3. CAIRS-LMS

This is a different software package, which is commonly used in some of the libraries abroad. The package is known as CAIRS/LMS or CAIRS Library Management System.

CAIRS has been developed by Leatherhead Food Research Association (LFRA), U.K. It differs from other packages in two important aspects. Firstly, CAIRS has been developed by information scientists who continue to depend upon it to run an information service and a series of databases at the Leatherhead Food Research Association. In other words, CAIRS staff brings an understanding of library operations which is not the case with other packages. Secondly, CAIRS staff is committed to developing the software for their wider business, and is very responsive to the suggestions made by their customers to improve the product.

CAIRS may be considered as an ideal package for any information centre or a library looking for a totally integrated solution to its library housekeeping and information retrieval requirements. It provides the advantages of the more conventional relational database for immediate transaction processing. CAIRS includes one of the most powerful indexing and retrieval environments available in any software package. The package also offers solutions to cataloguing requirements where bibliographic abstract and added keyword indexing are used. Readymade modules are available for acquisitions, cataloguing, borrowers, suppliers, issues/returns and renewals. It has facilities for serials holdings and interlibrary loans. CAIRS also provides facilities for user defined catalogue structure.

Standard features in all the modules include command and menu driven modes. The package has expert searching capabilities, full data entry and editing facilities, free text and keyword indexing, interactive error reporting, free format control, current awareness services, SDI bulletin generation, accounting aids and statistical management aspects.

In conclusion, it may be said that CAIRS appears to offer a great deal of flexibility. The package is under constant revision and development and a good relationship between the supplier and the user group exists. All these aspects attract library professionals towards use of CAIRS.

4. TECHLIB Plus

This is yet another comprehensive package based on BASIS Plus, one of the world's leading document DBMS and Text Retrieval Systems. It is designed to streamline and facilitate all day-to-day operations of a fully electronic library.

The package provides facilities for patron access, catalogue maintenance, circulation, serials management, acquisition, processing and MARC cataloguing. One of the most significant features of this package is that image references can be stored directly on the databases created through TECHLIB Plus. In other words, users can access images and information stored in databases developed using BASIS Plus DBMS and Text Retrieval System. The package also provides direct access to information contained in Current Contents. TECHLIB Plus is flexible and is simple to customise. It conforms to your library's unique profile and then maintains that profile in new releases of the software. It is built to accommodate continued growth and diversion both in document collection and computing requirements.

TECHLIB Plus is a proprietary item of Information Dimensions Inc., U.S.A and is marketed in India by the National Informatics Centre, New Delhi. Further information relating to this package can be obtained from NIC.

5. Softlink Library Automation Software Package

This is an international software package which is marketed through a number of agencis. In our country (India), Softlink Library Automation Package is marketed by Softlink Asia Pvt. Ltd., New Delhi.

Recently, the company has taken a decision to call this software with two names OASIS for DOS version of the package and Alice for Windows version all over the world to maintain consistency in nomenclature.

The Softlink Library Automation Package is available to all the customers in four distinct versions. These are:

(i) The public library version
(ii) The special library version
(iii) The academic library version
(iv) The school library version

It is a modular package and has a number of salient features. Some of these are:

(i) It enables a library to purchase only those modules which suit its immediate requirements.
(ii) It facilitates a library to undertake its automation activities in stages.
(iii) The package allows the automated library to expand its services.

(iv) The package has inbuilt capabilities to enable libraries to respond to the changing needs of their clientele.

The modules of the software package have been categorised into standard modules, advanced modules and special modules. For the management of day-to-day functions in any library, it is necessary to have all the standard modules. These modules are:

1. Management, Reports and Utilities.
2. Circulation.
3. Inquiry (OPAC).

On the other hand, the advanced modules facilitate the extension and the usability of the automated library. These modules comprise Acquisitions, Periodicals, Communications, Journal Indexing and Remote Inquiry. Special modules are useful to libraries which have specialised needs. In this manner, there is a certain amount of flexibility and freedom to the libraries to acquire only such modules of the software which are essential and of immediate use to them.

Hardware Requirements: The software operates on any IBM compatible micro-computer using MS or PC-DOS, equipped with 5 MB of RAM and 150 MB hard disk. The software also operates across Local Area Networks (LANs) which support DOS record locking. This includes Novell's NetWare and NetWare Lite and many other platforms. Both OASIS and Alice can also run on Windows NT. Training facilities and after sale support services are provided by the company for those who go in for this software package.

5.15. INDIAN LIBRARY SOFTWARE PACKAGES

In India, the application of computers for library and information centres, though started in 1960s, has geared up only recently, i.e., after the introduction of computers into the market in mid 1980s. In the last two decades, several attempts were made in India at the institutional level for computerisation of library and information services. Most of these efforts were piecemeal and are not backed up by long term planning. However, a number of R & D organisations are now making efforts in this direction.

1. Software Development at Institutional Level: INSDOC (now NISCAIR) takes the credit for being the first institution to experiment with the application of computer in the library sector. From the available literature, we can say that during the first half of 1960s, INSDOC developed a software for the IBM 1620, Model 1 computer to produce a union catalogue of scientific serials. Later, at the fag end of the 1960s, owing to some technical problems, INSDOC had to redesign the entire project relating to the Union Catalogue and execute it on IBM 360, Model 44 available at Delhi University. A software package of 15 programmes has been developed in Fortran IV and PL/I for complete processing of data relating to National Union Catalogue of Scientific Serials (NUCOS). This effort was followed by a series of experiments of INSDOC regarding processing data relating to a Roseter of Indian Translators, a production of author and subject index of Indian Science Abstracts, and for producing similar other information products.

During the same period, Documentation Research and Training Centre (DRTC), Bangalore conducted a series of experiments in Document Finding System (DFS). Under the guidance and supervision of Prof. A. Neelameghan this proejct was accomplished and a set of programmes were developed and implemented on IBM 1401 computer system.

The effort made at Bhabha Atomic Research Centre (BARC), Bombay in developing AFSARI software system in COBOL for the provision of Current Awareness Service and SDI and the effort at Tata Institue of Fundamental Research (TIFR) for developing a software for generating their library catalogue based on annual acquisitions, occupy important positions in the history of library automation in India as early contributions towards the subject.

There have been several attempts at the institutional level to develop software for housekeeping operations in libraries such as acquisitions, serial control, circulation and catalogung. Major libraries like BHEL, Hyderabad; RRC, Kalpakkam; NAL, Bangalore; ICRISAT, Hyderabad; NISCAIR (INSDOC) Delhi , TIFR, Bombay; IDL Chemicals, Hyderabad; IIT, Dehradun and so on, have worked in this direction.

More recently, national and regional organisations like DESIDOC, NISSAT, DELNET have shown interest in assisting the libraries by sharing their expertise by way of involving themselves directly or indirectly in the development of a software and distributing it at an affordable price. SANJAY, MAITRAYEE, DELWINDOWS are the examples of the library software which have the support of DESIDOC, NISSAT and DELNET respectively. The small libraries in particular will greatly be benefited by this gesture, as the software by these organisations is developed by experts in the field and available at relatively low prices.

2. Softwares Available in India: There are a number of Commercial Software Packages available for library automation in India. Each package has its own unique features & limitations. Some of them are:

S. No.	*Name of the Software*	*Software Developer /Marketer/ Vendor*	*Place*
1.	Alice for Windows	Softlink India	New Delhi
2.	CDS/ISIS	NISSAT	New Delhi
3.	DELDOS	Developing Library Network (DELNET)	New Delhi
4.	DELSIS	Developing Library Network (DELNET)	New Delhi
5.	Grandhalaya	NISCAIR	New Delhi
6.	Liberator	CMC Ltd.	Kolkata

7. Librarian	Soft Aid	Pune
8. Librarian Management	Raychan Systematic	Bangalore
9. Librarian Suite	Soft Aid Computers	Pune
10. Library Manager	System data control (P) Ltd.	Mumbai
11. Libris	Frontier Inst. of IT	Hyderbad
12. Libsoft	ET&T	New Delhi
13. Libsys	Libsys Corporation	Gurgaon
14. Maitrayee	CMC Ltd	Kolkata
15. MINISIS	SNDT Women's University	Mumbai
16. Nettlib	Kaptron India (P) Ltd	New Delhi
17. NIRMALS Thiruchitrapalli	Nirmal Inst. of Computer	
18. NLIS	Asmita Consultants	Mumbai
19. Salim	Uptron India Ltd	New Delhi
20. Sanjay	DESIDOC	New Delhi
21. SCIM	Algorythms	Pune
22. SOUL	INFLIBNET	Ahmedabad
23. Suchika	DESIDOC	New Delhi
24. Techlib Plus	National Informatics Center (NIC)	New Delhi
25. Troodon	Comtek Service (P) Ltd.	New Delhi
26. TULIPS	Tata Unisys	Mumbai
27. Wilsys	Wipro India	Bangalore

Software Standards : There are no specific standards and specifications for library software. However the software should follow some technical standard as those of National Information Standards Organization (NISO) of U.S. American National Standard Institute (ANSI), Internationl Standard Organization or International Electrotechnical Committee, etc. Some of the important standards are (1) Information retrieval (Z39.50), (2) Electronic Manuscript Preparation and Markup (ISO 12083), (3) Information Interchange Format (Z39.2 or ISO 2709), (4) CD-ROM file structure (ISO 9660), (5) Common Command Language

(Z39.48), (6) International Standard Serial Numbers (Z39.9) (7) Library Performance Indicator (CD 11620).

Software Selection : There are no common hardware and software which will satisfy all the requirements of the libraries. Libraries have to choose appropriate software depending on their requirement, budget, etc. The software should satisfy atleast 80% of the requirements of the library. The software should allow to migrate from one software to another without any limitations. One has to enquire about the software features from the vendors as well as from their clients. The software has to be acquired on trial basis atleast for a period of three months and then it should be procured on finding satisfactory results.

Criteria for Evaluation

There is no specific procedure for evaluating a library automation software. An attempt has been made to prepare a check list for evaluation of library software by NAARAM. Checklist for Micro Computer Based Library Software (CMBLIS) of Library of Congress, Nicolet Library System's Comprehensive Request For Proposal (RFP) for an Automated Library System Wisconsis, James E. Rush Associate's Weightage for library software may also be used as tools for evaluation of a software.

6
Library Automation : Computerisation of Library House-keeping Operations

6.1. INTRODUCTION

Computer has gained its importance in every field of human activity because of its speed, accuracy and capability of large scale processing. It is space saving device as well because information stored on computer readable devices takes much less space than the conventionally stored systems.

The term "Computerisation" means mechanisation of library activities. The activities like acquisitions, classification, cataloguing, circulation, maintenance, information retrieval, etc., known as House Keeping Operations which are labour intensive can well be operated using computer.

The term 'automation' can be used, for the sake of historical reasons, synonymously with 'mechanization' (i.e., application of machines to carry out an operation/activity). The usage, however, of the term in this sense is not in vogue in the modern library science literature. On the other end of the spectrum, it would be convenient to equate 'automation' with 'computerization'. When a computer is used to support a library operation, that is when a computer performs some of the basic processing tasks in an operation such as acquisitions, circulation or serials control- a computer-based or automated library operation results.

6.2. NEED FOR LIBRARY AUTOMATION

The reasons which favour automation of library activities are: Exponential growth of knowledge and information (information now is largely available in machine-readable forms), emergence of information networks at national and international levels etc., require computerisation for access, greater possibility of online remote database searches, and resources sharing among libraries.

Hence, library automation is very much essential to control the ever increasing knowledge/information; establish links between library/information systems; provide speedy and accurate services as well as save the time of the readers; increase the performance efficiency of the library staff; provide customised services to readers; facilitate electronic browsing and retrieval; avoid duplication of technical processing and help obtain and maintain multiple records/files; eliminate wastage of labour; generate useful and accurate statistics for decision-making, etc.

6.3. STEPS IN LIBRARY AUTOMATION

Automation requires planning, designing and implementing. Planning involves identification of the activities to be automated, assessment of the volume of information to be handled, selection of software, selection of compatible hardware systems, training and retraining of the library staff and educating the users.

Systems designing requires a careful discussion among librarians, programmers/systems experts as to the purchase of computer(s) with suitable configuration including peripherals, software packages put up by vendors/agencies or alternatively developing suitable packages, etc.

Systems implementation is the process of making the newly designed system fully operational. This can be done by any of the three methods, viz., direct, parallel and pilot conversation methods.

In direct conversion, the new system simply replaces the old one on a decided data. The parallel conversion method means running the old and new systems paralle-lly for a specified period. In pilot conversion, only one selected area is tested with the new system. If it works properly the other areas are converted to the new system in a phased manner.

6.4. LIBRARY HOUSE-KEEPING OPERATIONS

A library, will have to perform minimum number of basic operations. There operations are conventionally referred to as "House-Keeping operations". Library activities can be grouped into two broad categories : house keeping operations and information storage and retrieval.

House-keeping operations acquisition, classificaiton, cataloguing, circulation, serial control, stock maintenance and administrative work. Information storage and retrieval services performed by computer are: General Collection information. Current awareness service, S.D.I., database and information transfer services.

6.4.1. Computer Aided Acquisition

Acquisition, is an essential library operation which is critical to the achievement of a library's mission. Acquisition, as you know already, involves a great deal of detailed and exacting paper work; materials handling in large quantities, reconciliation of orders, invoices and materials received; fiscal control and so on. Acquisition, thus, is, highly labour intensive, and therefore, a prime candidate for automation support.

As defined by ***James E. Rush,*** 'Acquisitions' encompasses all aspects of the procurement of all types of library materials whether by gift or exchange, from the request stage through transfer of materials to cataloguing.

Advantages of automaed acquisitions are many. Automation benefits acquisitions through more accurate, timely and complete records of orders, order status, fiscal data, vendors/suppliers directory, and so on. Further, automation support for acquisition eliminates much of the 'forms' preparation and paper handling required in manual system and, thus reducing the presonal time and efforts required to do this work. A most important benefit of computerization of acquisitions work is the powerful, cost-effective monitoring capability it affords to library management.

(i) Objectives of Automated Acquisitions: The purpose of acquisitions is to manage and control the expenditure of funds for materials that meet the collection development criteria of the library and the needs of its clientele. This means that acquisitions process must be accurate, efficient and responsive to the demands of library users.

The main objectives of automated acquisitions system are as follows:

(a) To reduce labour and paper-intensive work involved in manual acquisitions;

(b) To maintain up-to-date information/record of all activities involved in acquisitions;

(c) To have effective and efficient control over ordering, claiming and cancellation functions;

(d) To provide accurate and timely financial information, and

(e) To provide necessary management information reports, whenever they are required.

(ii) Functions of Automated Acquisition System: Acquisition System is concerned with finding book selection sources, searching and selection of books required, placing of orders with a wide range of suppliers, keeping track of orders, receiving the recording of their receipt, settlement of invoices and maintaining detailed accounts of funds.

In a manual acquisition system, one finds that the library has to maintain several paper files and records. Examples of files and records necessary in acquisition are records (usually on cards) of books on order, files of purchase orders, correspondence with vendors, records pertaining to advance payments and follow-up pertaining to non-supplied items, etc. In addition, acquisition involves a number of activities like checking for duplication, generation of purchase orders, filing of on-order records, monitoring of expenditures and preparation of budgets, receiving of books ordered, passing of invoices for books received, accessioning, etc. Some of the tasks involved in the administration and management of the acquisition function are of a routine or clerical nature e.g. filing of cards, typing of purchase orders, passing of bills, etc. Further, the same data is re-entered several times, for e.g., when placing a purchase order the bibliographical details (author, title, etc.) are required to be types on the purchase order, again the same information is required to be typed in a follow-up reminder to the vendor.

These routine works can be easily conducted with the help of computers, relieving the professional staff for qualitatively better work, e.g. better books selection, better budgeting, more interaction with users for better selection of books.

6.4.2. Computerised Cataloguing

One of the major tasks in libraries is cataloguing. In manual cataloguing, say, card catalogue, requires multiple entries (author, title, subject, series, etc.). This means repetitive work.

Automation of cataloguing is one time operation. There is no repetition. There is no need of sorting or alphabetical or other kind of filing. The computer does it if properly programmed. It can also generate printed catalogue cards.

Cataloguing is one of the important functions, which links user's requirements to the documents in a library. Computerized catalogue is the most efficient tool in retrieving information about the documents in library easily and quickly. A good catalogue enables both the users and the library staff to utilize the library collection effectively.

The cataloguing functions require the professional as well as clerical skills on the part of the cataloguer such as typing of headings, sorting of cards and alphabetization, filing etc.

The computer has been used in a variety of ways in cataloguing. The most elementary use of computers for cataloguing is to minimize data-entry of keyboard effort. After all data elements for cataloguing of a given publication are entered, it is possible to use the data to produce a full set of catalogue cards for it. Once the entered data is verified, all cards produced are error-free. It can also help in producing book cards and spine lables.

Computers are also useful in producing book catalogues i.e., catalogue records arranged in the form of a list of entries and bound as books. Computer can, also be utilized for centralized cataloguing e.g., MARC project of the Library of Congress.

(i) OPAC (On-line Public Access Catalogue) : According to Kaske, and Ferguson "OPAC is a catalogue which provided at minimum the bibliographic record content, the retrieval function and access points similar to and understandable in terms of a card catalogue."

According to Library of Congress (LC), "It is an access tool and resource guide to the collection of library or libraries which contain interrelated sets of bibliographic data in machine readable form and which can be searched interactively on terminal by users". This is a tool in library software to provide access to the library's holding through various catalogue and indexes, such as the author catalgue, the title catalogue, the subject catalogue, the classified catalogue, publishers index, conference place index and KWIC/KWOC indexes. Also possible are combination searches using Boolen operators that yield highly satisfying and precise results however complex the query. OPAC also provides the facility to request acquisition of title, to reserve materials and send personalized SDI overdue/recall/collect notices and messages by email.

(ii) WEB OPAC (web Online-access catalogue): This provides an advanced GUI (Graphical User Interface) to enable searching of the library database through an industry standards web browser, such as Netscape Internet Explorer, etc.

6.4.3. Classification

Computers can also be used in classification. As a matter of fact, the DRTC, Bangalore experimented the use of the Colon classification. Dewey Decimal Classification, Library of Congress Classification, etc. are in operation as retrieval languages.

6.4.4. Circulation Control

In libraries, the circulation system conventionally managed consists of charging, discharging, overdue control, reservation, renewal and appropriate records maintenance. These operations are quite amenable to automation. An automated circulation system acts as in interface between the user and the information system with other backup services like acquisition, cataloguing, serial control and house keeping chores. The system can perform such functions as issues/returns; renewals; reservation; notification of delinquent borrowers; calculation of fines, notices and receipts of fines; recall notices; borrowers' information (name, address, telephone number, identification number, etc.); document status information (on issue, in bindery, missing, damage, etc.); circulation statistics; stock verification reports; etc.

The use of technological devices such as computers, barcode scanners and its software in circulation helps in performing these routine operations easily and quickly.

Functions of Circulation Control

Charges/Issues: Charges/Issues is one of the fundamental functions in a circulation control system. For charging an item, the Patron Identification Number (PIN) and Document Identification Number (DIN) are identified to the system (through OCR (Optical Character Recog- nition) or keying in the data or by some other means) which are eventually validated by the system for the correctness. Only if both are through with the validation check, the system records the transaction and allows the patron to borrow the item. The validation should not only check whether the entered code (PIN or DIN) is correct but also see whether the total number of items borrowed is within the borrowing privilege of the patron.

In the interest of efficiency, the system should support for having different patron types with different borrowing periods. Further, it should allow different types of items to be loaned for different loan periods as prescribed by the library. A good system allows multiple books to be borrowed in a single transaction. This will, of course, save the time required for each transaction.

If needed, the system should print due date slip also. The due date calculation should be done by the system taking into account the general and special holidays as applicable to that library.

Discharge/ Return: The discharge function basically involves receiving the item back into the library and updating the patron's record to reflect the returning of the item and producing an acknowledgement for returning the item, if required. As in case of charging, even in discharging the PIN and DIN are identified to the system. The system after suitable validation, updates the concerned records suitably.

An efficient system allows for discharging multiple items in a single transaction, back dating the discharge so as to prevent fines from being accumulated against a patron (this has to be allowed only to the authorised staff), and handling of some exceptional situations.

Renewal: This function allows for the patron to extend the loan period. This function may be thoroughly controlled by the patron type, material type, the reservation status of the book, and other conditions as applicable to a individual library. As many times, renewal has to be done with or without the presence of the patron and/or item, the control has to be exercised by the system automatically.

In case the item to be renewed has a hold (reservation) or recall outstanding, the renewal should be denied, of course depending on the library policy. Again, depending upon the library policy, successive renewals may be restricted.

Holdings/Reservation: This function helps the operator to reserve a document which is on loan. It is usual practice in libraries to maintain the holds queue on first-come first-serve basis. Even in this function, before actually recording the holds, the system has to govern the hold placement by material type, patron type and other conditions as required by the library policy.

Upon the discharge of an item, the system should produce a notice to be sent to the patron at the head of the queue. If the patron does not claim the item within a specified time, the system should automatically send the notice to the next patron in the queue.

If the situation demands, the system should allow authorised persons to modify the holds queue and/or to cancle the holds to any patron. The system should be flexible enough to accommodate the handling of exceptional as and when it may arise.

Recall: It is not an unusual situation in libraries to recall the items borrowed by a patron. Even in this function, the system may allow recall to be governed by patron and material type. Though, normally, an item is recalled if it is overdue and/or is reserved by some patron, there may be other conditions for recall such as that item is required for some purpose in the library, the item has to be sent binding and so on.

Overdue: An item is said to be overdue, if it is not returned to the library on or before the date established at the time of charge or renewal or recall. The sytem should detect the overdue items and produce suitable overdue notices to the patrons. When required, the system should be able to provide listings of overdue items and patrons having overdue items.

Fines/Overdue Charges: In order to ensure the prompt returning of items, it is usual practice in libraries to levy fines against patron for failure to return items by due date. Generally, the fine accrued will be calculated upon the discharges of an overdue item. While calculating fines, it is necessary for the system to consider (as per the library policy) the type of items, the patron class, and other specifications as applicable in individual library. Further, the system should take into account the holiday list during the calculation of fines.

If the library policy allows, the system should allow for partial payment of fines also. An efficient system allows suitably authorsied staff for waiving of the fines and levying of fines for document(s) mutilated by the patron.

6.4.5. Application of Bar Code-Technology

Bar code has found varieties of application in different fields, including libraries and informatin centres. The familiar symbol of general masses due to their appearance in all personal products, book, food and grocery packets, garments, other records, etc; the application of bar code technology in circulation system of a library and information center is most successful due to its speed, accuracy and reliablity. The Kentish Town Branch of CAMDEN Public Library made pioneering efforts for application of this technology in library and information service, in 1972, which used the plessey Light Pen System. Since then, this technology of automatic identification has found acceptance in the libraries and information centers worldwide. Bar code be defined as a self-contained message with information encoded in a series of black bars of varying breadths and white spaces between every two of them. It is a way of representing a series of number of letter. There are many kinds of bar codes, but most of them represent each character by a different combination of wide and narrow bars. Another way to think of a bar code is like a font. Some dark shapes on a light background represent each character. Bar code provides ease of recognition by an optical device. These are read by a scanner, which sends messages to the computer, identifies bars as 0s and 1s (zeros and ones) O and white blanks as 'offs' or ons'. Thus, a barcode is series of 0s and 1s, representing characters as computer can identify digits in such a form only.

Types of bar code symbologies : A code is a combination of character and number that represents an entity. The symbology is the language used to represent the code in a machine-readable form. The set of patterns comprising the total character set for a particular bar code is known as its symbology. In other words, the code represents by a combination of bars and spaces of varying widths are called the bar code symbology.

6.4.6. Serials Control

The term 'Serials' denotes those publications which are issued in successive parts on a recurring basis, usually, but not necessarily, at regularly scheduled intervals and usually having numerical or chronological designation. The term `Serials control' refers to those task which support the procurement and management of serials collection in a library.

Objectives of Automated Serials Control: The major objectives of automated serials control system may be summarised as follows:

(i) To record and maintain accurately and timely the serials holdings data;

(ii) To have effective and efficient control over subscriptions, claiming and cancellations activities;

(iii) To have a good control over binding and related activities;

(iv) To provide accurate and timely financial information;

(v) To provide necessary management information reports, whenever they are required; and

(vi) To reduce labour and time consuming work involved in manual serials control system.

Functions of Automated Serials Control: You know the various functions involved in manual serials control. Though, the basic principles remain the same in automated environment also, special features involved in automated systems are described below. Only common major functions that can be expected of an automated serials control system have been described in the following sections.

Check-in: One of the most important feactures of a serials control system is its check-in capability. Because it is a highly repetitive operation, it must be fast and "friendly" to be useful to the library.

There are two basic methods in which the system can be devised to check-in serials. They are by editing holdings statement and by prompting for expected issues. In the first method, the operator has to input the check-in data into the system every time. While, this method is very flexible, it can be inconvenient and time consuming. In the second method, the system can predict the expected issue. If the predicted issue matches with the one in hand, with minimum number of keystrokes, the issue can be checked-in. This is, of course, a quick method. However, this method is possible only for those serials which have predictable pattern of publication and the expected issue can be predicted based on some frequency cycle. Thus, the system must allow for manual input of issue date also for the journals for which prediction of next expected issue is not possible or is quite unreliable.

If the checked-in issue is not the one expected but is a later one, the system automatically marks the gap. On the other hand, if the checked-in issue is not the expected one but earlier one, the system should be able to find out whether the issue details correspond to missing (gap) or whether it is a duplicate issue. In either case, the system should be able to update suitable file/ records with minimum operator intervention.

A good system supports the check-in of multiple copies of an issue on a single check-in transaction even when these copeis are accommodated in separate copy records. In the interest of efficiency, the system should also support check-in of special issues, combined issues, supplements, "come with" issues and so on. It is helpful if the system provides a link to the full bibliographic record since there will be occassions on which the checker must consult the bibliographic record to resolve some problems like variations in title or other bibliographic data elements.

Claims: The most frequently faced problem in serials management is the non-receipt of the journal issues in time.

In manual system, it is a difficult and time-consuming process to identify the non-receipt of journals for sending claim notices for them. With automation, identification and claiming for such issues becomes facile and accurate and takes much less staff time to accomplish the task.

The system should automatically identify the issues that should be claimed. Some claims may be automatic and may cause the system to trigger claim notice production without or with minimum staff intervention. Other claims will be semi-automatic in the sense that they require staff review prior to claim notice production. Certain situations demand for forced claim i.e., claming for an issue through operator initiation. The system should have facility to handle all the three situations.

The system should be able to automatically identify and produce claim notices for relevant issues on:

(i) Failure to receive a new order within a library in a specified period.

(ii) Failure to receive the next issue with the expected time frame.

(iii) Receipt of an issue later than the expected time frame.

(iv) Receipt of fewer number of copies in case the library is subscribing for multiple copies.

(v) For items that do not have predictable pattern of frequency or enumeration, claims have to be sent for those items for which there has been no check-in activity within a library-specified period.

To be really useful, the system should generate follow-up claims. The criteria for generating such claims may be one suitable to the individual library's practice. Although the system may support issuance of any number of claims, generally a maximum limit is fixed since the probability of receiving the issue after that limit is low.

Binding: This function is particularly important in serials control system. It is a common practice in libraries to bind the completed volumes for archival storages. An automated system shold able in indicate when an item is ready to be sent for binding. The system might support a variety of approaches for determining binding readiness, including:

(i) upon full receipt of a specified number of issues;

(ii) upon receipt of the final issue in a specified level of enumeration hierarchy; and

(iii) at regular intervals specified by the library.

At any point of time, the system should be able to provide on demand the lists of serials that are candidates for binding.

Binding orders should be prepared by the system upon instruction from the authorised staff. The binding orders may contain relevant details like type of binding (material, colour, method, etc.), information to be recorded on bound material, type of lettering (typeface, colour, etc.), the mode of inclusion of index/content pages and so on.

A good system provides the staff the capability of deferring bindery orders when circumstances dictate, and to indicate to the system a time in future when the binding order should be produced for reveiw. The provision of facilities like cancellation of orders, production of claims notice for non-receipt of bound issues as well as non-receipt of invoices, etc., will add to the efficiency of the system.

Upon the receipt of the bound volumes, the system should allow to record the receipt and other details suitably.

Acquisitions: Acquisition, in serial control system, refers primarily to the task involved in making new subscriptions, re-subscriptions, re-subscription renewal and cancellation of subscription. In order to handle the acquisitions work efficiently, the system should maintain in-process file and a vendor file. The in-process file may contain the bibliographic and order data, as well as invoice data if required.

The system should be able to produce automatic subscription renewal alert. Acquisitions through gifts and exchanges should also be supported by the system. The system should provide support for production of orders, claims, cancellation notices and other communications required in this function.

Fund Accounting: Automated systems are particularly valuable in fund accounting and audit trial. A good system maintains correct and current financial records. Obviously, this function must be sufficiently flexible so as to operate within the library policies and changing fiscal management requirements.

One of the main features in this function is that the system should allow to maintain funds under different budget heads as required by the library from time to time. The maintenance of funds encompasses creations of funds, closing of funds or modification of funds by suitably authorised persons.

On payment for the new subscription and renewal of subscriptions, the system should adjust the funds appropriately. It should record the actual price paid, postage, foreign exchange, etc., as appropriate to each serial.

Other features related to accounting function include alerting duplication of accounts, calculation of foreign currencies and handling of exceptional situations.

Maintenance of a full audit trial particularly for financial transaction is essential. The audit trial details should be recorded in such a way that they should identify the person effecting the transaction, the date, the time, nature of transaction carried out, etc.

It is highly useful, if the system provides some support

in the work related to payment of subscription also. The assistance from the system includes maintenance of record of all payments made (by payee), maintenance of cheque register (if the library staff is authorized to write cheques), voucher register, etc. Though very rarely seen in practice, the system may be made to write the cheques also.

Reports: A well designed system provides a variety of reports required for day-to-day, as well as occasional work/ decision making process. The system should provide both statistical as well as management reports.

A good system is capable of producing daily activity reports (number of issues checked-in, number of items claimed and so on), vendor performance reports, financial reports and so on.

Thus, serials control is a major operation. Computerized system helps handling the operation more easily, quickly and economically. It performs such tasks as data entry, (title of the serial/journal, periodicity, date of issue, individual article and author, locus, abstract and key words, etc;) order of new serials; renewal of subscription for titles on current subscription list; cancellation of subscription; recording receipt of issue; sending reminders; outputting of various lists (like periodicals received during a specified periods); holding with status (on shelf, on bindery, on circulation, etc.) budget control; binding control; etc.

6.4.7. Stock Verification

Stock verification is generally considered a sensitive, controversial and unwanted evil. But it is necessary and unavoidable.

An automated system with bar coding facilities is not only easy but is also foolproof. Many companies produce bar-coding strips, readers and softwares.

By reading/clicking the 'Bar Code' reader, the accession number of the library books are stored into the computer memory. The accession numbers read by the bar code readers are compared with the book database accession number. The numbers in the book database which are left without matching are identified as 'missing'. A missing list can initially be printed out to do the tracing following it.

6.4.8. Administration

Office routines, circulars, reminders, enquiries, etc., can be handled with efficiency. Some of the software packages which are useful in managing administrative routines are: word star, banners, high presentation graphics, page maker, amipro, foxpro, etc.

6.4.9. Library Statistics

Statistics of all library activities like total holding of number of journals, books, etc., holdings of back volumes, serial titles on current subscription list, visitors, circulation details (per day, week, etc.), membership details, books status (lost, cost, recovered, damaged, condemned, etc.) overdue, furniture and equipment details, staff data, etc., can be generated and maintained. Most of the records/forms such as approval form, overdue notice, reminders to the delinquent borrowers, purchase slips, reservation slips, etc., being routine/repetitive in nature, the same could be programmed easily and for one time.

The most important house-keeping activities associated with any modern library comprise acquisition, cataloguing, circulation and serial control. The success of a library depends to a large extent, on the efficient and effective organisation of these house-keeping activities.

7
Computerised Information Services

7.1. NATURE AND TYPES OF SERVICES

The use of Information Technology facilitated libraries to develop services that would have been impossible to offer earlier. Computers can be used in two ways in libraries and information centers in providing information services. The first option is to design a local (in-house) information storage and retreival system, which is limited to the resources available in a particular library or information center and render services to the users. The other is to use the computer as an access tool and obtain information from externally operated storage and retrieval systems. Generally, a local information system is designed to serve the requirements of users of a library based on its own resources. Now-a-days, the same computer is used to access information from external sources globally located anywhere in the world, using modern telecommunications facilities. Modern libraries provide a variety of computerised information services. These information services can broadly be categorised into anticipatory and responsive services. Some of the significant services are Current Awareness Services (CAS), Selective Dissemination of Information (SDI), online search services, printed indexes, database product and services, document delivery services and CD-ROM database products and services.

Thus, computer-based information services can conveniently be categorised in the following types:

7.1.1. Current Awareness Service

Current Awareness Service helps the user to keep him up-to-date with the progress within a subject area. It involves a process of reviewing the publications immediately on receipt, selecting information pertinent to the programme of the organisation served, as well as recoding individual items to be brought to the attention of those persons, to whose work they are related. CAS has the characteristic feature of bringing the new information continuously to the notice of the scientists. The techniques used for providing CAS are as follows:

* Telephone calls.
* Periodicals routing.
* Maintaining card files of references of information by manual or machine methods.
* Recording individual references and forwarding them to the concerned persons.
* Issuing of CAS bulletin from the library.
* Circulation of contents pages of periodicals.

7.1.2. Selective Dissemination of Information (SDI)

"SDI service is personalized CAS service which is provided within an organization that concerns itself with the channeling of new items of information from whatever source to those points within an organization where the probability of its usefulness is high". SDI service was developed mainly to provide the research scholars and scientists individually at regular intervals, a list of carefully selected publications, in their areas of interest. This service can be provided manually as well as in a mechanized form.

With the help of computers, a number of large abstracting and indexing services have produced machine-readable files of large volumes of document records. These files are usually in the form of magnetic tapes, which are commercially available and can form very convenient databases for large-scale SDI services. Some of the well known database are the CAS (Chemical Abstract Service), ISI (Institute for Scientific Information), MEDLARS (Medical Literature Analysis Retrieval System), etc. The development of CAN/SDI service offered by the National Science Library of Canada is another effective move in this direction.

7.1.3. Printed Indexes

One of the first applications of the computer to information retrieval was in the production of printed indexes. Computers were used, both for the preparation of in-house indexes to reports, local abstracting and indexing bulletins, patent lists, etc., and also for the production of indexes for the major abstracting journals like Chemical Abstracts, Biological Abstracts, etc. Originally, indexing was an isolated operation. Now-a-days, indexes have become one of the range of database products.

Most of the indexes consist of a series of lead terms usually arranged in alphabetical order. Each lead term may be qualified and must have a link that leads the user to other list or documents. Computer generated indexes mostly rely on automatically assigned index terms. They might also be based on intellectually (manually) assigned terms.

There are different types of computer produced indexes. One such category is keyword based indexes. Under this category fall the following types: KWIC, KWOC, KWIT and KWAC. All these are based on the keywords but are differently formatted.

7.1.4. Citation Indexes

Citation indexing is one of the means of producing an effective index by the effective use of computer for arranging and reformatting entries. The input to this indexing system comprises the references of recent articles published in the core journals of any discipline. For each article, a list of work (documents) that it referes to is also compiled. In other words, a citation index lists 'cited' documents, together with a list of those items that have cited them (i.e., citing articles). The most important example of citation indexes is that of Science Citation Index (SCI) produced by Institute of Scientific Information. The speciality of this type of indexes is that given one document (cited) in a field, the searcher should be able to trace other related documents. Citation links provide a valuable additional approach to the identification of related documents. This type of indexing could become feasible only through the use of computers.

7.1.5. Online Search Services

Online search service system that provides access to a large number of database, generally convert those databases into uniform format with some standarization features so that the basic commands and search techniques apply across all the databases offered by a given vendor. Naturally, the intending user needs to be aware of the range of search services that are available. It might so happen that one database may be availble from several search services (vendors). Access to that database may be considerably cheaper, especially once the telecommunication charges have been taken into account, via one search service than the other. Moreover, a different vendor may offer search facilities which support much more effective searching for a specific (given) topic than might be possible via another search service (vendor). Some services might offer customers other benefits such as ease of searching, processing speed and competitive pricing.

There are a number of different types of such services such as: i) The traditional Super market online search services; ii) Specialist online search services; iii) Publishers ' search services; iv) Platform independent services; and, v) Bibliographic utilities.

In recent times, online service suppliers are attempting to respond to the long felt need of devising common interfaces to tool such bibliographic and directories including directories of websites, which indicate the location of infomration and the full text of the document which contains the information. Some of the sophisticated online search services are also trying to offer access to other information channels, such as database mounted by the other vendors, the contents of other websites, information collections such as libraries, and people as information channels. This new aspect of the service is described as an Integrated Information Solution (IIS). Some of the examples of the services which seek to generate integrated information solution are: i) K. R. Science Base for the WWW, ii) DIALOG Web, iii) Engineering Information Village, etc. Such IIS need to be targeted to meet the needs of specific groups, and the service supplier must understand those needs, not only in terms of the type of the database to be accessed, but also in terms of specific features of interfaces and the most acceptable pricing strategies.

The link between the user terminal and the host computer is often via a packet switched networks. The flow of data is in one direction, from the keyboard to host (requests), and, in the other direction from host to visual display screen (information). In this dialogue, the host computer imposes constraints on what the searcher can do and when. For example, commands must be constructed in exactly the required format and often it is necessary to wait for a reply from the host before entering the next command even though the content of the command may not be dependent on the answer to the previous command.

7.1.6. Document Delivery Services

Document delivery is considered as one of the

important elements of providing access to information. It involves the integration of document discovery, the location of a supplier, request and delivery.

Document delivery is a complex process, which spans time and distance between customer and suppliers. It takes many forms. For example, it may involve documents in a variety of forms and involves a number of intermediaries. In other words, document delivery involves authors, publishers, subscription agents, document delivery services, book suppliers and librarians. Since information is generated in different formats, and their production involves different agencies, it is but natural that there are many options for document delivery. Many of these agencies may be involved in both electronic and print-based document delivery. Librarians, publishers and other document delivery services are concerned with the complexities of document delivery in an environment in which conventional document delivery is coupled with electronic document delivery.

Categories of Document Delivery Services

There are different agencies concerned with document delivery service. Some of the services are:

(i) Library networks and consortia, including national libraries and document delivery services. The central focus of these networks being resource sharing and the creation of shared bibliographic and catalogue database. Such agencies may also offer a range of other value-added services.

(ii) Document delivery on CD-ROM, which is particularly appropriate in the context of books, encyclopaedias and other lengthy documents.

(iii) Commercial Document Delivery Services, which operate with alliances with online search services and draw on the resources of a number of other libraries.

(iv) Library suppliers and serials supplier agents, who have used networks and EDI, (Electronic Data Interchange) to improve the document ordering process and associated process such as altering invoicing and book processing.

(v) Electronic journal publishers and suppliers. It may be noted that there is a limited number of e-journals at present, but significant efforts are being made in the digitization of journals that have been previously distributed in the printed form. This effort would certainly enhance the electronic document delivery service efforts.

Some important aspects relating to the above mentioned categories of document delivery services need to be understood properly. For example, library networks and consortia usually create catalogue database as a means of accessing and sharing the resources of a group of libraries. Though, any type of document could be exchanged, the main emphasis is on printed documents. Similarly, CD-ROM suppliers of full text and multimedia databases, would be more helpful as document delivery service vendors only for the the supply of bulky documents such as encyclo- paedias, etc., their services may be availed only when such documents are to be delivered for.

In conclusion, it may be stated that document delivery service is one of the important aspects of information dissemination. This service will continue to be delivered in a range of different electronic as well as print formats for years to come. Different formats are appropriate for different purpose.

7.1.7. CD-ROM Database Products and Service

CD-ROM is a derivation of the compact digital audio disc. All the optical formats use a set of laser pick-up optics. CD-ROM uses the digital audio compact disc (CD) system for storage and retrieval of machine readable (digitally encoded) information.

Optical storage technology uses optical scanning techniques to store massive amount of information in a compact area. The use of laser allows an optical storage device, such as CD-ROM disc, to function as a high density, compact, portable, and easy to use computer storage device. The CD-ROM disc can be used in a standalone disc drive or a disc drive that is about the same size as a floppy disk drive with a single computer interface.

Optical discs, specifically in the form of CD-ROM, have become increasingly important as medium for storage and dissemination of information since the 1990s. In the present context CD-ROMs represent a means of access to information. They may be used as an alternative to online access to external database via telecommunications networks, including WWW. If in case the database recorded on the CD-ROM is a full-text of a document like an encyclopaedia, it can be searched any number of times conveniently and portions of its text can be copied for use.

The basic stand-alone workstation provides a single user with access to a single disc. The basic components of the stand-alone configuration are:

(i) A stand-alone PC.

(ii) A CD-ROM drive.

(iii) Appropriate software.

(iv) A printer.

Most PCs have an integral CD-ROM drive, but if this is not available, the PC needs a spare expansion slot via which the drive can be linked. If in case, hard copies (printouts) of the results of a CD-ROM search are required, then a printer is essential. The choice of the printer depends upon the requirement and the relative priorities.

On the software side, in addition to the operating system of the micro-computer, it is also necessary to have the following:

(i) Device driver software (which tells the computer that a CD-ROM drive is connected and how to communicate with the drive).

(ii) Retrieval software, which supports searching of the CD-ROM database (this will be supplied by the producer of the CD-ROM database).

(iii) Installation software, which controls the installation of the database on the user's equipment, and supports the setting up of configurations such as user-defined passwords, and equipment specifications.

But the ideal CD-ROM configuration offers a multi-user access to many databases in a way that allows the integration of databases on CD-ROM with other database used by the information seeker. This is facilitated by network configuration. These include network file servers and jukeboxes, pre-catching and internet access.

8
Communication Technology

8.1. INTRODUCION

Communication is the process of transferring messages from one point to another. As shown in Figure 8.1, the three basic elements of any communications process are:

1. A sender (source) which creates the message to be transmitted.
2. A medium which carries the message.
3. A receiver (sink) which receives the message.

For example, when you speak to your friend on the telephone, you are the sender. The telephone line through which your voice is transmitted is the medium and your friend is the receiver. This is a simple example of voice communication. The same concept holds good for data communication also. Data communications is the function of transporting data from one point to another. In this case, the sender and the receiver are normally machines, in particular, computer devices (computers, terminals, peripheral devices like printers, plotters, teletypes, disks, etc.), and the transmission medium may be telephone lines, microwave links, satellite links, etc. However, the messages that are transmitted are data, not voice conversation. Thus, the electronic systems that transfer data from one point to another are called data communications systems. Unlike computers, that process and rearrange data, data communications system transmit data from one point to another without any change.

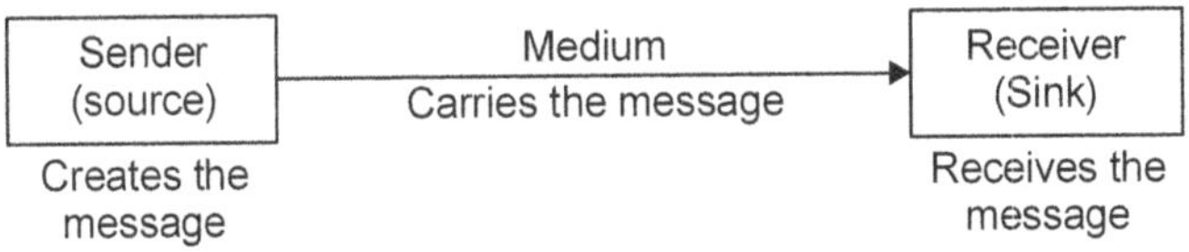

Fig. 8.1 : Basic elements of a communication system.

Telecommunication is an important area of Information Technology. The rapid developments in telecommunication over the past years have been an essential component in the growth of computer-based library and information systems and services. Communication systems are classified according to the channel used or frequency of transmission, Accordingly, we have the following communication systems:

1. Radio Communication.
2. Microwave Communication.
3. Satelite Communication.
4. Coaxial cable Communications.
5. Fibre optic Communications.

8.2. TELECOMMUNICATION : CONCEPT AND DEFINITION

'Data Communication', 'Communication technology', 'Computer telecommunications', 'Communications' 'Telecomputing', etc. are just some of the terms we come across in our current literature on the subject. Most of these terms are used to described a process, that of transmitting a message from one point to another by electronic means, and the devices used to achieve this process. The process is well known and we engage in this process daily as we speak to one another. We call this the communications process. Therefore, "Telecommunications may be defined as the transmission of representations of information between remote locations by electronic means. This information may be in the form of voice, video, or data generated by a computer" A telecommunication process, thus, consists of data to be transmitted (our messages), devices called terminals to send and receive message, and a communication channel.

8.3. DATA TRANSMISSION MODES

There are three ways or modes, for transmitting data from one point to another. As the shown in Figure 8.2, these are simplex, half-duplex, and full-duplex.

Simplex: If transmission is simplex, communication can take place in only one direction. Devices connected to such a circuit to either a send-only or a receive-only device. For example, a data collection terminal on a factory floor (send only) or a printer (receive only). At first thought adequate for many types of applications in which flow of information is unidirectional. However, in almost all data processing applications, communication in both directions is required. Even for a "one-way" flow of information from a terminal to a computer, the system will be designed to allow the computer to signal the terminal that data has been received. Without this capability, the remote user might enter data and never know that it was not received by the computer (due to some problem somewhere). Hence, simplex circuits are seldom used because a return path is generally needed to send acknowledgement, control or error signals.

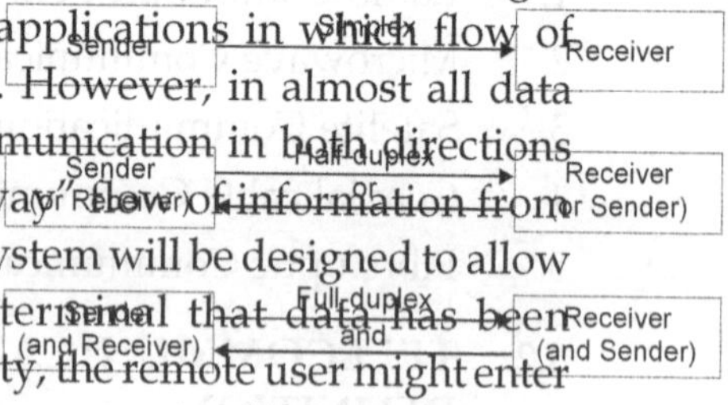

Fig. 8.3 : Modes of data transmission

Half-duplex: A half-duplex system can transmit data in both directions, but only in one direction at a time. Thus, a half-duplex line can alternately send and receive data. It requires two wires. This is the most common type of transmission for voice communications because only one person is supposed to speak at a time. It is also used to connect a terminal with a computer. The terminal might transmit data and then the computer responds with an acknowledgement.

Full-duplex: In a full-duplex system, the line must be "turned-around" each time the direction is reversed. This involves a special switching circuit and requires a small amount of time (approximately 150 milliseconds). With high speed capabilities of the computer, this turn-around time is acceptable in many instances. Also, some applications require simultaneous transmission in both directions. In such cases, a full-duplex system is used, that allows information to flow simultaneously in both directions on the transmission path. Use of a full -duplex line improves efficiency as the line turn-around time required in a half-duplex arrangement is eliminated. It requires four wires.

8.4. TRANMISSION MEDIA

The sender-medium-receiver concept has actually been with us for a very long time. For example, shouting to another person does in fact involve voice transmission over a distance via the medium air, which carries the sound wave. Needless to say, the use of telephone line, as a transmission medium, considerably enhances the possible distance. Like telephone lines, there are several types of physical channels (communication media) through which data can be transmitted from one point to another. Some of the most common data transmission medium are briefly described here.

8.4.1. Twisted Wire Pair

A twisted pair wire consist of two bunches of thin copper wire. Wire pairs are commonly used in local telephone communication and short distance (upto about 1 km) digital data transmission. They are usually made of copper and a pair of wires are twisted together to reduce interference by adjacent wires.

Wire pairs are normally used to connect terminal to the main computer. Data transmission speed of upto 9600 bits per second can be achieved if the distance is not more than 100 meters. However, for longer distance, local telephone lines are used. In this case, typical speed of digital signal transmission is 1200 bits per second.

Wire pairs are an inexpensive medium of data transmission. They are easy to install and use. However, their use is limited because they easily pick up noise signals which results in high error rates when the line length extends beyond 100 meters.

8.4.2. Coaxial Cables

Coaxial cables are groups of specially wrapped and insulated wire lines that are able to transmit data at high rates. They consist of a central copper wire surrounded by a PVC insulation over which a sleeve of copper mesh is placed. The metal sleeves is again shielded by an outer shield of thick PVC material. The signal is transmitted by the inner copper wire and is electrically shielded by the outer metal sleeve.

Coaxial cables offer much higher bandwidths and are capable of transmitting digital signals at very high rates of 10 mega bits per second. They are extensively used in long distance telephone lines and as cables for closed circuit TV. They are also used by telephone companies to transmit data. In many cases, coaxial cables are packaged into a very large cable that can handle over 40,000 telephone calls simultaneously. Further more, coaxial cables have much higher noise immunity and can offer cleaner and crisper data transmission without distortion or loss of signal.

8.4.3. Microwave System

Another popular transmission media is microwave. This is a popular way of transmitting data since it does not incur the expense of laying cables. Microwave systems use very high frequency radio signals to transmit data through space. However, at microwave frequencies the electro-managnetic waves cannot bend or pass obstacles like hill. Hence, it is necessary that microwave transmission is in a line-of-sight. In other words, the transmitter and receiver of a microwave system, which are mounted on very high towers, should be in a line-of-sight. This may not be possible for every long distance transmission. Moreover, the signals become weaker after travelling a certain distance and require power amplification.

In order to overcome the problem of line-of-sight and power amplification of weak signals, microwave systems use repeaters at intervals of about 25 to 30 kms in between the transmitting and receiving stations. The first repeater is placed in line-of-sight of the transmitting station and the last repeater is placed in line-of-sight of the receiving station. Two consecutive repeaters are also placed in line-of-sight of each other. The data signals are received, amplified, and re-transmitted by each of these stations.

Microwave systems permit data transmission rates of about 16 Giga bits per second. Furthermore, it can carry literally thousand of voice channels at the same time. The link can support 50,000 voice channels. However, the capital investment needed to install microwave links is very high and hence they are mostly used to link big metropolitan cities with heavy telephone traffic between them.

8.4.4. Communications Satellite

The main problem with microwave communication is that the curvature of the earth, mountains, and other structures often block the line-of-sight. Due to this reason, several repeater stations are normally required for long distance transmission which increases the cost of data transmission between two points. This problem is overcome by using satellites which are relatively newer and more promising data transmission media.

A communication satellite is basically a microwave relay station placed in outer space. These satellites are launched either by rockets or by space shuttles and are precisely positioned 36000 kms above the equator with an orbit speed that exactly matches the earth's rotation speed. Since a satellite is positioned in a geo-synchronous orbit, it is stationary relative to earth and always stays over the same point on the ground. This allows a ground station to aim its antenna at a fixed point in the sky. Hundreds of satellites are now in orbit to handle international and domestic data, voice, and video communications needs. The Indian satellite, INSAT-1B, is positioned in such a way that it is accessible from any place in India.

In satellite communication, microwave signal at 6 GHz (read as gigahertz Hz) is transmitted from a transmitter on earth to the satellite positioned in space. By the time this signal reaches the satellite it becomes weak due to 36000 kms of travel. The satellite amplifies the weak signal and transmits it back to the earth at a frequency of 4 GHz. This signal is received at a receiving station on the earth. It may be noted that the re-transmission frequency is different from the transmission frequency in order to avoid the interference of the powerful re-tranmission signal with the weak incoming signal.

The main advantage of satellite communicatin is that it is a single microwave relay station visible from any point of a very-very large area. For example, satellites used for national transmission are visible from any part of the country. This transmission and reception can be between any two randomly chosen places in that area. Moreover, transmission and reception costs are independent of the distance between two points. In addition to this, a transmitting station can receive back its own transmission and check whether the satellite has transmitted the information correctly. If an error is detected, the data would be re-transmitted. However, a major drawback of satellite communication has been the high cost of placing the satellite into its orbit. Moreover, a signal sent to a satellite is broadcast to all receivers within the satellite's range. Hence, necessary security measures are to be taken to prevent unauthorised tampering of information.

8.4.5. Optical Fibers

A potential cost-effective earth alternative to satellite communications for the future will be the use of optical fiber's. The Bell Systein of U.S.A. has tested small half-inch-diameter cables that could transmit as many as 50,000 voice messages simultaneously by means of advanced optical techniques based upon laser technology.

In fibre optics, semiconductor laser transmit information in the form of light along hair-thin glass (optical) fibers at 186,000 miles per second (the speed of light), with out significant loss of intensity over very long distances. The system basically consists of fiber optic cables that are made of tiny threads of glass or plastic. Towards its source side is a converter that converts electrical signals into light wave. These light waves are transmitted over the fiber. Another converter placed near the sink converts the light wave back to electrical signals by photoelectric diodes. These electrical signals are amplified and sent to the receiver.

Some of the interesting features of optical fibers are:

(i) They provide high quality (low error rate) transmission of signals at very high speeds. Digital transmission speeds of 1 giga bits per second have been used with error less than 1 in 10^9 bits. Some transmission that take about an hour over copper wires can actually be sent through optical fibers in under one second.

(ii) A normal fiber in a glass fiber cable is about the size of a human hair. In some large cities, there simply is no room for additional bulky copper wires. The conduits used to house the copper wires are typically of a fixed size, and replacing existing conduits for more copper wires would be too expensive. In this case, the use of smaller fiber optical data communications system is very effective.

(iii) Optical fibers may be used to communicate either analog or digital signals. In analog transmission, the light intensity is varied continuously, whereas in digital transmission the light source is turned on or off.

(iv) Fiber optical transmission is not affected by electromagnetic interference. Hence, noise and distortion are also reduced with fiber optic.

(v) Optical fibers are most commonly used for point-to-point one way communications links because it its extremely difficult and expensive to tap a fiber optic cable at various unauthorised tampering of information.

While experts agree that the optic transmission will be widely used in the future, there are still some technical difficulties to overcome. For instance, optical fibers do not currently allow complete switching or routing of light signals. As a result, at switching points, optical signals must be convered into electrical signals for routing and then back into light for further optical tranmission. Despite such glitches, however, fiber-optic transmission system are already on the market, and their popularity is growing rapidly.

8.4.6. Digital and Analog Transmission

Data is propagated from one point to another by means of electrical signals which may be in digital or analog form. In an analog signal the transmitted power varies over a continous range, for example sound, light and radio waves. The amplitude (v) of analog signals is measured in volts and its frequency (f) in hertz (Hz). The higher is the frequency of the signals, the more number of times it crosses the time axis. However, a digital signal is a sequence of voltage pulses represented in binary form.

Computer generated data is digital, whereas the telephone lines used for data communication in computer networks are usually meant for carrying analog signals. When digital data are to be sent over an analog facility, the digial signals must be converted to analog form. The technique by which a digital singal is converted to its analog form, is known as modulation. The reverse process, that is the conversion at analog signal to its digital form, at a destination device, is called demodulation.

Digital transmission of digital data is more reliable than analog transmission of digital data. However, digital transmission facilities are currently available only to a limited extent. For example, digital signalling is impossible for satellite and whenever feasible the communication systems are converting to digital. The advantage of digial over analog for data transmision are:

1. Lower cost.
2. No modems required.
3. Higher transmission speed possible.
4. Lower error rate.

It is expected that the years ahead will see ever-increasing digital transmission capabilities.

8.4.7. Asynchronous and Synchronous Transmission

Data transmission on a communication line is normally carried out in two different modes: asynchronous and synchronous. Asynchronous transmission is often referred to as start-stop transmission because of its nature, that is, the sender can send a character at any time convenient and the receiver will accept it. This is the characteristic of many terminals. When a terminal is connected to a computer and an operator manually pressess keys on the terminals, the time spent between succesive keystrokes would vary. Thus, in asynchronous transmisison, data is transmitted character by character at irregular intervals.

In order to enable the receiver to recognize a character when it arrives, the transmitter "frames" each character. Preceding the character is a start bit and following the character will be one or two (depending upon the system) stop bits. Thus, for the 7 - bit ASCII code, for each character the transmitter transmits the seven character bits, one parity bit, one start bit and one or two stop bits for a total of either 10 or 11 bits. Note that as each character is "framed" by a distinct start signal and a stop signal, the time taken between transmitting any two characters can be any length or none at all. Thus, the computer might send a continuous stream of data to the terminal.

Asynchronous transmission is well suited to many keyboard type terminals and paper tape devices. The advantage of this method is that it does not require any local storage at the terminal of the computer as transmission takes place character by character. Hence, it is cheaper to implement. However, since the transmission line is idle during the time intervals between transmitting character, if the lines are short, this is not bad because line cost would be low and idle time not expensive. Even though less efficient than synchronous transmission, it is also used with devices such as card readers and printers simply to reduce cost.

Synchronous mode of data transmission involves blocking a group of characters in somewhat the same way records are blocked on magnetic tape. Each block is then framed by header and trailer information. The header consist of synchronized information which is used by the receiving device to set its clock in synchronism with the sending end clock. The header also contains information to identify sender and receiver. Following the header is a block of characters that contains the actual message to be transmitted. The number of characters in a block may be variable and may consist of hundreds of characters. The message characters in the block are terminated by a trailer. The trailer contains an end of message character followed by a check character to aid detection of any transmission error. Thus, with synchronous transmission, entire block of characters is framed and transmitted together.

Synchronous transmission is well suited to remote communication between a computer and such devices as buffered card readers and printers. Here, the logical data block length would by 80 or 132 characters. It is also used with buffered terminals and for computer to computer communication.

The primary advantage of synchronous transmission is its efficiency. Not only does it eliminate the need for invidual start-stop bits on each character, but much higher data rates can be used than with asynchronous tranmission. The period between blocks is kept small and the block itself is sent at nearly the maximum line speed. This ensures efficient utilisation of the transmision line. The main disadvantage is the need for local buffer storage at the two ends of the line to assemble blocks and also the need for accurately synchronized clock at both ends. As a result synchronous equipment usually costs more.

8.4.8. Frequency and Bandwidth

Let us try to understand a little about how information is transmitted. The information may be in the form of sound (human voice, music) or it may be visual (printed page, microfilm, video picture) or it may be digital data. Whatever, may be the form, it must be converted to electrical signals (electromagnetic waves) before it can be transmitted over a given medium. Such signals very often cannot be sent over a channel as they are, but must be modulated in some way to fit them into the carrying medium. The frequencies of the electromagnetic waves are normally radio frequencies which vary range from low frequencies capable for carrying only small amounts of information to millimeter waves, which can carry large amounts. Above the radio frequencies lies light frequency, which can be modulated to carry even larger amounts of information. In other words, the amount of information that can be sent over a given channel in a given time is dependent on the bandwidth. The bandwidth available increases with increasing carrier frequency. Thus, generally speaking, the wider the bandwidth, the larger the amount of information which can be carried and the faster its speed. Therefore, we can provide a definition to the concept of frequency as under.

Frequency is the rate at which a wave or cycle alternates between high and low (analog mode) or on and off (digital mode). For example, the lowest buzz notes reproduced on a good stereo set may emanate a wave pattern as slow as 30 times (cycles) per second, while very high notes cause wave patterns to alternate as often as 20,000 times per second.

One cycle per second is called a Hertz (HZ). The table below shows some frequencies for telephone and other electronic transmission media.

Electronic Transmission Frequencies

Media	
Sub-voice	30-30 Hz (Hertz)
Voice	300-300 Hz
High Fidelity Equipment	3-30 KHz (kilohrtz)
Radio Broadcasting	30-3000 KHz
Television Broadcasting	3-30 MHz (megahertz)
VHF Television	30-300 MHz
UHF Television	300-3000 MHz
Satellite Communication	3-30 GHz (gigahertz)
Microwave communication	30-300 GHz
Laser, fiber optics	300 GHz Tera hertz Range

Bandwidth

Bandwidth is the second concept important for transmission. This concept can be explained with the help of the traffic network mentioned earlier. If there is a two-way street, consisting of two single lanes, one in each direction, only one line of vehicles can travel in each direction. On a superhighway, however, there may be three or four lanes in each direction; cars may travel along these lanes, in parallel, each at its own rate of speed. We have a wider 'band' of highway which can accommodate more cars traveling in the same direction at the same time. In the same way, the width of the electronic path determines how many cycles or bits can travel along this given path at any given time; the more bandwidth is available, the more bits may be transmitted, and the better the quality of transmission. In a simple telephone conversation, we use a bandwidth of about 3000 bits per second or KHz. Television needs more bandwidth to accommodate audio and visual signals, and uses approximately 4,500,000 Hz or 4.5 MHz.

Frequencies and bandwidth occur from low to very

high along a continuous range of frequencies called the spectrum. To keep transmission from interfering with one another, each type (voice, radio, television, satellites, etc.), is allocated a bandwidth in this spectrum. Allocation is determined for any nation by its communications commission and internationally by the International Telecommunications Union (ITU) to avoid competition for the same bandwidths by different carriers and countries.

When bandwidths are allocated, sufficient extra space is provided between frequencies to prevent electronic interference in so far as possibe. This safety precaution might not always work, when we hear or see overlap among radio broadcasts or television programmes.

8.5. COMMUNICATIONS PROCESSORS

In a data communication network, the task of network designers is to select and coordinate the network components so that the necessary data are moved to the right place, at the right time, with a minimum of errors, and at the lowest possible cost. A number of communications processors (typical micro or mini computers) are used by network designers to achieve their goals. The functions of some of the commonly used commu- nications processors are briefly described here.

Multiplexers: There are many applications in which several terminals are connected to a computer. If each terminal is operating at 300 bits per second over a communication line (channel) that can operate at 9600 bits per second, then we see a very inefficient operation. It has been found that the capacity of a channel exceedes that required for a single signal. A channel is an expensive resource. Hence, for its optimal utilisation, the channel can be shared in such a way so as to simultaneously transmit multiple signals over it. The method of dividing a physical channel into many logical channels so that a number of independent signals may be simultaneously transmitted on it is known as multiplexing. The electronic device that performs this task is known as a multiplexer.

A multiplexer takes data communications lines or signals and converts them into one data communications line or signal at the sending location. For example, there may be four terminals connected to a multiplexer. The mul- tiplexer takes the signals from the four terminals and converts them into one large signal which can be transmitted over one communications line. Then, at the receiving location, a multiplexer takes the one large signal and breaks it into the original four signals. Without multiplexers, you would have to have four separate communications lines.

Thus, with multiplexing it is possible for a single transmission medium to concurently transmit data between several transmitters and receievers. There are two basic methods of multiplexing channels. They are frequency division multiplexing and time division multiplexing.

1. **Frequency Division Multiplexing (FDM):** The bandwidth or range of a medium exceeding that of any given signal. This fact is utilised for frequency division multiplexing. In FDM, the available bandwidth of a physical medium is split up (divided) into several smaller, disjoint logical bandwidths. Each of the component bandwiths is used as a separate communiactions line (channel).

   The best example of FDM is the way we receive various station in a radio. Each radio station is assigned a frequency range within a bandwidh of radio frequencies. Several radio stations may be transmitting speech signals simultaneously over the physical channel which is "ether" in this case. A radio receiver's antenna receives signals transmitted by all the stations. Finally, the tuning dial in the radio is used to isolate the signal of the station tuned. In FDM, the signals to be transmitted must be analog signals. Thus, digital signal must be converted to analog form if they are to use FDM.

2. **Time Division Multiplexing (TDM):** The bit rate of a transmission medium always exceeds the required rate of the digital signal. This fact is utilised for time division multiplexing. In TDM, the total time available in the channel is divided between several users and each users of the channel is alloted a time slice (a small time interval) during which he/ she may transmit a message. The channel capacity is fully utilised in TDM by interleaving a number of data streams belonging to different users into one data stream. Streams of data sent through the physical channel must be demultiplexed at the receiving end. Individual chunks of message sent by each user is reasembled into a full message at the receiving end.

TDM may be used to multiplex digital or analog signals. For communications of digital data, it is more convenient to transmit data directly in digital form and thus, TDM is more appropriate. Moreover, communication between computers occurs is short fast bursts. Each burst thus, needs the full channel bandwidth which is available to a signal in TDM. Besides this, TDM is generally more efficient as more sub-channels can be derived because it is upto the networks designer to allocate time slots to different channels. It is common to have 32 low-speed terminals connected to one high speed line.

Whether or not to use multiplexing usually depends upon economics. The cost of high-speed modems and multiplexers is very high compared to the cost of low-speed modems. However, if line costs are high due to long distances, then multiplexing is cost-effective. One serious disadvantage with multiplexing relates to the transmission line failure. If the line goes out, everything is dead. With individual lines only one terminal is likely to be lost.

Concentrators: A concentrator performs the same function as a multiplexers, but concentrators have the ability to actually reduce the number of signals. For example, 100 signals from different device coming into the concentrator could leave as only 70 or 80. The signals are concentrated to form a fewer number of signals. This requires intellignece. This intelligence normally takes the form of microprocessors or even minicomputers. Thus, a concentrator is basically an intelligent multiplexer.

The advantage of using a concentrator is that devices of varying speed and types are connected to the concentrator which in turn is connected to the host computer by high speed lines. Concentrators are especially useful where data communications cost are high, such cocentrators are more expensive than multiplexers. For some long-distance and international data communications applications, however, the use of concentrators is cost justified.

Front End Processors (FEP): If information is to be moved from point to point in a computer networks, then some type of control is necessary. Network processing (also known as communications processing) is the control of information movement between the various locations of the network. This is a substantial task.

In the early network days, the communications processing job was handled by the main computer. This began to place heavy additional loads on the CPU. Thus, the ability of the computer to do information processing, that is, the job for which it was intended, was seriously derated. As a result, manufactures introduced front end processor. This is a separate CPU designed specifically to handle the network processing task.

A front end processor is usually installed in the same location as the host computer. Its primary purpose is to off-load communications processing task from the host computer, thereby the host computer can be dedicated for applications and data processing jobs. It virtually acts like an intelligent terminal or like a secretary/receptionist to the main computer.

8.6. SWITCHING TECHNIQUES

In its simplest form, data communication takes place between two devices that are directly connected by some form of transmission medium-twisted wires, coaxial cables, microwave and satellite links. Often, however, it is impractical or uneconomical for two devices to be directly connected. Instead, communication is achieved by transmitting data from source to destination through a network of intermediate nodes. These nodes provide a switching facility they move data from node to node until the destination is reached. There are three different methods of establishing communication links between data sources and receivers in a communication network. These are: circuit switching, message switching and packet switching.

1. Circuit Switching: It is the simplest method of data communication in which a dedicated physical path is established between the sending and the receiving stations through the nodes of the networks. This method is used to connect two subscribers in a telephone conversation. Computers and terminals connected through a telephone network also use this method of establishing communication path among them.

In the method of circuit switching each rectangle represents a switching node for the communication network. When a message is to be communicated, a physical path is established betweeen the sending station and the receiving station by physically connecting switching nodes that fall on the path. Once a circuit is established between the two stations, it is exclusively used by the two parties and the dedicated physical link between both ends continues to exist until the call is terminated either by the sender or the receiver. As soon as the connection is terminated by one of the two stations, the dedicated resources are deallocated and can now be used by other stations also.

Thus, circuit switching involves three phases- circuit establishment, data transfer and circuit disconnection.

Advantages

1. The main advantage of circuit switching is that once the circuit is established, data is transmitted with no delay other than the propagation delay which is negligible (typically of the order of 6 msec. per 1000 km.)
2. It is suitable for low speed communication between a terminal and a computer because the method is simple and requires no special facilities.
3. Since a dedicated continous transmission path is established, the method is suitable for long continuous transmission.

Disadvantages

1. Prior to actual data transfer, the time required to established a physical link between the two stations is of the order of 10 secs. or more depending on the distance. For many computer applications, e.g. point of sale verification, this lapse time is too large and unsuitable because communication among computers occurs in burst-for-short period with long silent period in between, during which the communication line is not used.
2. Since the physical link is a dedicated one, the channel capacity is dedicated to one source for the entire duration of a connection. Hence, the network resources are not properly utilised.

3. The method proves to be very uneconomical when used for communication between computers that are connected using expensive high speed lines.

2. Message Switching: A message is logical unit of information and can be of any length. In this method, if a station wishes to send a message to another station, it first appends the destination address of the message. After this, the message is transmitted from the source to the destination either by store-and-forward method or broadcast method.

In the store-and-forward method, the message is transmitted from the source node to an intermediate node. The intermediate node stores the complete message temporarlly, inspects it for errors, and transmits the message to the next node based on an available free channel and its routing information. The actual path taken by the message to its destination is dynamic as the path is established as it travels along. When the message reaches a node, the channel on which it came is released for use by another message. If a message is to be transmitted from station A to station B, it may take either path 1-2-3-4 or 1-5-4 depending on the availability of a free output path at that particular moment.

In broadcast method, the message is braodcasted over a common medium known as broadcast channel. All the stations check the destination address of each message as they pass by, they accept only those addressed to them. The routing delays inherent in store and forward method are eliminated in this method. However, this method requires that all stations must be connected to the broadcast channel.

Advantages

1. In message switching, no physical connection is required between the source and the destination as it is in circuit switching.
2. As channels are used only when messages are

transmitted, this method uses the channels very effectively.

Disadvantages

1. As the message length is unlimited, each switching node must have sufficient storage to buffer messages. In many cases this storage space may be under-utilised.
2. In message switching, a message is delayed at each node for the time required to receive the message plus a queuing delay waiting for an opportunity to retransmit the message to the next node.
3. The method is too slow for interactive/ real time applications. Hence, it is used when message delays are not critical.

3. Packet Switching: This method works in a similar fashion as message switching. However, it overcomes the disadvantages of message switching techniques because in this method routing is done on packet basis and not on message basis.

A message is split up into 'packets' of a fixed size (of the order of one or few thousand bits.) Besides the block of data (part of a message) to be sent, a packet has a header that contains destination and source addresses, control information, message number, number of current and last packets, synchronisation bits, acknowledgement and error checking bytes, etc. Like message switching, the packets may be routed from the sender node to the destination node either by store-and-forward method or by broadcast method. In the store-and-forward method, the packets are stored temporarily at the intermediate nodes for error recovery purposes and is routed to next node based on an available free channel. The actual path taken by the packet to its destination is dynamic because the path is established as it travels along. Thus, it is possible that different packets of the same message can be routed across different paths leading to the same destination depending upon line availability and congestion.

Advantages

1. Unlike message, packets are of small and fixed size. Hence, the storage requirement for buffering the packets at intermediate nodes is minimal.
2. Since the routing is done on packet basis, the intermediate nodes do not have to wait for the entire message, hence the transmission is very fast.
3. The methods is fast enough for interactive/ real time applications. It is thus, most suitable for "bursty" communication among computer and is widely used in wide area networks.

Disadvantages

1. There is no guarantee of how long it takes a message to go from its source node to its destination node, because the time taken for each packet depends on the route chosen for that packet, alongwith the volumes of data being transferred along that route.
2. Due to the need to buffer each packet at every intermediate node and to reassemble the packets at the destination node, the overhead incurred per packet is large.

8.7. TERMINAL TO LINE CONNECTION

Use of Modems: Computers handle and produce digital signals. While using the ordinary telephone lines, the digital signals are to be converted to analog wave format. Similarly, the receiving unit has to do the reverse operation. This process of conversion and reconversion is called modulation and demodulation. A Modem or acoustic coupler is used for this purpose. Modem is a construction of Modular-DE Modulator. There are two types of Modems: internal and external. An internal modem comes on a printed circuit board that is placed inside the computer, whereas, an external modem is connected to the computer via a cable attached to the computer.

8.8. TELECOMMUNICATIONS STANDARDS AND PROTOCOLS

Standards are crucial in the telecommunications if data is to be transmitted successfully between different manufacturing equipment. The International Telecommunication Union (ITU) and its attached organization Consultative Committee for International Telegraphy and Telephones (CCITT) have been concerned with standardization of telecommunications. Broadly speaking, the approach of ITU is to consider the problems of both advanced and developing countries. According to CCITT, standarlisation avoids many problems in the process of data communications, such as:

1. The use of the existing telegraph and telex network for data communications.
2. The use of the public switched telephone network.
3. The use of a separate network dedicated to 'Data services' (public data network).
4. The use of an integrated service digital networks.

As far as India is concerned in the field of telecommunication, we are near the advanced countries while in many others fields we are more like developing countries than advanced ones. We have however, a long way to go in developing over data communication networks.

Protocols are rules governing the limitation and maintenance of data flow. These are implemented in different ways for different types of equipment and networks. Information professionals are most likely to encounter these when setting up their software and hardware for online searching.

8.8.1. Wireless Communication

(i) Free space: Free space communications, often simply called radio, employ electronic magnetic waves propagated in the open rather than the flow of electrons through a wire or light through a lightguide. Many communications thought of as wired (for example, switched telephone circuits) actually are often transmitted via microwave or high-frequency radio.

Radio can be an alternative to other communications media, especially when access to telehpone is awkward or non-existent, such as in vehciles. It is convenient to divide radio communications into local communication (which involves direct reception of a transmitted signal and which are relatively inexpensive ways of covering areas the size of a city or perhaps, a county) and remote communications (which, by using apparatus that receives, amplifies, and retransmits the signal, are capable of covering much larger areas).

(ii) Local: Local communications via radio fall into two primary categories: communication using frequencies assigned specifically to public service organisations, and communications using frequencies available to private citizens for personal communications.

(iii) Utility Band: Using frequencies assigned to public services has the advantage of being relatively secure (bearing in mind that no radio communication truly can be considered secure) and generally free from interference, both natural and artificial. The utility band provides dependable communications over the areas of library and information science (LIS) organizations are likely to cover, such as countries. The equipment however, is fairly expensive, and the licensing requirements, while not complex or technical, do require care.

(iv) Citizen's Band: The common citizen's band (CB) radio also may be used for local communications. Such apparatus is much less expensive than the typical utility band equipment and is available from more sources. It is also easier to obtain licenses for such equipment. Countering these advantages are potential disadvantages. Because the citizen's band is open to the public, communication frequencies are sometimes crowded and are subject to interference (sometimes malicious interference) by the other operators. The citizen's band's total lack of security may be either a disadvantage or free advertising, depending on the mission of the communicator.

(v) Ground-to-Groun : Direct communications over long distances by individuals or LIS institutions are seldom accomplished by radio today. Nonetheless, private microwaves facilities should not be ruled out, especially for data communications, since appreciable savings over private wired systems may be possible. When such ground-to-ground communications are used, the preferred method is via line-of-sight transmission using very high frequency signals, or microwaves, with repeaters strategically spaced to receive, amplify, and retransmit the message as needed.

(vi) Via Satellite: While only a few years ago, satellite communications by small organizations were only a science fiction scenario, they are well established, if not common, today. Satellite communications are especially attractive when long distances are combined with a need for certainty of access, that is, when private or leased telephone lines would be the alternative. Obviously, they are almost necessary when organisations must hold frequent, lengthy communications with, for example, the Pacific Islands. While few LIS institutions can purchase and deploy their own satellites, commercial communications companies like COMSAT will lease channels in time.

(vii) Cellular Telephone: An interesting and potentially useful melding of communications technologies is the cellular telephone (sometimes called cellular radio) services that are beginning to become common in large population centres. The service, commonly called mobile telephone, normally uses a single high-power transmitter to reach a local area often specified artbitraily as fifty miles. Each conversion occupies the transmitter, and in order to add additional circuits, additional transmission frequencies are required. This is expensive.

Cellular telephone services, on the other hand, use many low-powered transmitters. Each transmission site contains several transmitters that communicate with remote transreceivers (transmitter/receiver units). Each service area is divided into many cells, each of which can handle several simultaneous conversations; therefore, the number of telephones that can be active over the entire area is much larger than in a traditional mobile telephone network. Indeed, cellular systems are said to be able to handle almost one hundred times the number of simultaneous conversations that conventional systems can handle.

The cost of this increased service is increased complexity. A sophisticated computer at each cell transmission site keeps track of where the remote unit is and, at the appropriate time, hands that unit over to the adjacent cell. To accomplish this function, each transreceiver is a double system capable of sending and receiving signals over two frequencies at the same time; one for voice and one for data, as well as a microprocessor. The cell ties, in turn, are controlled by a single switching office that links the radio signals to the ordinary telephone service.

9
Network Technology

9.1. INTRODUCTION

"Information is valuable only if it is used, communicated and transformed into knowledge and action. Networks provide the pathways to achieve this end in that regard, an information society is a society of information networks".

The purpose of networks is to interconnect computers and other devices so that data can be transferred from one location to another. As far as the use of communication technology is concerned, though the networks operate behind the scene, they exert a profound influence on the application of communication technology. Access to remote information systems, the operation of electronic mail and the world telecommunication services are increasingly becoming dependent on the networks.

A communication network consists of a number of channels and a switching equipment that help in connecting these channels in various ways so as to meet the needs of its users. The structure of networks could be categorized into various types depending on the ways the terminals are connected and the way in which the users can gain access to them. The basic network topologies are as follows:

A fully connected network topolgy is one in which there is a channel between every pair of terminals and therefore no switching equipment is required. In a star network, there is a channel between every terminal to a central location. In a star network, the number of channels required is minimum. The central location must contain all the switching equipment in the network which can permit communication between any terminal with any other. In a partially connected network, some terminals are connected directly and others are not. Partially connected networks also require some sort of switching. In a ring network, all terminals are connected together in a ring and messages travel in one direction. In this topology, none of the terminals have overall control of access to the network. In Tree topology, the terminals are connected together by a branching communication channel and there are no loops in the network. In a bus topology, a single channel is shared by all the terminals but they are not joined together to form a loop. Each terminal uses the bus to communicate with other terminals in the network. Loop topology is a combination of ring and star structures. In this topology, all the terminals are connected together in a ring but one of the terminals controls the rest of the terminals.

In a fully connected network, each pair of terminal has its own channel over which communication can take place. Thus, no switching equipment is necessary. In a star network the number of channels is the minimum, one for each terminal. The central location must contain all the switching equipment in the network, which must have the ability to permit communication between one terminal and other. Similarly, in partially connected ring, tree, bus and loop networks, some sort of switching mechanism is required.

A communication network is therefore a combination or arrangement of the channels, the terminals and the switching mechanism.

In any kind of multiple network there are two ways of relaying information: circuit switching and packet switching.

A network that allows its channels to be connected physically in order to establish a single continuous channel for the transmission of signals between any two of its terminals is known as circuit switching. Packet switching is in fact a variation of message switching where messages are switched from their source towards their destination using channels as and when they are available. The messages are stored at intermediate point till the channels are available. In packet switching the difference is that the messages are divided into small portions of standard length, called packets. Packet switching reduces data transmission overhead by attaching codes to each item of data sent through the network. The codes identify the source and the destination of each item and hence no end to end connection is required. Packet switching is a relatively new technique in data networks which is now being used worldwide. Packet switching systems are being used on a variety of transmission media including local area network, metropolitan area network, Integrated Services Digital Networks (ISDN).

Recently, packet technologies based on fiber optic transmission have been developed which can operate at a higher speed and are better suited for larger metropolitan area networks.

Another important development in the network communication system is the Integrated Services Digital Networks (ISDNs), which permits both voice and data to be carried in digital form across an international switched digital backbone. The advantags of the ISDN are: separate networks are not required for transmission of voice data and image, modems are not required, two different types of messages can be transmitted over the same line simultaneously ever more faster, cleaner and error-free. The ISDN is now in the early stages of growth and it is going to revolutionize the networking of the entire world. Apart from the high speed network development underway, researchers are working also on the possibilility of wireless digital networks that will permit mobile workstations to be part of global network. The wireless global network is going to be similar to the cellular telephone networks in which computer carried in briefcase, cars, ships, etc. will be able to maintain link and send and receive data.

Another important development in the network technology is the internet, a procedure that interconnects different kinds of packet networks. Special processors called gateways are required to connect two or more networks, so as to pass the packet traffic from one network to the next. Advancement of micro electronics has now made intelligent data networks possible. Current research in the use of artifical intelligence techniques for telecommunications is primarily on expert systems.

9.2. NETWORKS

Networks imply putting together sub-sets of information centres and libraries in order to act in a cooperative manner with a predetermined obligation. Networking is a common concept, which concerns itself with mutual co-operation and co-ordination between systems of information for exchange of resources, services, facilities, etc. This exchange is termed as a network when these activities are performed in a systematic pre-planned manner. A network can be defined "as group of individuals or organizations that are interconnected. The linking must include a communication mechanism, and many networks exist for express purpose of members. It offers potential for increased access to larger resources and for a greater measure of service than the sum of all the constituent parts. In the library world, institutions form networks primarily to achieve better sharing of resources consisting of bibliographic information and of collections,and better service of patrons."

The Oxford English Dictionary states that a network is an "interconnected chain or system of immaterial things". On the other hand the National Commission on Libraries and Information Science (NCLIS) USA defines network as "Two or more libraries and/ or other organizations engaged in a common pattern of information exchange, through communications, for some functional purpose. A network usually consists of a formal arrangement whereby materials, information and services provided by a variety of types of libraries and/ or other organizations are made available to all potential users. Libraries may be in different jurisdictions but agree to serve one another on the same basis as each serves its own constituents. Computers and telecommunications may be the tools used for facilitating communications among them" (ALA year book, 1986, p. 248).

UNISIST II working document defines Information Network as: "A set of interrelated information systems associated with communications facilities, which are operating though more or less formal agreements and institutioanl arrangement in order to jointly implement information handling operation with a view to pooling their resources and to offer better services to user. They generally follow identical or compatible procedures."

Thus, a library network can be briefly called a systematic organization and co-ordination of interconnected libraries for achieving greater economy and efficiency.

The main objective of a library network is to promote avenues for the effective utilization of information through sharing of resources by a group of libraries based on acceptable agreements and policies. The use of computer technology and telecommunication has added new dimensions to the concept of networking in the libraries.

9.2.1. Types of Networks

There are basically three types of networks:

(i) Local Area Network (LAN): Networks used to connect computers in a single room, rooms, within a building or buildings on site are normally called local area networks (LANs). LANs normally transmit data in a digital form with typical transmission speeds upto several megabytes per second. Local area networks link computers in the same general area for the purpose of sharing information and hardware.

According to Murthy and others, the configuration of LAN can be a star, a ring or simple devices attached along a length of cable. The typicl LAN connects computers located with a half a mile from each other. The computers attached may be of different types and perform a variety of functions such as data processing, word processing and electronic mail.

(ii) Metropolitan Area Networks (MAN): These types of networks generally cover specific metropolitan area and provide to them all the services.

(iii) Wide Area Network (WAN): The term wide area network (WAN) is used to describe a computer network spanning a regional, national or global area. In contrast to LAN which only has a few components, WAN involves a large number of devices between the source and destination of data.

According to Muthy and others, it provides the communication over long distances, covering a large geographical area and are also called remote networks. It cover a large city or metropolitan area. Such large networks are turning to be a necessity for carrying out the day to day activities of many business and governmental organizations and their users.

WANs are typically created using specially conditioned telephone lines, microwaves or satellite data transmission.

Developments in Network Technology include the increasing use of computers to control switching and information flow. Most significant is the modernisation of the public network so that voice and data can be carried over a single network. This type of single network is referred to as Integrated Services Digital Network.

Need for Networking: As a universal phenomenon, libraries the world over are facing two major problems. These are:

(a) Information explosion.

(b) Price escalation of library documents.

(c) Increased cost of library services.

The number of publications in various disciplines, especially in Science and Technology is alarming. It is estimated in the past that the primary source of literature in the field is doubling in every 10 years. According to UNESCO statistics of World Book Production, about three lakh books are published every year. The number of learned journals in the field of science and technlogy alone has now come to the tune of 60,000 adding at the rate of 1000 journals a year approximately.

Another important problem librarians/information professionals are facing is the constant increase in the prices of library documents.

Another problem is increasing cost of library services as costs of library services have skyrocketed, libraries have realized that through cooperative arrangement there is the possibility of providing new services whose cost would be spread over many institutions. The concept of cooperation proves much effective and satisfies the user needs in a better way.

Thus, we may notice that in order to find a solution to the problems faced by libraries/information centers regarding information explosion and costs, library networks have been established for co-operation and resource sharing among libraries so that one individual library may not feel burdensome while handling vast amount of information and price escalation of library documents and services.

Present Scenario of Library Networking in India

The present status of library networking in India is that most of the libraries covered by some network are creating databases of their holdings and in automating the library activities. Generally, periodical holding is attempted first in building up the databases as it takes less time than for the other types of library documents. This is followed by the databases of holdings of books, reports, dissertations, standards, etc. The Library Network Centres, i.e., the co-ordinating agencies of the networks also are concentrating on equipping them to provide the user with access to the total records. They provide such access either by email or online through the telephone network. In addition, these centres also try to provide a common software for database development and automation of library activities and services.

9.3. LIBRARY AND INFORMATION NETWORKS

Table below gives the details of status of some important librarys networks in India.

Table. 9.3

Name	*Year of starting*	*Promoting Agency*	*Whether registered as a society*	*Database development & other activities*
ADINET (Ahmedabad)	1993	Society, INFLIBNET & NISSAT	Yes	Library holding database in progress, Library automation in progress, Training programme Database of current periodicals in member libraries

Name	*Year of starting*	*Promoting Agency*	*Whether registered as a society*	*Database development & other activities*
BALINET (Bangalore)	1995	NISSAT	Yes	Activity will start after getting financial support from NISSAT
BONET (Mumbai)	1994	NCST & NISSAT	No	Online union catalogue of periodicals, online reqeust system of ILL E-mail and Internet access, online searching of foreign database Database on computer and as are software CD-ROM database searching, database of contents of Indian periodicals Soft ware for OPAC.
CALIBNET (Calcutta)	1992 (1986)	NISSAT	Yes	Library automation in progress. Access to Internet ad Dialog CD-ROM database searching.
DELNET (Delhi)	1990 (1988)	Society, NIC & NISSAT	Yes	Book database Multilingual book database. E-mail service. Union list of current periodicals. Database of Indian specialists. Online searcing of foreign databases.
INFLIBNET,	1991 (1988)	UGC	Yes	Union Catalogue of 50,000 records. Database of periodicals (30,000 records). Contents with Abstract Services (COPSAT). Training Programme for university library staff.
MALIBNET (Chennai)	1993	Society & INSDOC,	Yes	Current serials database. Journal contents database (1,00,000 records). All INSDOC databases on MALIBNET. Automative engineering database (4,500 records). Access to Internet and Knight

Name	*Year of starting*	*Promoting Agency*	*Whether registered as a society*	*Database development & other activities*
				Riddger (Dialog) database. CD-ROM database searching.
MYLIBNET (Mysore)	1994	Society, Mysore Library Consortium & NISSAT	Yes	Library automation in progress.

From the above table, it can be seen that except DELNET and INFLIBNET, most of the other library networks have yet to develop databases of library holdings in a significant way. Even these two networks have to go a long way, to cover in their databases, the entire holdings of all the participating libraries. Unless this is achieved, the networks would not be able to achieve significant resource sharing as well as rationalization in library acquisitions. Most of the networks are, however, making efforts towards this end by conducting training programmes for the staff of the participating libraries in data capturing, database development and automation of library activities and services.

9.3.1. ADINET

Ahmedabad Library Network (ADINET) is a network of libraries in and around Ahmedabad. ADINET was registered as a Society in October 1994. It was sponsored by National Information System for Science and Technology (NISSAT), Department of Scientific and Industrial Research, Government of India, until March 2003. ADINET aims to bring about cooperative mode of working amongst the libraries and information centres in and around Ahmedabad. The main objective of ADINET is to promote sharing of resources and disseminate information among member libraries by networking them and creating a centralized

Union catalogue of their holdings. A centralized database of periodicals, books & non-book materials available in libraries of Ahmedabad is being created by ADINET.

9.3.2. BONET

Bombay Library Network (BONET) was created in 1994 as a joint project of NCST, Mumbai, and NISSAT, New Delhi. BONET has created a database of 15,000 items on computers and software technology. It has a Union Catalogue of periodicals available in 25 libraries of the region, accessible through email. A number of CD-ROM databases are available on Novell server and are accessible on Local Area Network.

9.3.3. Developing Library Network (DELNET)

In Delhi, libraries have been growing very fast in respect of number and size and they cater to the specialized and general clientele of various types. These include the libraries of the universities, colleges, schools, research institutions, government libraries, public libraries and departmental libraries. Now a days, increase in information has led to increase in the demands of the users. It is pointed out that in the era of information explosion, libraries in India are generally ill-equipped to handle and retrieve information effectively. In most of the libraries, the financial resources and the space requirement for housing library collections are limited. The only option left with the librarians is to promote the sharing of resources by automation and networking. With this objective, the India International Centre initiated efforts for the establishment of Developing Library Network (DELNET) (formerly known as Delhi Library Network) in January 1988.

DELNET is the first operational library network in India sponsored by the National Information System for Science and Technology (NISSAT), Department of Science and Technology, Government of India. It was started as a project of India International Centre in 1988 and later officially registered as a society in June 1992.

The main objectives of DELNET are optimum utilization of funds through sharing of resources, creation of commonly usable databases and communication between libraries with the help of automation and networking. It will network 35 libraries in Delhi area. A packet switched network is envisaged with each cluster of libraries being serviced by a packet switching exchange. All databases created cooperatively are expected to reside on a central computer system and dial-up access will be provided to all participating libraries. This network will have email, file transfer, union catalogue of serials, database of holdings of individual libraries, bulletin board facilities, etc.

Activities of DELNET

(i) DELNET, a major resource sharing library network in South Asia connecting more than 863 libraries in 30 States and UTs in India and six countries outside India.

(ii) Goal to provide better and efficient services to the libraries both in and outside India.

(iii) Offers access through Internet to around 45 Lakh ctalogue records of books and also half million records of periodicals, articles, thesis and dissertations among other database.

(iv) Promoted by National Informatics Centre (NIC), Ministry of Communication and Information Technology, GOI and India International Centre (IIC), New Delhi.

(v) Registered as a society on June 30, 1992.

(vi) Recognized by Council of Scientific and Industrial Research (CSIR) as a scientific and research organization during 1993.

(vii) Governing Body members are reputed academicians/ Heads of various reputed Universities and Libraries/ Head of various GOI departments viz. Culture, Education and Information technology etc.

Objectives

(i) To promote sharing of resources among the libraries by developing a network of libraries by collecting, storing and disseminating information and by offering computerized services to the users.

(ii) To extensively provide Interlibrary loan and Document Delivery Services.

(iii) To coordinate with other regional, national, international network libraries for exchange of information and documents.

(iv) To develop specialized bibliographic database of books, serials and non-book material.

(v) To establish/facilitate the establishment of referral and/or research centers, and maintain a central online union catalogue of books, serials and non-book materials of all the participating libraries.

(vi) To offer technical guidance to the member-libraries on collecting, storing and disseminating information.

(vii) To develop a database of projects, specialists and institutions.

Benefits for Members

(i) Access to DELNET database.

(ii) Resource sharing.

(iii) Adoption of international standards.

(iv) Save on acquisitions.

(v) Professional service/training.

(vi) ILL online facility.

(vii) Wider subject coverage.

(viii) Assistance in retro-conversion.

(ix) Institute promotion through INTERNET.

(x) Concession to member-institutions.

DELNET-AICTE Initiative

DELNET and AICTE have signed on MOU to:

(i) Promote access to more relevant information in each library of AICTE approved technical institute.

(ii) Give training to library staff so that they get familiar with database creation work using international bibliographic standards.

(iii) Create union catalogue of resources available within the technical colleges and institutions for resource sharing purpose through DELNET.

(iv) Locate resource of national importance through DELNET online databases and make them available through inter libraryloan.

(v) Provision of a facility which "enables students and educators to publish their projects, writing and curriculum materials in a way that is both similar to and different from, traditional methods".

(vi) Providing support for collaborative working with various researchers.

The role of the DELNET is highly revolutionized with the use of Internet. The user who had geographical limitations can now have access to information available anywhere in the world.

9.3.4. INFLIBNET (Information and Library Network)

The University Grants Commission (UGC) in its attempt to establish networking has taken the initiative and decided to develop a network of academic libraries to effectively manage and administer the resources of these libraries and provide efficient library services to a large number of users, using modern computer and communications technologies. As a consequence of UGC's efforts INFLIBNET, a network of university and college libraries in India was established in 1988.

The network became functional in 1991. Over the years, the programme has progressed well. Beginning May 1996, the INFLIBNET is recognized as an independent autonomous Inter-University Centre (IUC) under UGC to co-ordinate and implement nationwide high-speed data network using state-of-the-art technologies for connecting all the university libraries in the country. INFLIBNET is set out to be a major player in promoting scholarly communication among academicians and researchers in India.

The ***objectives*** of INFLIBNET as envisaged in its Memorandum of Association are:

* To promote and establish communication facilities so as to improve capability in information transfer and access, to provide support to scholarship, learning, research and academic pursuit through cooperation and involvement of agencies concerned.
* To establish INFLIBNET as a computer communication network for linking libraries and information centres in universities, deemed to be universities, colleges, UGC information centres, institutions of national importance and R&D institutions, etc. avoiding duplication of efforts.

In order to fulfil the broad objectives listed above, the, INFLIBNET performs the following functions:

(i) To evolve a national network of libraries and information centres in the country and to improve information handling capability.

(ii) To provide reliable access to document collection

through online union catalogue;

(iii) To provide better access to bibliographic information sources with citation and abstracts through online accessing of international databases held by international information networks and centres;

(iv) To provide document services by establishing resource centres around libraries having a rich collection of documents.

(v) To promote information resource utilisation through shared cataloguing interlibrary loan service;

(vi) To computerise operations of libraries and information centres in the country following a uniform standard;

(vii) To facilitate communication among scientists, engineers, researchers, social scientists, academics, faculties and students through electronic-mail.

(viii) To enable users regardless of location and distance to access information;

(ix) To create online information service and

(x) To encourage cooperation among libraries.

As one of the steps towards achieving the laudable objectives mentioned above, the INFLIBNET has initiated the automation process by funding 54 university libraries. It appears that only 17 of these libraries which received financial assistance from INFLIBNET have so far acquired the hardware to commence the automation activity. Even the progress in respect of resource sharing during the period is stated to be rather slow.

INFLIBNET has also taken a number of other measures which facilitate the realisation of its objectives some of the significant steps in this direction are: (i) for the purposes of promoting resource sharing activity, it has alrelady created a union catalogue of 50,000 records. It may be mentioned here that union catalogue is one of the important tools which facilitates the resource identification, location and sharing aspects of resource sharing activity as a whole among members of the network; (ii) INFLIBNET has also took great initiative in the creation of database containing 65,000 records of thesis/dissertations and also a periodicals database having 30,000 records. These are some of pioneering efforts undertaken by INFLIBNET to realise its basic objectives.

The network has developed a standarised software, SOUL.

INFLIBNET is operating at four levels:

(i) National (a National Centre to coordinate the activities and services of the network)

(ii) Regional (four regional centres each housed in a university library in the region)

(iii) Sectoral (Various Sectoral Information centres)

(iv) Local (about 400 nodes at colleges, departments, universities, and R & D centres). In addition, about 100 Document Resource Centres located in the universities and R&D organizations are also proposed to be set up for document delivery service.

Services

INFLIBNET programme is a multi-service network planned to offer catalogue based services, database services, document supply services (Fax/Non-Fax), collection development, referral services, email, bulletin board, audio & video, computer conferencing services and facilities. More services might be included as the network progresses.

The participating institutions can gain in many ways. Each library becomes richer with access to large information resource. Exhaustive search becomes possible, precise retrieval of information is ensured, speedier dissemination of information and fast document delivery service are accomplished and communication with experts and like minded academicians becomes a reality. The network will provide gateway to international systems.

The UGC INFONET

On behalf of the UGC, the INFLIBNET is executing the UGC INFONET project in collaboration with the ERNET. Formally inaugurated by the Hon'ble Prime Minister on 28th December, 2002, under UGC INFONET initiatives, university campuses are being modernized with state-of-the-art campus wide networks. The UGC is setting up its own nationwide communication network called UGC-INFONET. The UGC-INFONET is being overlaid on ERNET infrastructure to provide assured quality of service and optimal utilization of bandwidth resources. The project is being funded by the UGC with 90% capital investment and 100% recurring cost during the X Plan period. A Joint Technical and Tariff Committee (JTTC), consisting of leading experts in the country has been set up to guide and monitor the entire project. INFLIBNET Centre, an autonomous IUC of the UGC, is the nodal agency for co-ordination of the UGC-INFONET and facilitates linkage between ERNET and the universities. UGC-INFONET will be a boon to the higher education system in several ways.

UGC's E-Journals Consortium

The UGC's E-Journals Consortium aims at providing online access to electronic journals and databases in all disciplines to the universities in India. All universities which come under the purview of UGC will be beneficiary members of the programme. The scheme would be gradually extended to colleges as well. The programme is being executed by Information and Library Network (INFLIBNET) Centre, Ahmedabad. Access to various electronic resources have formally commenced from January 1, 2004, initially for 50 universities and has been extended to 100 universities with effect from January, 2005.

The programme aims at increasing accessibility of electronic resources to the universities. It will go a long way in mitigating the severe shortage of periodicals faced by university libraries for several years. The E-Journals programme is a cornerstone of the UGC-INFONET effort, which aims at addressing the teaching, learning, research, connectivity and governance requirements of the universities. The E-Journals programme demonstrates how communication networks and computers can be used to stretch and leverage available funds in furthering these aims.

9.3.5. CALIBNET

Calcutta Libraries Network (CALIBNET) is the result of the initiative taken by NISSAT to ensure better utilization of the available science and technology information resources in this metropolitan city through resource sharing.

CALIBNET was planned to link 38 science and technology libraries of various sizes located in the Kolkata Metropolitan area in two phases (eight in the first phase and the remaining thirty in the second phase). All these libraries as a prerequisite are first to be computerised and then linked into a network.

Functions

All functions, e.g., cataloguing, serials control, acquisition, fund accounting, circulation and local user services in the participation libraries are computerised.

Services

The network is intended to provide such services as current awarneess, SDI union catalogue, partial databases and access to the national and international networks.

Main Features

The main features include on-line/ off-line input, editing and retrieval of records. CALIBNET eventually will be connected to all other metropolitan networks (Delhi, Mumbai, Chennai and other cities) through packet-switched data network.

9.3.6. PUNENET

Following the launching of DELNET and the creation of CALIBNET a feasibility study of Automation and Networking of Libraries in Pune Metropolitan Area (PUNENET) was made which recommended implementation.

Objectives

PUNENET is planned for implementation in four phases with the objectives of better utilization of funds through sharing of resources by creation of commonly usable databass and communication between libraries and automating the functions of the individual libraries.

Services

The network services to be offered are union cataloue, current awareness, SDI, authority data, acquisition and fund accounting, serials control, books and journals maintenance, circulation, user services, interlibrary loan services, document transfer/copy, access to national/international databases.

Other metropolitan area networks planned and initiated are BONET (Bombay), MALIBNET (Madras), HYLIBNET (Hyderabad), ADNET (Ahmedabad).

9.3.7. DESINET

Defence Science Information Network (DESINET) is a library and information network proposed for DRDO to cover unclassified and technical information. The DESIDOC, Delhi is involved in planning and implementing this network. As it is intended to cover defence information needs, it will serve the concerned scientific research and defence communities in the country. This network will also be linked with similar other networks.

9.3.8. ERNET

ERNET is developed as a computer network for educational and research institutions in India. ERNET started with 8 leading institutions (the five Indian Institute of Technology, the Indian Institute of Science, the National Centre for Software Technology (NCST), and the Department of Electronics (DOE)).

Objectives

The main objective of ERNET is to enhance "National capabilities in the areas of design, development, research, education and training on the state-of-the-art concepts of computer networking and related emerging technologies".

(i) Its immediate aims are to progressively set up a nationwide network for academic and research communities starting with eight participating premier institutions.

(ii) undertake design, development and advanced research in computer networking and related technologies.

(iii) conduct education, continuing education, training and consultancy programmes to generate critical manpower needed by the industry and the clients.

Services

ERNET offers e-mail, file transfer, remote log-on, database access, bulletin board, etc., and other communication services.

9.3.9. SIRNET

The Scientific and Industrial Research Network (SIRNET) was planned by the Council of Scientific and Industrial Reserch (CSIR) as a computer communication network for exchange of information among its 40 laboratories and R & D institutions. The NCST, Mumbai was commissioned to undertake the feasibility study.

Objectives

The main objectives of the SIRNET are to harness the vast scientific information resources available with national laboratories; to ensure and make possible resource sharing among them; and to link the entire scientific community of the country with the national library system and to facilitate international scientific communication.

Coverage

SIRNET will help organizing indigenous online database services on different subjects such as leather technology, food technology, natural products, chemistry, radio-physics and medicinals plants.

Architecture

SIRNET is planned as a four layer system consisting of backbone nodes (constituting the first layer to span the length and breadth of the country), city nodes (as the second layer to function as cleaning house for the traffic originating/ terminating in the cities having more than one laboratory and not provided with backbone), laboratory nodes (Third layer provided at the individual CSIR laboratories that may be directly connected either to the city or backbone nodes), and local end users (constituting the fourth layer linked to laboratory, city or backbone nodes).

Services

Keeping in view the data exchange needs and resources sharing and information requirements of CSIR scientists, SIRNET will make available services such as electronic mail (already implemented in the first phase using high pitch response from all CSIR laboratories and other

R&D institutions coming up on the network), file transfer (Transfer of different files from one machnie to another); document transfer/ILL (using facsimile transmission for exchanging or processing copies of documents); and database access (to access NISCAIR produced indigenous databases, viz., *National Union Catalogue of Scientific Serials in India, Current Contents of Indian Journals, Polymer Science Database, Material Science Bibliographic Database, Catalogue of Scientific & Technical Conference Proceedings, etc.)*

Inter Networking

SIRNET has at present only one mail node (CSIR Mail node) located at NISCAIR, New Delhi. Connected to a larger network, ERNET (Education and Research Network) set up by the DOE with financial assitance from UNDP, provides e-mail facility to 20 non-CSIR institutions. ERNET being connected to the international network, UUNET (Unix User Network) other international networks like BITNET, DSNET, JANET, etc., are also accessed. Direct access to more than 6,000 databases is available through Geteway Packet Switching System (GPSS) of the Videsh Sanchar Nigam Ltd. (VSNL) from Delhi, Mumbai, Channai, Bangalore, Hyderabad, Pune and other cities. NISCAIR has established access to over 1800 international databases on 15 different hosts through VSNL-GPSS facility. The I-NET (Set up by the department of Telecommunications, Govt. of India) offers facilities for interlinking terminals and computers through packet switches located in important cities of the country. Eventually, SIRNET will operate through I-NET, the main national data network I-NET also provides access to international databases through GPSS-VSNL, Mumbai.

9.3.10. Vidyanet

VIDYANET is a proposed dedicated communication computer network for meeting the needs of scientists and research workers in the leading laboratories and research institutions of the country. The suggestion for VIDYANET came from the scientists of the Tata Institute of Fundamental Research, Mumbai.

Objectives

One of the VIDYANET's major objectives is to stimulate corporate research, day-to-day exchange of research information and the execution of joint projects and publications. It also intends to allow users to develop databases on specialized areas like bio-technology, superconductivity and supernova research. It aims at providing rapid means of communication by linking computers at various institutions in India to similar networks outside, like EARN (European Academic Research Network, Ganeva), and BITNET.

Services

VIDYANET can provide facilities such as transfer files of any type (Data, programmes, documents); receiving and sending electronic mail to one or more users; exchange of immediate messages; sharing of computer resources and access to remote applications, databases, libraries etc. In its first phase VIDYANET will link up about ten institutions from all over the country.

9.3.11. BTISNET

It is a specialised information network. The Department of Biotechnology, Government of India, is setting up ten specialised information centres in genetic engineering, plant tissue culture, photosynthesis and plant molecular biology, cell transformation, bio-process engineering, etc.

Facilities

The facilities assured are making available international scientific information; easy access (through NICNET) of current information in bio-technology by R&D centres, universities and other scientific sections situated in the remote parts of the country; data processing using applications software in an interactive mode from the specific resident node; wide distribution of databases covering various aspects of biotechnology, provision of access to specialised applications software on remote location to obviate the need for duplication of software and facilities at each location; and establishing of online communication access with international networks through a gateway from the apex node of BTIS.

The entire system would be superimposed on the NICNET to take advantage of the telecommunication facilities and the powerful computing system of NIC installed at Pune, Hyderabad and Delhi. The nodes of BTIS and the user centres will be provided with facsimile facility and core staff to main the centres. Under the BTIS programme, the computerised services will be available for retrieval of bibliographic information.

General Networks

The following are the general data networks which have some bibliographic applications as well.

9.3.12. NICNET

The National Information Centre (New Delhi) established the National Informatics Centre Network (NICNET) based on satellite technology. NICNET is concerned with government departments and public sector organizations for data transmission. All state capitals have been connected with compatible computer systems to the respective district headquarters. Eventually, this network would facilitate flow of information among the four national and regional nodes, 32 states and union territory nodes and all the districts nodes in the country.

Bibliographic Applications

In collaboration with the ICMR, National Informatics Centre established ICMRNIC centre for biomedical information. Access to international biomedical databases will avoid unnecessary duplication in research, provide vital information for patient care and bring about improvement in health services. NIC has succeeded in establishing MEDLARS in India, the only country in South-East Asia to receive MEDLARS information. Thus, this network is offering services to MEDLARS database and several others on CD-ROM. NISSAT is working with NICNET to mount Chemical Abstracts database.

9.3.13. INDONET

Developed by the CMC Ltd. in 1986 it is the first commercial computer network designed for intercity data communication. It provides such facilities as ACME for advanced store-and-forward messaging techniques; file transfer from computer to computer; distributed data processing; special purpose software; international gateway; database access, etc.

Bibliographic Applications

In addition to the above services INDONET has also some bibliographic applications which are useful for library and information world.

Both INDONET AND NICNET have undertaken to put the National Union Catalogue of Scientific Serials in India database (NUCSSI) online. INDONET also collaborates with NISCAIR and the NISSAT centre at CMTI, Banglore to create facilities for SDI and retrospective search services on COMPENDEX.

9.3.14. VIKRAM

The Department of Telecommunications, Government of India has piloted VIKRAM as packet switched public data network with its Network Management Centre at Delhi. All the eight switching nodes and 12 remote access points will be connected by telecommunications system.

Bibliographical Applications

Like NICNET and INDONET, VIKRAM also has bibliographical applications. It has offered its infrastructure to NISSAT for pilot experimentation on library networking in the country.

CONCLUSION

During the recent period, quite a large number of libraries and information centres are seen actively trying to apply IT and federate into networks. In addition to the public data, general and specialised networks described, many other specific/ special networks for Railways, Airways, Banking, Steel, Coal etc., are also coming up fast. India is thus on the threshold to a new era of computer communication networks both for general purposes and for library and information purposes. NISSAT, although plays a key role, there are many tasks that it has yet to tackle. These tasks relate to better hardware and software systems on one hand and manpower planning and development on the other.

While the special libraries and the information centres of major national laboratories as well as R&D institutions have registered considerable progress in automation, the other libraries, such as academic libraries and public libraries are still conventionally managed. The high profile INFLIBNET which came into being in 1991 is still far behind the targets. Among the other networks DELNET is perhaps the only one that is in operation having achieved the targets satisfactorily. The other networks like BONET, HYLIBNET, MALIBNET, BALNET, ADINET are yet to make headway. It is felt that CALIBNET has not created any value-added products as yet and has not fulfilled the basic objectives of library network like INTERNET, CD-ROM search, etc. facilities made available at CALIBNET and other similar nets are not so very important because any institution/Library can acquire these facilities. What is more important is creation of databases for the library resources. The situation calls for rethinking and application of appropriate measures to ensure effective and efficient network systems in the country.

10
Network Topologies

10.1. INTRODUCTION

A network is a logical extension of a data communication system. In a computer network, two or more processors or computers are linked together with carriers and data communication devices for the purpose of communicating data and sharing resources. The term *'topology'* in the context of a communications network, refers to the way in which the end points or stations of a network are linked together. It determines the data paths that may be used between any pair of stations of the network. Although, the number of possible network configurations is seemingly limitless, there are three major network configurations. They are the ***star network, the ring network***, and the ***completely connected network***. In practice many networks are composite networks which interlink network with different topologies and protocols. The inference between the networks is provided by a gateway switch.

10.1.1. Star Network

In a star configuration of computer network, there is a host computer which is attached to local computers through multiple communication lines. As shown in Figure: 10.1.1, local computers are not linked directly to each other and can communicate only via the host computer. The routing function is performed by the host computer which centrally controls communication between any two local computers by establishing a logical path between them.

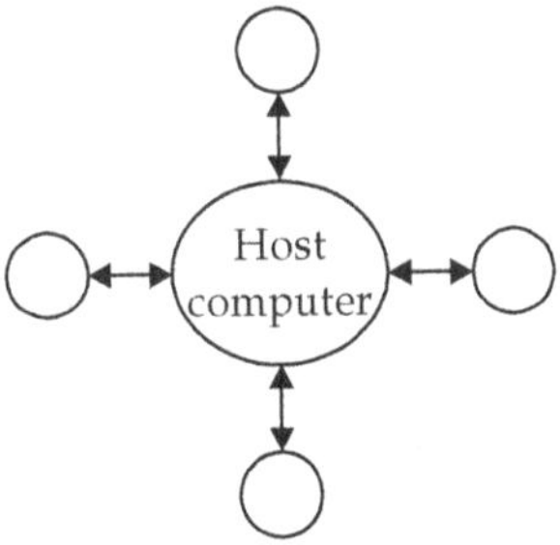

Fig. 10.1.1 : A star configuration of computer network

Advantages

1. Star topology has minimal line cost because only n-1 lines are required for connecting n nodes.
2. Transmission delays between two nodes do not increase by adding new nodes to the network because any two nodes may be connected via two links only.
3. If any of the local computers fail, the remaining portion of the network is unaffected.

Disadvantage

1. The system crucially depends on the central node. If is the host computer fails, the entire network fails.

10.1.2. Ring Network

This configuration is a no-host or ring arrangement of communicating equals. That is, there is no main or controlling computer in the network. Figure:10.1.2 illustrates the circular or ring arrangement of a computer network. Each ring processor has communicating subordinates, out within the ring there is no master computer for controlling other computers.

Thus, each node of a ring network must have simple communication capability. A node receives data from one of its two adjacent nodes. The only decision a node has to take is whether the data is for its use or not. If it is addressed to it, it utilises it. Otherwise it merely passes it on to the next node.

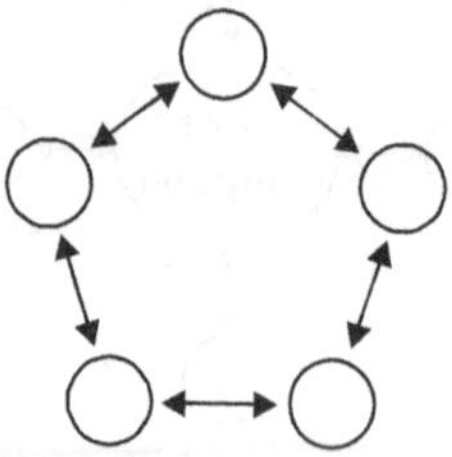

Fig. 10.1.2 : A ring configuration of computer network

Advantages

1. The ring network works well where there is no central-site computer system. It is a truly distributed data processing system.
2. It is more reliable than a star network because communication is not dependent on a single host computer. If one line between any two computers breaks down, or if one of the computers breaks down, alternate routing is possible.

Disadvantages

1. In a ring network, communication delay is directly proportional to the number of nodes in the network. Hence, addition of new nodes in the network increases the communication delays.
2. The ring network is not as popular as star network because of its more complicated control software.

10.1.3. Completely Connected Network

As shown in Figure: 10.1.3, a completely connected network has a separate physical link for connecting each node of any other node. Thus, each computer of such network has a direct dedicated link, called a point-to-point link with all other computers of the network. The control is distributed with each computer deciding its communication priorities.

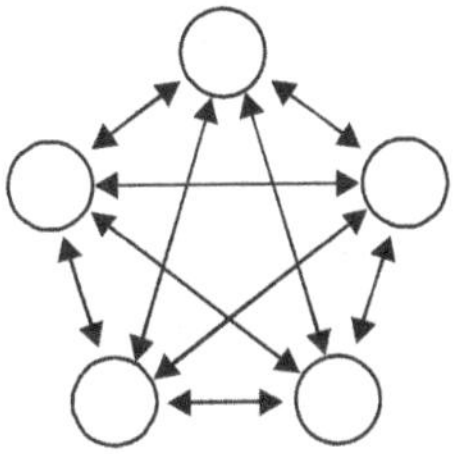

Fig. 10.1.3 : A completely connected computer network

Advantages

1. This type of network is very reliable as any line breakdown will affect only communication between the connected computers.
2. Each node of the network need not have individual routing capability.
3. Communication is very fast between any two nodes.

Disadvantages

1. It is the most expensive system from the point of view of line costs. If there are n nodes in the network, then n(n-1)/2 links are required. Thus, the cost of linking the system grows with the square of the number of nodes.

10.1.4. Hybrid Network

The choice of topology for installing a computer network depends upon a combination of factors such as:

1. Reliability of the entire system.
2. Expandability of the system.
3. Cost involved.
4. Availability of communication lines.

5. Delays involved in routing information from one node to another.

Different network configuration have their own advantages and limitations. Hence, in reality, a pure star or ring or completely connected network is rarely used. Instead, an organisation will use some sort of hybrid network, which is simply a combination network. The exact shape or configuration of the network depends on the needs and the overall organisational structure of the organisation involved. In some cases, the hybrid network may have components of star, ring and completely connected networks. A typical network of this type is shown in figure 10.1.4.

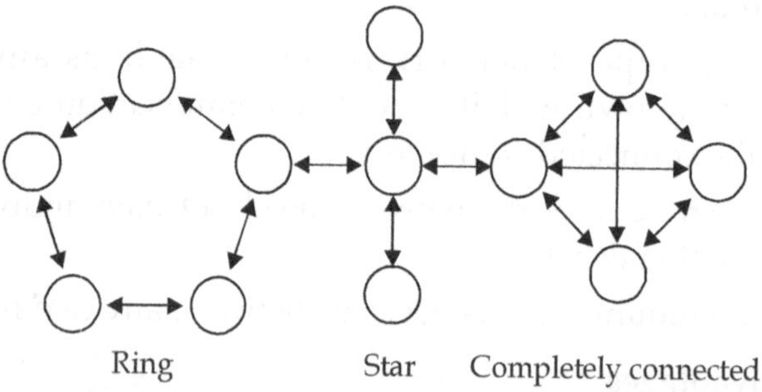

Fig. 10.1.4: A typical hybrid network having a combination of ring, star, and completely connected network configurations

10.1.5. Multipoint Network

There is yet another method of linking computers together in a network. In this method, a single transmission medium is shared by all nodes. As shown in Figure: 10.1.5, all the computers are attached to the same line. When a particular computer wants to send a message to another computer, it appends the destination address to the message and checks whether the communication line is free. As soon as the line becomes free, it broadcasts (places) the message on the line. As the message travels on the line, each computer checks whether it is addressed to it. The message is picked up by the addressee computer which sends an acknowledgement to the source computer and frees the line. This method is known as 'multipoint' or 'multidrop' linkage of computers. It is also known as a 'broadcasting' network. This method is appropriate for use in a local area network where a high speed communication channel is used and computers are confined to a small area. It is also appropriate when satellite communication is used as one satellite channel may be shared by many computers at a number of geographical locations.

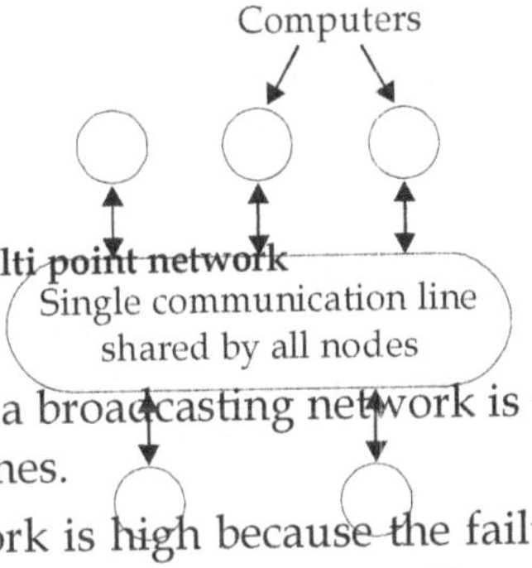

Fig. 10.1.5 : A multi point network

Advantages

1. The main advantage of a broadcasting network is the reduction in physical lines.
2. The reliability of network is high because the failure of a computer in the network does not effect the network functioning for other computers.
3. Addition of new computers to the network is easy.

Disadvantages

1. Each computer connected to the line must have good communication and decision making capability.
2. If the communication line fails, the entire system breaks down.

10.2. LOCAL AREA NETWORK (LAN)

A *local area network* (LAN) is a digital communication system capable of interconnecting a large number of computers, terminals and other peripheral devices within a limited geographical area, typically under 1 Km. LANs normally operates within a compact area such as an office building or a campus and is owned by the using organisation. The configuration of a LAN can be a star, a ring, or simply devices attached along a length of cable. In LAN, transmission channels generally use coaxial or fiber optic cables and special interface units rather than telephone lines and modems. Thus, the transmission speed is very high. The attached computers may be of different types and be performing a variety of functions such as data processing, word processing, and electronic mail. The two main purposes of the local area network are to link computers within an organisation or campus so that they may share expensive peripheral devices, for example high speed printers or magnetic disks holding the data base, and to allow these computers to communicate with each other.

Ethernet, developed by **Xerox** Corporation, is a famous example of a LAN. This network uses a coaxial cable for data transmission. Special integrated circuit chips called controllers are used to connect equipment to the cable, and small boxes called transceivers transmit and receive cable data at each station. Each station can exchange data with any other station or group of stations. This particular LAN can tie together **Xerox** computer systems, copiers and other devices. Furthermore, devices made by other computer manufactures can also be made compatible with Ethernet.

Omninet, developed by Corvus systems, is another example of a LAN. This particular network has the ability to interconnect micro-computer systems. Radio Shack, Apple and other micro-computer systems can be interconnected using Omninet.

10.2.1. Characteristics

The various characteristics of LAN are as follows:

(i) It links multiple different types of user computers together.

(ii) In a LAN, computers are spreaded over a small geographical area ranging from few meters to few kilometers.

(iii) It avoids degradation of performance.

(iv) In a LAN, communication channels are usually privately owned and hence, not regulated by telecommunication departments and are of relatively high capacity and are error free.

(v) It reduces dependence on a central system and helps to share resources like hard disk, CD, printers etc.

(vi) It also helps to implement online applications at high speed rate.

(vii) It is generally operated in the Mbits (Megabit per second).

10.2.2. Advantages

There are various advantages of LAN among which important ones include the following:

(i) It provides a cost effective and increased computer effectiveness environment.

(ii) It is obsolescence proof, flexible and growth oriented.

(iii) It allows resource sharing.

(iv) It provides foolproof security system against illegal access of data.

(v) It is redundancy supportable.

10.2.3. LAN and Library and Information Services

Various housekeeping operations and technical services as acquisition, cataloguing, circulation and serial controls and information services can be managed through

LAN. According to Selvi and Butler (1975), there are five characteristic features for library resource sharing network.

(i) A dependent system which is operated multilaterally in response to the common desires of a group of member libraries.

(ii) A duplex element which enables two way communication which separates a network from publication of information service which is one-way.

(iii) Digital, which involves some use of computers or digital machines.

(iv) The distribution of information, which may take many forms such as catalogue cards and print out etc.

(v) An independent organisation, separate from the administrative, political and fiscal bounds of its members.

Like other modern technologies, the LAN can also be used as an important tool for resource sharing in information handling.

By establishing a local area network of the local libraries, their different primary and secondary sources, databases, computer based information services can be shared besides cataloguing and classification etc. This will not only save the time of technical staff but also be economic for them, if all the processing is done under local control of a workstation. With the use of a LAN, we can provide right information to the users at the right time at a lower cost on his desk.

10.3. WIDE AREA NETWORK (WAN)

A *wide area network* (WAN) is a digital communication system which interconnects different sites, computer installations and user terminals, and may also enable LANs to communicate with each other. This type of communication network may be developed to operate nationwide or worldwide. In a WAN, the transmission medium used are normally public systems such as telephone lines, microwave and satellite links. Packet switching is most effective as public connection services are available for packet switched WANs. A WAN is also knwon as a *log haul network*.

The ARPANET of the Advanced Research Projects Agency of the U.S. Department of Defence is an example of WAN. This network connects about 40 universities and research instituions throughout the United States and Europe with about 50 computers ranging in size from minis to supercomputers. Another example of a WAN is the INDONET which is being planned by the Computer Maintenance Corporation, India. It links three IBM/4361 systems one each at Mumbai, Kolkata and Chennai and a PDP 11/44 system at Delhi. It is a network of large computer centres to give nationwide access and processing facilities.

Difference between LAN & WAN

1. A LAN is restricted to a limited geographical coverage of a few kilometers, but a WAN spans greater distances and may operate nationwide or even worldwide.
2. The cost of transmitting data in a LAN is negligible since the transmission medium is usually owned by the user organisation. However, in case of a WAN, this cost may be very high because the transmission medium used are leased lines or public systems such as telephone lines, microwave and satellite links.
3. In a LAN, the computers, terminals and peripherical devices are usually physically connected with wires and coaxial cables. Whereas, in a WAN there may not be a direct physical connection between various computers.
4. Data transmission speed is much higher in LAN than in a WAN. Typical transmission speeds in LANs are 0.1 to 100 mega bits per second. On the other hand, in a WAN the data transmission speed is normally of the

order of 1800 to 9600 bits per second.

5. Fewer data transmission errors occur in case of a LAN as compared to a WAN. This is mainly because in case of a LAN, the distance covered by the data in negligible as compared to a WAN.

10.4. COMMUNICATION PROTOCOLS

In a computer network, how are computers and related devices actually able to send information across data communications lines? The answer is ***data communication software***. In fact, it is the data communication software that is responsible for holding all data communications systems together. It instructs computer systems and devices as to exactly how the data is to be transferred from one place to another. These procedures embedded in the software are commonly called ***protocols.***

Thus, in data communication, a *protocol* is a set of rules and procedures established to control transmission between two points so that the receiver can properly interpret the bit stream transmitted by the sender. It provides a method for orderly and efficient exchange of data by establishing rules for the proper interpretation of controls and data transmitted as raw bits and bytes.

Roles of Protocol

In any computer network, data communication software normally performs the following functions for the efficient and error free transmission of data:

1. Data sequencing: It refers to breaking a long transmission into smaller blocks and maintaining control. That is, a long message is split up into smaller packets of fixed size. These packets are further fragmented into data frames. This techniques is widely used in conjunction with error control techniques to reduce the amount of data that must be retransmitted in case of detected error.

2. Data routing: Routing algorithms are designed to find the most efficient route between sources and destinations. They can handle varying degrees of traffic on the present network configuration with optimal time utilisation. Normally, they are dynamic enough to accommodate network changes and growth.

3. Flow control: A communication protocol also prevents a fast sender from overwhelming a slow receiver. It ensures resource sharing and protection against congestion by regulating the flow of data on the communication lines.

4. Error control: Error detecting and recovering routines are also an important element of communications protocols. The most common method for correcting errors is to retransmit a block. This method requires coordination of the two stations so that the block having error is discarded by the receiving station and is repeated by the transmitting station.

5. Precedence and order of transmission: There are well defined rules to condition all stations about when to transmit their data and when to receive data from other stations. It is ensured that all stations get a chance to use the communication lines and other resources of the network depending upon the priorities assigned to them.

6. Connection establishment: When two stations of a network want to communicate with each other, the communication protocol establishes and verifies a connection between the two.

7. Data security: Providing data security and privacy is also built into most communications software packages. It prevents access of data by unauthorized users because it is relatively easy to tap a data communication line.

8. Log information: Data communication software can also develop log information which consists of all jobs and data communications tasks that have taken place. Such information is normally used for financial purposes and the various users of the network are charged accordingly.

11
Internet : Genesis, Growth and Development

11.1. INTRODUCTION

The Internet consists of a large number of linked computer networks forming a global network. This is largely open and free, allowing users to communicate with each other for work and recreational purposes, and for corporate and personal reasons. Because the Internet is so vast and is without regulation or hierarchy, the network is a treasure-trove of information from many sources. Resources are available in all subjects; mailing is possible for all the participants; documents can be forwarded and delivered across the world and directories and journals abound. Developments such as the World Wide Web (WWW) combine friendliness of user interface with enormously powerful information retrieval capability. Electronic mail is one of the most important services offered through the Internet, with each person having a personal mail address, enabling them to link up to another user anywhere in the world and communicate within seconds. In other words, it is easier to view the Internet in two related but distinct parts : it is the communications network, which is the immense web of interconnected local and wide area networks, telephone lines, cables, fibre-optics and satellite links which provide the medium for the transfer of information around the Internet, and the computers and computing sites which actually hold and process the data which is available to be transmitted across the network. It may be metioned that while the communications networks part of things are well integrated and for the most part operates transparently to the user, the same cannot be said about the data end of the business.

It may further be stated that the communications network is basically a physical networks of connections, which provide the means of passing signals from one place to another. The adoption of a common set of protocols, or standard "ways of talking" makes it easy to use. In other words, these protocols enable data to be passed coherently and easily from one place on the network to another. TCP/IP (Transmission Control Protocol/Internet Protocol) is at the heart of Internet Communications. The TCP/IP must be thought of as a common langauge and rules for the behaviour in the communications environment which all parts of the Internet share and understand. All the computer systems connected to the Internet must be in a position to communicate in TCP/IP langauge. We can say that communicate in TCP/IP langauge or have some arrangement to interpret and translate TCP/IP instructions. The end users need not know anything about how TCP/IP works. Users can communicate or talk through their local operating systems such as Windows, DOS, UNIX, etc., and programmes will take care of translating user's requirements into a form which complies with the protocol. However, the users must remeber that the TCP/IP common langauge is concerned with one thing only, that is communication. All it does is to make it easy for one machine to contact another to be able to pass data from one place to another. It has nothing to do with controlling, specifying or standardising the content of the data which may be transmitted. Therefore, as an answer to the questions, 'what is Interent?' We may state that Internet is a collection of interlinked computer networks, or a network of networks. Currently, Internet connects over one million different computers and the rate of increase in use and new subscribers is growing everday. The Internet provides global connectivity via a mesh of networks based on the TCP/IP and Open Systems Interconnection (OSI) protocols. Historically, the Internet was essentially an academic network for communication between eminent research centres, but is also accessible to colleges, businesses and libraries throughout the world. In other words, the Internet offers a gatway to a myriad of online databases, Library catalogues and collections, and software and document archives in addition to e-mail.

Technically speaking, "the Internet is a massive, searchable, dynamic, widely available, distributed, multip-platform information system which possesses a number of general capabilities." In looking at the Internet objectively, most librarians feel that it has opened up wide vistas of sources (including graphic sound and text materials) on a global basis that previously were unavailable to the average library or individual searchers. Of course, it assumes that the searcher has the proper equipment, software and Internet connection before anything happens, and even then, retrieving material might be slow, or impossible to achieve in certain cases because there is so much traffic on the system. In other cases, the searcher may quickly discover great quantities of materials of interest or perhaps a single item that is very valuable to retrive. Therefore, the Internet can be a very useful system for enlarging sources of data of a library.

11.2. CONCEPT AND DEFINITION

Internet is the abbreviation of Internet work system and is described as a network of networks. To some people, it is source of entertainment, to others it is a research tool, yet to others, it is a gold mine of money-making opportunities.

Different computer experts, however, define 'Internet' differently. To Pinaki Ray, one of the known experts in the field, "the buzz word to end all buzzwords is Internet". He prefers to call Internet as cybermocracy which has no class, no creed, and no political borders.

Mr. H. R. Mohan, Systems Manager, defines 'Internet' as the network of networking computers facilitating easy transfer of information across computers".

Internet, according to Joe Abernathey is 'a network of all kinds of computers that use myriad operating systems. Packets of data travel from system to system along the Internet until they reach their destination. Internet designers required a linguafranca, the system could understand, so that packets could get where they were supposed to go, even if, some links in the net were down.'

M. Ganapathy, described 'Internet' differently. According to him, "Internet is a global collection of people and computers, all linked together by many miles of cables and telephone lines, all able to communicate because they talk a common language- the Transmission Control Protocol/ Internet Protocol (TCP/IF).

Mark Butler remarks that computer alone cannot keep the Internet alive. On the one hand, internet is a vast collection of large and small interconnected computer networks extending all the way across the world, while on the other, it is all the people whose active participation make the Internet, a valuable information source.

The Internet's world wide web is, therefore, a vast electronic library, made up of millions of pages of informration stored in hundreds of thousand of linked computers arround the globe. With the proper computer software and the right internet connections, PC users can flip from page to page browse from one electronic document to another just by pointing and clicking on the computer screen in least possible time, Thus, internet, a worldwide entity, could technically be defined as a set of all interconnected networks. In other words, internet is a federation of networks or network of networks that speak the same protocol.

11.3. GENESIS, GROWTH AND DEVELOPMENT

During 1969, the U.S Department of Defence, through their Advanced Research Project Agency (ARPA) created an experiment. This was a Packet Switched Network over telephone lines. Out of this initial network, Advance Research Project Agency Network (ARPANET) on of the early forerunners of Internet was born. During 1970s the ARPA developed a set of rules, called protocols, that helped in connecting different networks having different host computers. The number of networks connected to ARPANET continued to grow over the years. The American Defence Department inavdvertently created this electronic commune as a way of military researchers to make contact with each other. This world-wide network of networks having its origin in the U.S Defence Department's ARPANET (Advanced Project Research Administration/Agency Networks), one of the early fore-runners of internet, has now become an electronic global village ARPANET allowed scientists, researchers, and military personnel at diverse sites to communicate through email. Subsequently, the other sites which were not connected to ARPA Net, began to see the advantages of electronic communication. Many of these sites found ways of connect their private networks to the ARPANet. Most of these private networks were not having a similar host computer and hence, it led to the need of hooking-up computer systems to host computer systems that were fundamentally different from each other (say, IBM and non IBM machines). During 1970s, the ARPA (Advanced

Research Project Agency) developed a set of rules, called protocols that helped in connecting different networks having different host computers. Before the close of the decade, the craze spread in such a way that many networks all over the world were connected to ARPANet and the number of such networks continued to grow. During 1982, ARPANet joined with MILNet (the military network) and a few others, and it is said that Internet was thus born from this consolidation of networks.

11.3.1. Growth and Development

While internet was started origianlly at U.S.A in 1969 as a defence project, in India it started as a ERNET project in 1987-88. While describing the hidden clues of the growth of WWW, a study aptly remarked that given the growth and increasing commercialism of the Web, it is easy to forget that the system was created only in 1989 to help scientists to share information. The study states further that, though Internet itself was set up in 1969, graphical browser, software programmes that help users mouse-click their way around the web, were first developed in 1993 and the popularity of Netscape Communication's Navigator browser caused an explosion of activity in 1994. However, Internet was made available in its full blown version in India only on 15th August 1995 by Videsh Sanchar Nigam Limited (VSNL), a Government of India enterprises. Thus, Internet, the largest computer network of networks in the world has witnessed a spectacular growth particularly during last few years. The study conducted by Andrew Pollack (1995) on the growth of Internet shows as to how fast the world community got addicted towards this much debated cybermocracy.

According to Toney Rutkowski, Executive Director of the Internet Society (a group that oversees development of network), half of the internet domains at present are outside the U.S. It has been estimated that internet connects around 20 million users world-wide today and is growing by more than a million users each month. However, the study conducted by Chandrasekhar shows that, internet has now about 2 million computers connected with over 40 million users world wide- thus, having a growth rate of 10 percent per month. On contrary to this, estimates that, Internet comprises around 30,000 different networks spread over 180 countries across the globe having more than 50 million users growing at a rate of 1.5 million a month.

Netcom, one of the biggest internet companies in the world, however, claims to have more than, 1,30,000 individual consumers which it serves under 'Internet Service' for individuals.

The traffic on the internet, according to study, is growing at a phenomenal rate of 12% per month. Internet has grown from a small, closed, and highly specialised system to a world wide network providing service to about 6-7 million people across the globe.

The Internet Society, on the other hand, estimates that the number of host computers worldwide to have increased from half a million in 1991 to four millions at the end of 1994. The number of users, estimated at 20 millions today, is expected to increase to 250 millions by the year 2007 AD.

The study conducted by M. Govindarajan shows that, 'Internet' is actually a collection of 48,000 public and private networks spread all over the world, to which computer owners from 77 countries have gained access.

A recent survey of 1,258 respondents conducted by Yahoo, a provider of Internet search engine in London (U.K) dispels the myth that, 85% use Internet in the office and at home; 97% communicate by E-mail; 73% use the Internet daily; and 59% spend atleast six hours a week using the Internet.

11.4. INTERNET TECHNOLOGY

Among all networking technologies, the internet

technology is most useful and economically viable in the era of present communication system. The term "Internet" comes from a concept called inter-networking that denotes interaction between networks of computers. It is a vast collection of large and small inter-connected networks extending all the way across the world. The Internet world wide web (www) is, therefore, a vast electronic library made-up of millions of pages of information stored in hundreds of thousands of linked computers around the globe. It is basically a network of inter-connected computer systems spread throughout lengths and breadths of the globe and which is largest networks of computers in the world providing major information services. Thus, information supply highway enables the following:

(i) User from any part of the world can connect or access information irrespective of time and space factors.

(ii) Users on this worldwide network can exchange electronic mail with one another within a few seconds.

(iii) Users can talk with one another online.

Internet is thus, an international network of networks. More than 30,000 networks are connected among 71 countries through internet. In each of these countries, there is at least one backbone computer which operates at a very high speed to carry the bulk of traffic load. In India, VSNL's Gateway Internet Access Services (GIAS) networks is working as the backbone for other networks. India has its main internet access node at U.S.A via satellite media and to internet node in Europe via submarine cable media.

LANs, WANs and Network Connections: The two basic types of networks are local area networks (LANs) and wide area networks (WANs). A LAN links computers that are physically close to each other and usually 'hard wired' together via cables. Typically, LANs are used in single organizations at single sites. WANs, however, can over large distances, within and beyond national boundries; they are generally connected through telecommunications links, which may use a mixture of advanced technologies such as fibre-optic cables and satellites. It is the wide area networks that are of most concern here.

Computers handle digital data in the form of discrete bits (binary digits, taking one of two values) and bytes (groups of 8 bits, taking 256 values). Networks transmit data in one of two forms, either analogue (a continuous signal) or digital (a stream of bytes). Most networks, like the Internet, use dedicated digital telecommunications lines, Organisations that make heavy use of an external network may install leased telecommunications lines to provide permanent digital links from their in-house multi-user machines or LANs to external network services. Individual and private users make a dial-up connection to an access provider via ordinary telephone lines. This is almost invairably an analogue connection and requires translation of data between analogue and digital forms. This translation is done by a modem.

Bandwidth

Dedicated network lines, especially if they are made of optical fibre, can handle more data than an ordinary telephone line, even using the latest, fastest modems. The limit on data transfer, the bandwidth of a telecommunications line, can still be reached even on the fastest of lines when lots of users try to move vast amounts of data. In U.K, the Internet noticeably slows down during the day as Americans start using it in ever-increasing numbers throughout their day-light hours.

Protocols

Networks require a common framework of routines and rules to allow computers to communicate with each other. These are called protocols. Protocols are technically complex, but very simply put they specify, for example, how data are to be encoded for transmission, the physical transmission media that are allowable, the conventions for addressing items of data so that they can be delivered to the correct networks destination, and the applicaitons (the types of tasks) that are to be supported on the network.

A variety of protocol suites have emerged both in properietary networks, as for example IBM's system network architecture (SNA) and also in academic networks with TCP/IP (transmission control protocol/Internet protocol) for the Internet and the Coloured Book protocols on the original JANET service. The OSI (open system interconnection) reference model, first proposed by the CCITT (then the Consultative Committee on International Telegraphy and Telephony), was an attempt to impose international standardization, but has never achieve universality. A variety of different protocols continue to proliferate, although more and more users are moving to TCP/IP.

Networks using different protocols need a method of exchanging data. This is done through gateway services, which effectively 'translate' data from one set of protocols to another. Some gateways are more sophisticated than others. Ideally, the user should not be aware that the gateway exists: in other words, the commands and operating procedures on either side of the gateway, and the facilities offered, are, from a user's point of view, identical. Such gateways are said to be transparent or seamless.

Packet Switching

Most WANs (including the Internet) user packet switching techniuqes. The first to do so were X.25 networks. A protocol breaks a message down into small packets. Each packet includes some of the data from the message, together with a sequence code identifying where those data fit into the complete message. Each packet also has an address of the recipient computer and an address for the sending computer. Packets are totally hidden from users.

There are many advantages to using packets. They can be routed in a variety of ways between sender and recipient computers, thus bypassing any network failures or bottlenecks. Packets can be received in any order, as the sequence codes enable the origianl message to be re-assembled. A recipient computer can check the sequence codes of packets it receives to work out if any have been lost. The main advantage of packets is that they cannot handle (easily) information that must be delivered in 'real time' (i.e. according to timing restrictions). Thus, sound or video can be transmitted across networks like the Internet, but a user will notice jerkiness in playback.

The Clinet/ Server Model

Any use of a network involves at least two computers; the one the user is on, and another one that is being accessed for some purpose via the network. The user's computer may be a personal computer directly connected to the network, or a multi-user network host to which the user connects from their own machine, which acts as a terminal. Some networks, like FidoNet, operate on the peer-to-peer model. This means that no one computer is more important than any other. However, most networks, the Internet among them, operate the client/ server model. One computer, the client, on behalf of the user, requests services of another computer, the server. The speed and power of the server, and the bandwidth of the network connection, determine how quickly these services are fulfilled. At any one time a server computer can be dealing with any number of client computers. Thus, server computers tend to be more powe- rful than client computers, whose job very often entails merely the display of data passed along from a server.

This split between client and server is matched by a

split in the functions of network software. A database, for example, might consist of a server programme, which stores and retrieves data, and a client program, which generates the requests for data and displays the results. Each part of the system can be optimized for its job. The client program, for example, might operate using a graphical user interface (with mouse, windows and icons), to make things easy for the user. The server programme would need no such adornments. Finally, the server and client programmes can run on completely different makes and types of computer, which allows the formation of heterogeneous networks like the Internet, which can connect a user on an archaic IBM PC XT with a Cray supercomputer.

11.5. OBJECTIVES OF INTERNET

Every network has its own objectives. One of the vital objective of Internet is to acquire the capability of transforming its world wide web (www) into a powerful multi-communication medium, allowing free means of moving information instantaneously, uninterruptedly and democratically around the globe in least possible time without any threat to distance or distinction.

According to Dr. N. Seshagiri, Director General of the NIC, the basic objective of Internet is, "to bring the benefits of the Internet and, the global information and knowledge infrastructure to all scientific, economic and social professions in India". Scientists in India could now view images stored in distant databanks- perhaps pictures beamed down by satellites exploring the solar system and stored in databanks of the European or the US Space Research Organisations.

Amitabh Kumar, Chief General Manager (Planning) of VSNL is, however, of the opinion that, the terminal-based access to Internet using the services of a VSNL host computer aims to allow a user only to access all text-based services like, email, file-transfer, remote log-in etc., but not graphics, nor much browsing on the www. Thus, the ultimate aim of Internet is to meet the challenges of the information war through its WWW by transferring information from the point of generation to the point of the use by one and any where in the world. In addition to this, the full geographical interface and colour/multimedia effects are already available on the internet through full-fledged TCP/IP Account.

11.6. USES OF INTERNET ACCESS IN LIBRARIES

The Internet today gives access to an overwhelming amount of information, data and electronic information services provided by its ordinary users. At one end of the spectrum there are personal 'home pages' published by people the world over (for a name-searchable collection see Ahoy : The Homepage Gateway). At the other end is official government information, for example, that provided by the open government of India website, which provides a first point of entry for all India government and public sector information.

The Internet can be used to:

(i) Exchange personal messages with colleagues, friends or relatives at other networked sites.

(ii) Engage in group discussions, exchange information and ideas with people who share a common interest, and seek information from them.

(iii) Automatically receive information on world events, leisure interests, and technical, business, and professional matters by subscribing to electronic journals, conferences, newsletters and alerting services.

(iv) Look up information in reference works, databases and libraries worldwide.

(v) Retrieve journal articles, books, computer programmes and graphic images, and transfer them to a personal computer.

(vi) Make use of computer facilities that are not available locally.

(vii) Download new software or updates for existing applications.

(viii) Browse catalogues of goods and services and make credit-card purchases.

(ix) Participate in distance learning and academic conferencing.

(x) Engage in real-time 'chat' and multi-player interactive games.

(xi) Communicate with individuals or groups by means of voice only or voice and image.

(xii) Publish information for access by other Internet users.

Users of Internet Access in Libraries and a web site, may be in a position to offer some of the under men-tioned services to their users:

(i) The basic information relating to the functioning of the library can be provided through the Internet. This gives the users of the library an opportunity to establish direct email links which allow users to send messages,

(ii) New ways of access to library facilities such as remote access to catalogues,

(iii) New information services such as a home page linked to a collection of electronic texts, databases and other Internet resources,

(iv) Interactive home pages offering facilities such as reservation of library material and interlibrary loan and reference questions,

(v) Links to remote information and connections to information resources around the world.

Mounting web site on WWW does not require expensive or sophisiticated equipment. The basic components of a configuration may consist of an appropriate computer running under any operating system to use as a server. Computer systems running under DOS, Windows and UNIX can be used as servers for creating WWW documents, through network access dial-up. It is needless to mention that different types of software would be necesary for the purpose. Some of them are mentioned below :

(i) Server software to operate a server allowing client to interest with the information of your server.

(ii) Word-processing software for HTML work.

(iii) Gopher software to create images and icons, and

(iv) Scripting and programming software that allows the extension of the interaction between the client and the server.

It is also necessary to organise workshops on searching the Internet resources and allow users to develop their own skills in identifying, evaluating and selecting specific resources relevent to their interests.

11.7. ESSENTIALS FOR INTERENT CONNECTION

It is important to be aware that there are different kinds of connection to the Internet which substantially affect the way in which we will be able to work on it. There are two fundamental methods of connections: full connection or terminal connection.

Full connection actually makes the machine you are working on a part of the Internet. It is established either by direct connection, typically used by universities and corporate users, where a machine or network of machines is permanently linked by dedicated line to the net, and has its own address; or remotely by using SLIP (Serial Line Internet Protocol) or PPP (Point to Point Protocol) connections to a directly connected machine or router. With full connection, you can install any client software you like on your machine and use all the facilities of the net.

Terminal connection is where you local computer connects to another (host) computer which has a full connection, but acts only as a terminal on the host machine. The local computer is not part of the Internet: you simply use it to log on to the host, and then access the Internet from the (connected) host. There are three key differences to your working practice which result from these different types of connection. Firstly, with a terminal connection, your viewing is limited to the type of communication between yourself and the host, which is usually a text only link. If you want to use a graphic browser like Netscape and view pictures, you can't do it from a simple terminal connection (unless your host provides some special client/ server software, which is unusual). Secondly, since it is the host machine you are actually working from (the host is doing all the processing, your local computer is just a teminal on that machine), you are limited to running the specific application which is provided by the host. Thirdly, all the data you see and request is delivered to and stored on the host, not your local machine. If you want to hold or use the data on your machine, you must first transfer it from the host by a separate process. Likewise if you want to send data from your machine to somewhere else on the net, you must first send it to your host, only then can it be passed onto the Internet. By implication, you must have an account on the host machine to use a terminal connection although there are some sites (known as public access sites) which allow anyone to dial in and use certain facilities on their machine. Most commercial access suppliers providing terminal access provide an off-line mail reader, a program which lets you fetch e-mail from the host and send back mail you have previously written locally, off-line, with a minimum of fuss and connect time.

It is the norm today for commercial hosts to provide SLIP/ PPP connections, but not all do, especially those in areas where telecommunications facilities are poor and the

Internet is still developing, so make sure you know what you're getting if you're signing up. Also, be aware that configuring your system to run a SLIP or PPP connection isn't necessarily a simple task. The "Internet in a box" type of package, which sells you pre-configured, self-installing software plus a subscription to a service provider, can certainly help the technically inexperienced in setting up a full connection, but it's not always foolproof. Although, the sorts of package provided by major Online Servie Providers (OSPs-who offer emerged data services as well as basic connectivity, and usually charge by the hour) like American Online (AOL) and Computer Services are fully self-installing and pretty reliable, many of the smaller Internet Service Providers (ISPs-who only provide connectivity and basic services such as email and web servers, and typically have flat-rate monthly fees) do not offer such reliable "black box" setups when you sign up.

11.7.1. Requirement for Internet Connection

The minimum requirement to get the Internet connection is:

(i) A personal computer (PC).

(ii) A modem.

(iii) Appropriate communication software.

(iv) A telephone connection.

Besides above, the other essential peripherals required for an internet connection are:

(a) An STD telephone,

(b) A disk-antena,

(c) A Personal Earth Station (may be idealy connected to NISSA Satellite 2B or D),

(d) A router for routing TCP/IP,

(e) A hub,

(f) Computer ethernet cables and cords, etc.

However, a satelite-based internet connection, feel many, do not require a modem.

In India, Internet connections are provided by Videsh Sanchar Nigam Limited (VSNL) which offers both (i) Shell (for text-base service with no graphics or colour) or 'Terminal Dial-up', and (ii) 'TCP/IP' (for graphical user interface and colour/multimedia effect) connections.

11.8. INTERNET SERVICES AND ACTIVITIES

The services and actitivities of Internet are no longer restricted to information retrieval alone. In the recent past, internet has extended its scope to telephone sector, marketing, and various entertainments including sports, films, music, health-care and several such useful fields. Besides these, Yoga magazines, newspapers, and almost all home needs now have come on the WWW. Over 40 million surfers have made the internet a global market place.

Chandrasekhar enumerates the following services offered by Internet:

(i) E-mail/Bulletin Borads;

(ii) FTP (File Transfer Protocol) that enable the transfer of art work in electronic form);

(iii) Telnet (remote processing facility);

(iv) World wide web (WWW);

(v) Electronic publishing using WWW (useful for creating publicity material);

(vi) Gopher (mainly a menu based retrieval system where the information is presented as a directory or menu);

(vii) Internet-Relay Chart (IRC);

(viii) Usenet News Groups;

(ix) Remote log-in to the host computer;

(x) Archive; and

(xi) Mosaic (with internet access sofware), a graphical browser that respond to hypermedia links, etc.

In order to explore the nascent information or to keep track about the latest developments on any subject, one has to make use of any one of the browser or navigating tools available on the Internet. The most important among them are: (i) Gopher; and (ii) World wide web.

Gopher which is based on the concept of clients and servers is the first programme to browse the resources of the internet through a series of menus. While client software organizes information into menues, hypertext documents or any other format and transmits requests to get things done. Servers which may be located on the specific host computer or on any computer on the internet, on the other hand, helps to answer the requests received from the client software by transmiting the information/data sought by the client.

World wide web (WWW), the most exciting new tool for internet, is based on concept called, 'hypertext' as was developed by the researchers at the European Particle Physics Laboratory at Geneva. This helps to link words of one document with other documents. It is just like sitting with an encyclopaedia, as some one is reading one article, looking at a reference that intrigues him most, and flipping the pages to look up that reference. WWW is an ambitious attempt to link connected information, does not matter wherever the same is located on the internet and provides the user easy access to retrieve relevant files. Graphical WWW browsers, like 'Cello' and 'Mosiac" also respond to hypermedia links beyond just text.

Internet thus, can bring anything to anyone from anywhere in the world at any point of time- what a person only requires is, the access. One can send e-mail, play chess, chat with someone, copy from some other computer network connected on the internet, get information on any subject from any corner of the globe, advertise his own products at cheaper rates, and even do some shopping.

Internet, the gaint super network of 250 computer

networks world wide, can retrieve photographs, diagrams and other visual data in addition to the more conventional text-based data. This kind of multi-media document access from intenational databanks in diverse field has become possible in India through the world web information service and is still expanding the information highway of the National Informatics Centre (NIC) in order to widen its scope.

11.9. INTERNET GATEWAY /NODES IN INDIA

There are two such organisations in India that provides gateway service for access to Internet. These are (i) ERNET and (ii) VSNL.

11.9.1. ERNET (Education and Research Network)

ERNET was setup and managed by the Department of Electronics to cater to the academic community of the country since 1988. This network connects mostly the universities and research institutes and was used to exchange e-mails and access different libraries and journals on different subjects. Recently, it has been used to offer other services as well.

11.9.2. VSNL

Videsh Sanchar Nigam Ltd. has also branches into this area. Apart from exchanging email, VSNL does not offer yet much for serious internet users. Their system is reportedly outdated and slow. VSNL has allocated 16 lines for the users of Kolkata out of which, 5 lines are active. However, to increase the data transfer speed, VSNL has introduced new system in Mumbai and has started building a high capacity countrywide network for providing internet backbone in India. In order to spread the internet culture, VSNL has entered into a strategic alliance with Zee Education, a TV Channel; and Aptech, a computer education retailer with 270 outlets.

This high speed backbone network has started building with the state-of-the-art-end routers capable of supporting links at 34 bits per second (mbps) as well as ATM (Asynchronous Transfer Mode) technologies. This backbone routing network has initially six nodes, one each in:

(i) Mumbai
(ii) Delhi
(iii) Kolkata
(iv) Chennai
(v) Bangalore, and
(vi) Pune

On August 14, 1996, Lucknow became the seventh city to join the select band to Indian cities connected with internet services followed with a plan to provide internet service in six more places including Kanpur and Hyderabad in next two months, while the facility would be extended in 20 more cities by the end of the current financial year. Subsequently, this network is likely to be extended to other satellite cities of the country.

VSNL may soon, however, cease to be the country's sole gateway to internet with the Department of Telecommunications (DoT) planning to give private companies the right to offer internet access. But taking the strong infrastrctural background of VSNL, many experts feel that, VSNL will continue to provide the overseas links.

11.9.3. Other Networks having connectivity to Internet

Besides VSNL and ERNET, the other major networks in India which have connectivity to internet either directly or via other international networks include:

(i) SIRNET (Scientific and Industrial Research Network), setup and managed by NISCAIR on behalf of CSIR;
(ii) NICNET (National Informatics Centre Network), India's first high speed Information-highway, setup and managed by National Informatic Centre connecting networks in over 150 countries, commissioned on September 20, 1994;

(iii) INDONET setup and managed by CMC Ltd.;

(iv) I-Net, a public data network, setup and managed by DoT (Dept. of Telecommunication);

(v) RABMN (Rural Area Business Messaging Network), a satellite-based network setup and managed by DoT.

(vi) ICNET, a private electronic-mail network; and

(vii) UUNET-IN, the Indian component of the international Unix User's Network (UUNET) setup and managed by a private company.

11.9.4. WWW Through NICNET

Serving as a sophisticated gateway to international databanks, the www server is made available through the NIC information-highway, called NICNET which connected 15 cities in India as on January 1995 and now it has linked around 80 cities.

NICNET setup this information geteway in collaboration with Information Dimensions, Inc., of U.S who developed the BASIS Web Server underlying the design of the gateway. According to Dr. N. Seshagiri, NIC's Director General, NIC has weaved the entire country into a single communication entity to reach out to the world without any technical barries. With the powerful Ku-band-based NIC information highway, users can now go beyond Indian boarders as the network now connects them to over 200 networks in 160 countries.

11.10. SEARCHING ON INTERNET

A vast array of databases and services are available through the Internet. It is necessary to design interfaces that help users who search for information sources and services available on the Internet. This is because retrieval is recognised to be a complex and significant problem on the Internet. The reason for this is that the databases mounted on the net are in a wide variety of different formats, and different search retrieval software packages mounted on different computers and are providing access via different interfaces to subsets of the databases.

Tools used for searching the Internet often operate in client/server mode. Server software which enables the user to search the database in a more intuitive way has been set up on many computers on the Internet. The user's local system runs the equivalent client software which communicates with the server software and provides a homogeneous interface to the data. In other words, the user does not need to know where the data is stored or how to manage the server system's file store structure.

11.10.1. World Wide Web (WWW)

The WWW is the multimedia part of the Internet displaying a hyper text type of structure and search facilities. It was first developed for sharing documents between the nuclear physicists of the European Particle Physics Laboartory (CERN) in Switzerland in 1989, but the first commercial Web Software by Next in 1991, popularised this form of access to the Internet. The main characteristics of the WWW organisation and structure are:

(i) Organising documents into pieces of information (pages) using a set of rules which tag and format the documents, the Hypertext Mark-up Language (HTML).

(ii) Every individual document or page is assigned a unique address, called the Uniform Resource Locator (URL).

(iii) Each URL can be linked with a hypertext type link to other URL's and even pieces of information within each document (buttons) can be linked to URLs to other pieces of information.

(iv) These documents can be searched through interactive interface programmes which allow users to browse and navigate through the documents and are called Web browsers.

(v) The communication between the web browsers and the web servers is regulated by a common langauge using a standardised set of rules called Hypertext Transfer Protocol (HTTP). The HTTP allows the inerpretation of the HTML signs within each Web page in order to display correctly the page and to enable the transfer of files. A client programme or web browser provides the user with control over the retrieval process and also over the links to be activated.

Some individuals and organisations create home pages to present their own information or services. A collection of home pages located on the same server is called a web site. Access to these pages is via the Uniform Resource Locator (URL) using a browser. Some examples of browsers are Lynx, Netscape, etc., these address link the user to the host computer and their individual files, these are then displayed on the user's terminal (workstation). With the help of appropriate software users can read documents, view pictures, listen to sound, and retrieve information.

The hypertext structure of the web means that retrieval is done through following the links between different web pages through browsing and navigation. In indexing terms, the hyperlinks on the WWW that form the basis of the browsing network are controlled out humanly assigned indexing terms. There is no general control over which terms should be used as hyperlinks, but each hyperlinks is individually coded by the creator of HTML (Hypertext Markup Language). It may be mentioned here that though browsers encourage movement through a network of linked documents, browsing is not an efficient approach to the identification of specific information. Different search tools have been devised in order to assist people in finding information on the largest repository of documents in the world. These search tools can be divided into two main categories: 'subject directories' and 'search engines.'

11.10.2. Subject Directories

Subject directories, also known as subject guides, allow people to browse information by subject. They are hierarchically organised indexes of different subjects, with links to different web sites on each subject. The searcher can browse through the index in search of relevant subject and navigate to the relevant web sites by clicking on hot spots which represent those sites. Subject directories are built by human indexers.

Apart from general subject directories, there are also two other types of directories specialised subject directories and clearing houses. Specialised directories specialised in their specific areas and provide access to the most important sites and resources in those areas, where as clearing houses are collections of various specialised search directories, either by including the search directory on their web sites or by providing a link to the web sites of these speciliased directories. This facilities easy location of specialised information on the Internet.

11.10.3. Search Engines

Search engines are mechanisms which aid users to search the entire Internet for relevant information. They are based on allowing users to enter keywords that are matched against a database. Unlike subject directories, which use human indexes to build their indexes, search engines use software programmes which create automatically their own database containing lists of web pages. Search engines are composed of three different parts: (i) a program called a spider (or robot or crawler), (ii) a database with an index and (iii) a search software. Spiders wander through the web, crawling from site to site, following links between pages. Different search engines use different types of spiders, whereas some visit every possible site, others are based on more selective principles and visit only the most popular sites. The first type of spider finds a huge volume of information in a short space of time, the second type generates a smaller number of pages with perhaps more relevant information. Every page found by a spider is stored in a database and an index of its contents is built by extracting automatically words from the web pages and ranking them alphabetically using some principles which inverted file use. The index is, therefore, a list of every word (except stop words) with a pointer to its location on the database.

Again, different search engines will follow different principles. For example, some will index every single word on every web page, while other engines index only the title and top level phrases of a web site. The third element of the search engine is the search software, which is a program, which compares search queries keyed in by the users with the index, finds, matches and ranks them in order of relevance. The criteria for judging relevance will vary according to the search engine.

The different approaches, which search engines use in crawling the web, finding new pages and indexing them will produce totally different results. That is why when searching the same topic in different search engines, there can be differences in the results obtained. Due to the way the search engines operate, search engines are more oriented to find larger volumes of information and more specific information than subject directories. This is because they are based on searching Web pages and indexing automatically precise word from the sites rather than using a pre-defined index as subject directories do.

Examples of various search engines available with their sites as follows:

Search engine	Sites address
YAHOO	
[Hyperlink http://www.yahoo.com)	www.yahoo.com
ALTAVISTA	www.altavista.
[Hyperlink htt://www.altavista digital.com)	digital.com
EXCITE	
[Hyperlink http://www.excite.com)	www.excite.com
HOTBOT	
[Hyperlink http://www.hotbot.com)	www.hotbot.com/
INFOSEEK GUIDE	
[Hyperlink http://www.infoseek.com	www.infoseek.com/
LYCOS	
[Hyperlink htt://www.lycos.com)	www.lycos.com/
WEBCRAWLER	
[Hyperlink http://www.(webwww.webcrawler.com)	www.webcrawler.com
OPEN TEXT INDEX	
[Hyperlink http://www.opentext.com)	www.opentext.com
DEJANEWS	
[Hyperlink http://www.dejanews.com)	www.dejanews.com/
ALL-IN-ONE	
[Hyperlink http://www.albany.net\\allionon)	www.albay n.net\\
COMBINED SEARCH	
[Hyperlink http://www.search.com)	www.search.com/
Indian Search Engine (Khoj)	
(Hyperlink http://www.Khoj.com)	www.khoj.com/

As different search engines posses different strengths, new search tools have been devised recently, which enable users to search simultaneously the different databases of search engines, while using one single interface. These tools are called multi-threaded search engines. Though, these do not have all the search flexibility of individual search engines, they are very fast and can search through vast quantities of information. Some examples of multi-thread (meta) search engines are :

(i) Dogpile (http://www.Dogpile.com)

(ii) Metacrawler (http://www.Metacrawler com)

11.11. INTRANETS

An Intranet is internal communication mechanism of an organisation. It uses the Internet technology for the purpose. Generally speaking, Intranets utilise two of the key applications of the Internet: the web browsers with their graphical interfaces and email.

These are being used to support a wide range of information services, including access to document collections in document management systems and e-mail.

The applications to which Intranets can be put to use depends upon the type of Intranet. There are two categories of Intranets: (i) flat-conent Intranets, (ii) interactive Intranets. In the first category, files are simply requested from a storage location or server, received by the desktop computer and viewed through the web browser. Some applications of such Intranets are:

(i) Recruitement pointers to information available on the Internet;

(ii) Document distribution and updating;

(iii) Current awareness bulletins;

(iv) Electronic journal delivery;

(v) Internet subject resource listing; and

(vi) Information support material.

On the other hand, interactive Intranets provide many opportunities for two way communication within an organisation. However, the configuration of such Intranets is rather complex. For instance, when a user wishes to send, change, respond to or forward any kind of information to another location or person, a specific program is needed to process this information. Such programmes need to be held on an internal Web server, which utilises TCP/IP. In case an organisation's network does not run under TCP/IP, then the gateway may be used as an interface between the organisation's network protocol and the TCP/IP protocol. Applications with interactive type of Intranets are:

(i) email including message and attached documents;

(ii) video conferencing;

(iii) interactive services such as reservations;

(iv) online enquiry services; and

(v) access to library catalogue from the World Wide Web.

11.12. INTERNET SUPPORTING SOFTWARES

A consortium of American Computer Companies has developed a universal digital code known as 'Unicode' to allow computers to represent virtually all the world's languages. Software with fonts for everything- from Chinese ideographs and Russian Cyrillic to Sanskrit characters are also becoming more readily available (The Times of India op. cit. p. 14) for access to internet.

Several leading software firms including Netscape Communications Corporation, and Microsoft Corporation, are, however, trying hard to release easy-to-use computer programming language for internet access. Some of the notable softwares/programmes that give access to internet at present are tabulated as under:

S. No.	*Name of the Firm*	*Software*	*Features/ Significance*
1.	Microsoft Corporation, U.S.A	(i) Window' 95 (OS) (ii) Plus	An upgrade to Microsoft's existing Windows OS Software package most extensively tested. A distribution vehicle for a simple icon, or symbol on the computer screen.
2.	Netscape Communication Corporation	Browser	Claims to have used by the 80% of the www users or 17 million people.
3.	Sun Micro system & Netscape (Jointly)	Java Script	Distributed free over internet and is designed to allow even non-technical users to customise information

S. No.	*Name of the Firm*	*Software*	*Features/ Significance*
			accessible on www.
4.	Netcom	Netcruiser 1.6	Available only for computer using Microsoft Windows 3.1 and a version of DOS numbered 5.0 or higher. Easier to use and less expensive.

According to Tewari and Gupta, the Internet is a grab-bag of different tools, each of which is used to retrieve information. Some of such tools alongwith their functions are as under:

S. No.	*Software Tools*	*Applications*
(i)	FTP	Allows acces to millions of computer files stored world wide
(ii)	Archie	Helps to locate those FTP able files
(iii)	Gopher	A mena based file and service search and retrieval system.
(iv)	Lynx	A text-based access tool to the www hypertext (highlighted words that when selected,, branch off to other subject)
(v)	Telnet	Used to log-in and work in a remote computer availble any where in the world.
(vi)	Internet Relay Chat (IRC)	Allows an online interactive discussion and group discussions.

12
Electronic Mail and Its Usages

12.1. INTRODUCTION

The developments in the area of technology and its application to every sphere of human activity is rapidly increasing. The developments, particularly in the field of information handling, information technologies, viz. computer, communication and storage technologies have facilitated collection, storage organisation, processing analysis, presentation and dissemination of information. Libraries and information centres are concerned with the process of collecting, organising and disseminating the information to their end users have found it useful to make best use of modern sophisticated information technologies. As a result we are now seeing more and more libraries using reprographic machines, computers, communication technologies, like telephones, telexes, facsimiles, audio and video technologies, on-line access to data bases, CD-ROMs, etc. Now the trend is towards establishing a computer and communication based network of libraries for effective resource sharing. Electronic mail is one of these technologies which has become a very popular media in most of the developed nations for public and private message handling. Libraries and Information Centres have come to realise the effectiveness of this media and have slowly started using it for their routines.

12.2. ELECTRONIC MAIL: CONCEPT

Electronic Mail or the more popular term, E-mail, refers to the transmission of a message electronically through electrical signals. In other words, E-mail is a non-simultaneous interpersonal electronic communication.

In the E-mail system typically, the sender types the message using a computer keyboard and then the message is sent through a computer system by using telecommunication channels to a defined mail box (i.e. to the addressee) and there it can be stored in the receiving end computer memory for the delivery to the receiver.

E-mail systems allow the creation and transmission of messages which can be addressed to an individual or to a select group of individuals. The receipient can then read the message, answer it, store it or forward it to another individual, print it on a paper or delete it. It is basically a computer mediated communication system. Specialised message handling softwares are available which can be run on both PC-AT and mini or mainframe computers. These softwares help the E-mail users to edit, format the message during entry and send the mail to the distribution list.

12.3. USAGE OF ELECTRONIC MAIL IN GENERAL

Use of E-mail system has significantly increased during the past 6-7 years. The individuals and organisations who are part of the Academic, Research, Business, Library and Information Networks have started using this facility to a greater extent. E-mail has really become a very popular and faster mode of interacting with individual scientists and scholars. Academic Networks like BITNET (USA), JANET (UK) and ERNET (India) have been offering this E-mail facility to their users.

According to the Electronic Mail Association, there were about 5 million electronic mail boxes world wide in 1986. It was estimated that the number of messages transmitted during 2000 were more than 175 million. So the trend is towards an increasing degree of interconnection between the computer systems.

Recently Videsh Sanchar Nigam Ltd., Department of Telecommunication (DOT), Govt. of India has introduced a Gateway Electronic Mail Services (GEMS), which is based on CCITT X. 400 message handling system for easy access to International Databases and E-mail users. Access is provided through PSTN of PSPDN and initially this service is mainly being used for interpersonal messages and is currently available in four metropolitian cities, viz. Mumbai, Kolkata, Delhi and Chennai.

12.4. APPLICATION OF E-MAIL FOR LIBRARY AND INFORMATION SERVICES

E-mail has all the potentialities of using it for some of the Library and Information Services and has already become an integral part of the Libraries in the developing nations. Library and Information Centres which are part of Academic networks or independent information networks have started using it widely and extensively. Some of the major areas where the E-mail could be used as effective media are as follows:

(i) Inter-library Loan: Inter-Library Loan is one of the major activities of the Library and Information Centres. Due to the budget cuts and hike in prices of reading materials, libraries have been literally forced to use faster communication channels to share the resources available. E-mail is one of the better and faster means of communication. Through this system, libraries can forward its request for a document to one or more libraries at any time. It is even possible to check the availability of a document before confirming the actual document request and receive the response. This saves lot of time both for the librarian and the users.

(ii) Document Ordering: E-mails could be used by the libraries for ordering books, journals and other reading materials. It is possible to check the availability of certain titles with the publishers by sending a list through this system and on confirmation final orders can be placed. Journal claiming is another area where E-mails could be used more effectively. It would be much faster and unnecessary delays could be avoided. Many of the major publishers send their lists through this system and on confirmation final orders can be placed. Journal claiming is another area where E-mails could be used more effectively. It would be much faster and unnecessary delays could be avoided. Many of the major publishers in the west including Baker and Taylor, Ingram and Faxon and others are using this system.

(iii) Document Delivery: Document delivery is another application of E-mails in libraries. Orders for reprints from the document delivery alternatives such as UMI Article clearing house (UMIAC) can be accomplished through electronic means. These days many requests are generated (for documents) out of on-line searches and some of the online database owners are offering the capability as a part of their search protocols. Another aspect of electronic document delivery involves the advent of complete text databases, especially complete text of journal databases. There is another aspect where E-mails could be effectively used, i.e. databases can be searched and results can be downloaded and sent to the user mailboxes.

(iv) Professional Communication: Professional Library and Information Science Societies or Associations like many other National and International Professional societies have organisers located in different regions and in some cases world wide. E-mails can facilitate communication among these organisers. E-mails can also become a convenient means for professional membership to announce meetings and provide professional information to its constituencies. It also permits individuals having common interests to communicate without geographical restrictions. Libraries can collaborate on various projects, including bibliography compilation, collection development and policy making using electronic mail. Therefore, like inter-library loan, this applications will have great impact on inter-library co-operation and networking.

(v) Reference Service: E-mails are a more effective means in transmitting of reference requests and answers. It can be from Librarian to Librarian, Patron to Librarian, Librarian to subject specialists, etc. One need not visit the libraries to get the information on certain topics. If the answers are brief, it could be easily transmitted, instead of writing a separate letter. Besides, Electronic mail can also be used by the librarian on the campus and outside, to send the reminder notices, recent additions lists, etc. to the users. A regular news bulletin could be transmitted announcing various activities, of the library. Day to day correspondences could also be sent through an electronic mail. Users can give their feedback about the services through this media.

12.5. INTERNATIONAL SCENARIO

The E-mail has become an effective communication channel among the libraries in developed countries. In the recent past many libraries and information networks have come up bringing together different types of libraries and users. Most of these networks have been offering the E-mail facility to the participating libraries and their users.

The Joint Academic Network (JANET) set up in 1984 is a wide-area network linking together a large number of computers and users in British Universities, Polytechnics, Colleges, Research sites and British Libraries. Through JANET many OPACs database hosts and other information systems may be accessed. Its mail services have gateways to several other networks.

British Library Document Supply Centre (BLDSC) has an Automated Request Transmission (ART) Service, which accounts for about 40% of all the requests received. BLDSC offers various methods by which users of the loan and photocopy services can send requests using telecommunication facilities including the E-mail. E-mail share of the ART request is about 56%.

Library Association (UK) has launched its E-mail system called LA-NET in November, 1988. It had about 500 subscribers in May, 2000 and is offering these services to members of the Library Association. The LA-NET mail system gives access to scanning, reading and sending mails using different types of distribution lists.

Some of the major data base owners in USA and UK have their own E-mail systems. The most interesting system today seems to be Dialog's DIALMAIL. It is automatically available to all Dialog users. Besides offering all the normal options of an up-to-date E-mail system DIALMAIL has much used feature of delivering results from searching in DIALOG overnight at a cheaper rate.

American Library Association has set up its own network called ALANET for the benefit of members, libraries and end users. It currently has about 1900 mail boxes and provides services such as E-mail service, link to suppliers, noticeboard and gateways to on-line databases.

In Canadian libraries E-mails have been in use since 1982. Most of the requests for ILL and photocopy are sent through E-mail. Recently National Library of Canada has developed ILL protocol using OSI Reference model. It includes all functions necessary for location, lending and borrowing activities.

Australian Library Association has set up its own network called ILANET. It is basically a Library E-mail system. There are about 400 mailboxes of professional members.

12.6. INDIAN SCENARIAO

India has made a modest beginning in using the E-mail facility. In the recent past many networks have sprung up and many are in the offing. These are both general and specific purpose and are public, private and academic ones. Some of these networks which have started functioning are INDONET, NICNET, ERNET, INFLIBNET, CALIBNET, DELNET, etc. Most of these have E-mails as one of the basic functions.

ERNET the Educational Resource Network was initiated during seventh plan (1985-90) by the Department of Electronics with the assistance from UNDP with an aim to have network for academic and research community with the initial participation from eight leading academic and research institutions including the Department of Electronics. The E-mail is one of the services that this network has been offering. About 35 academic & research organisations have been connected to this facility. It also has a gateway facility through its main node at NCST which links to similar international networks. The proposed IITNETWORK for libraries proposes to use this facility extensively for its inter-library loan services among the five IITs.

Developing Libraries Network (DELNET) set up in 1988 with initial participation of 18 libraries in Delhi has launched an E-mail service. This service is supported by the NISSAT OF DSIR, New-Delhi. The purpose of introducing E-mail in this network is to promote library mailing, inter-library loan requests, distribution of questionnaires, activisation of professional contacts and demonstration of file transfer and connecting to national and international databases and networks.

SIRNET, the Scientific and Industrial Research Network which is a computer communication network, is set up for CSIR Laboratories. At present this network has one mail node (mail server) located in NISCAIR and a number of user nodes located at different major laboratories. It is right now being mainly used for communication between the institutions and individual scientists working in the various laboratories. It is connected to the international networks like UUNET through which other international networks like BITNET, JANET are accessible. NISCAIR has already started using this E-mail facility for some of its services within the CSIR laboratories and with other regional centres. In days to come most of the information centres attached to each of the laboratories will have an access to this facility and will start using it for their services.

Other networks, viz. INFLIBNET, CALIBNET, etc. which are in the very initial stages of their implementation also have proposal to make use of E-mail services for their selected library activities. The General networks like INDONET and NICNET have already started using E-mails for their day to day communications.

12.7. HARDWARE AND SOFTWARE REQUIRED

The following hardware and software are requied for initial setting up of E-mail service:

(a) A PC-XT 80386 UNIX machine with IBM RAM, 40 MB hard disk, 1.2 MB floppy disk, Rs. 232c ports and parallel port.

(b) A stand alone modem with error correcting facility at 1200 bps.

(c) A dial up line with STD/local dialing facility and

(d) Provision of Basic Networking Software, i.e. UUCP (Unix to Unix copy) with a standard UNIX package to communicate with other UNIX systems.

There are a few softwares which facilitate communication between computer to computer. They are - CROSS TALK, PROCOMM, and among them, the most recent message handling system is X. 400 of CCITT based on OSI.

12.8. ADVANTAGES AND DISADVANTAGES

Some of the advantages of this system is speed and realiability of delivery, security and privacy of messages. The messages can be sent any time of the day or even during night time when the charges are less and intruption will be less and one can get away with telephone tags, and above all it is easy to use.

There are some draw backs with this E-mail system. It can not handle graphics oriented information, lack of standard is another problem that affects easy communication. It needs initial investment and costwise it is not very cheap. Constant problems with local telephones is another problem that affects message communication and it is not easy for a lay man to use the system.

12.9. CONCLUSION

Electronic mail is growing fast. The days are not far off when we will be seeing every computer user having a link to one or more networks and using the E-mail facility for day to day communications. E-mails are going to be a part of library service media. Greater the use, lesser the delay in providing service to readers. Libraries need to take more interest in exploring the possibilities of introducing its capabilities into the library routines. The advancement in technology will continue to improve the effectiveness of the electronic mail, and no doubt it will be an indispensable media for handling the message between libraries and library patrons and vice-versa.

13
CD-ROM Technology

13.1. INTRODUCITON

Until recent times, the only major means of communication was conventional print. Then came micro print (micro film, microfiche, etc.). The advent of the computer has now not only revolutionised the printing technology but has brought into vogue electronic media like tapes, disks, etc. which has great potential storage and retrieval devices/means. These new media also, however, have proved inadequate and deficient. Optical storage media (capable of) containing textual and numerical information for high density of information storage and retrieval have been put up. CD ROM is one of such optical storage media. This medium is not a replacement for the existing print, film or magnetic media but is only a supplement.

Optical storage devices are based on mass storage devices that make possible faster access of information and saving of space. Of the various optical storage devices, the following three devices find application in information storage and retrieval:

(i) Compact Disc-Read-Only Memory (CD-ROM)

(ii) Write-Once Optical Discs (WORM)

(iii) Erasable Optical Discs (EOD).

CD ROM has established itself as an efficient, fast and cheap medium with 30 years of life. Now this projected life has been enhanced to 100 years by write once discs like Write Once Read many (WORM) discs and Direct-Read-After-Write (DRAW) discs. Then the erasable optic discs have come into existence and their development is going on. CD ROM and WORM discs are available for purchase. Write-once-and- erasable optical discs are believed to have a better future than CD ROM.

13.2. CD-ROM

CD-ROM, a Compact Disc Read Only Memory, are of size 12 cm in diameter and are made from polycarbonate substract and a reflective metalised layer. A disc weighs 26 grams. A typical CD-ROm can store about 650 MB of data. One would get a better idea of the size of the data that a CD can hold if we say that a CD can hold about 2,50,000 pages of text, each page containing some 2000 characters of 5000 video images. One would require more than 450 high-density floppy diskettes to store an equivalent amount of information that a CD can hold. The librarians need to develop skills to use CD-ROMs in saving library space, in preserving archival material and in providing effective time saving mechanism of identifying, selecting, loading and bringing the right CD-ROM database in connection with the right user. It has been extremely useful to the librarians in imparting the three main function of the library, viz. collection, storage and dissemination of knowledge.

CD-ROM has permeated the walls of all types of libraries throughout the world. Nielson and Maries (1989) reported that libraries and information centres account for the largest installed base of CD ROM drivers in the United States of America. The latest figure from Macler indicates that over 3,500 disc titles were available to the public in 1993, i.e. a ten fold increase in three years, these included multimedia CD titles which comprise 25% of all those on sale.

CDs are an indispensable source of information not only as they can hold large amount of information but also because they provide rapid responses to the researchers thus reducing much of the drudgery usually attendant on manual searching.

CD ROMs with its relative advantage of being compact in nature with its quick retrieval facility is becoming quite popular in libraries and information centres. Another advantage of a CD-ROM is the ability for networking. CD-ROM networks provide multiple access to many large database and this advantage has generated a higher level of usage.

Thus, there is now an increasing range of CD-ROMs which contain bibliographical records useful to libraries as sources of cataloguing data. The Library Corporation's Bibliofile launched in 1985, contains the complete Library of Congress catalogue of over a million MARC records on requirement than utilize them for their own system.

Over the years a number of databases have been made available on CD-ROMs. The British National Bibliography (BNB) has been launched on CD-ROM which is used by many libraries both a bibliographic tool and as a record source to generate orders and prepare catalogue records. A number of similar products are available on CD-ROM can be useful in reducing the amount of original catalgouing required.

We are passing through an era that can be aptly called as an era of knowledge explosion for the reason that information or knowledge that is so vital for the socio-economic progress of a country is expanding with a terrific speed. Knowledge is doubling within a span of a 10 year period on an average accumulated basis. According to UNESCO statistics about 3 lacs books are being published each year leaving aside other documents containing nascent thought such as seminars or symposia proceedings, research reports, theses, monographs and the learned periodicals in the field of science and technology alone, those numbers have now swelled upto 60 thousand, and are increasing at the annual rate of nearly 1000 periodicals. It is becoming increasingly difficult these days for an individual scientist or research worker to keep himself abreast with the latest developments and thoughts in one's field of specialization. Libraries adopting modern information retrieval techniques and offering intensive bibliographical and documentation service are the only means by which their valuable time and energy is saved from doing repetitive job/work.

13.3. USE OF CD-ROMS IN INDIAN LIBRARIES

CD-ROM database has been playing a very important role in bridging the information isolation between the developed and the developing coutries. In India CD-ROM was first introduced in 1987-88. It is only in the year 1990 that it caught up with the library and information professionals in India. The reason for the delay could be the high cost involved in producing the CD-ROM version of database and also certain difficulties in acquiring the international databases.

The CD-ROM puts multimegabytes of permanently stored databases at the user front end of a PC. Its only drawback is that the end user cannot put his own infomration on it.

The advantages of storing data on CD are: -

(i) high storage capacity (600 MB)

(ii) no head crash

(iii) low error rate, correctable data

(iv) long life

(v) random access

(vi) early transportable

(vii) independent file system

(viii) low cost

(ix) reliable medium

(x) less shelf space.

13.4. CD-ROM AND FUTURE DEVELOPMENT

The CD-ROM has proliferated most of the libraries and has become an intergral part of storage hardware, operating in conjuction with magnetic disc and tape. The use of more than one layer on a single platter and the development of the blue laser with a wave length of 430 nanometer will mean that CD-ROM capacities will increase to about 3 gigabits. With the development of efficient archiving software, libraries of the future will store most of the information on CD-ROM. Also with the falling prices CD- ROM database are gradually taking over from online databases. particularly those which are required in larger volumes thus amenable to mass production. Online searches and retrieval costs are generally not fully predictable by its very nature as in practice a lot of time is wasted on inefficient searches. It is also dependent on telecom links costing. On the other hand CD-ROMs are targeted on specific needs. It puts the power of searches back in the hands of the users.

Generally the CD-ROMs have on them powerful user-friendly search software with a pontential for complex searches. Multi-user access around already existing infrastructure of PCs and networks with addition of only CD-ROMs and drives makes the cost benefit ratio in favour of CD-ROMs judicious.

Procurement of CD-ROM databases (Off-line)

(a) CD-ROM Database: CD-ROM databases could have both reference and source database. It could be online or as well as offline. Its just media of storage, but it's quite popular due to its storage capacity, handling ease and transfer capacity from place to place. At best, CD-ROMs are most effective for offline storage. In addition, it is a mass storage for personal computers or scholar workstations for libraries.

(b) DVD-ROM Databases : The CD-ROM can deliver decent multimedia right now and the DVD with its maximum capacity of 17GB is currently the only credible true multimedia format. The advent of DVD and its gigabyte storage capacity has provided new potentials to expand the capacity of CD-ROM database, especially for multimedia applications. DVD-Digital Video Disc, or Digital Versatile Disc for the computer industry, is the next generation to Compact Disc in optical disc storage technology. DVD players can also read CDs. The DVD technology provides a storage capacity that is at least 6 to 7 times greater than a CD in the same aerial space. The main feature of DVD is the compression technology and storing data on multi-layer sides. There are varous kinds of DVDs like DVD-Audio, DVD-Video, DVD-Recordable, DVD-ER, etc.

For example, Silver Platter's MEDLINE Advanced bibliographic database with over 8 million citations and abstracts of articles from 3700 journals of 70 countries are stored on DVDs.

13.5. CD-ROM NETWORKS

CD-ROM has become an important medium for the storage and dissemination of information. Many information products are now available on CD-ROMs. CD-ROMs represent a means of access, to information alternative, to online access, to external databases via telecommunications networks.

The networking environment charges fundamentally with the use of CD-ROMs. A popular use of local networks, within a library and information service context, has been to make CD-ROM databases accessible to the network users from remote workstations. In fact, the development of CD-

ROMs has widened access to information, which was previously available through online searching systems.

The advantages of resource sharing which a local network of libraries can often become an attractive proposition as this does not involve telecommunications overhead and tends to be effective.

The basic components of a single CD-ROM workstation are a micro-computer and a CD-ROM drive. A printer will be necessary if you want to obtain a paper copy of searches and if you wish to do an online search to update CD-ROM, a modem and a telephone line will also be needed. If more than one person needs to use the system at a time, networking has to be taken recourse to. The ideal CD-ROM configuration offers multi-user access to many databases.

The advantage of putting CD-ROMs on networks is providing multiple concurrent access to information and help in streamlining of the disks themselves, which otherwise would be distributed and loaded manually.

CD-ROM networks are normally mounted on PC-based local area networks. Standards available LANs do not properly support the use of CD-ROMs, and require additional software add-ons to manage the optical drives. These are generally controlled by a separate optical file server (i.e., a computer adapted with CD controller cards to which drives are attached).

There are three alternative architectures for implementing CD-ROMs on a networks. These are:

(i) a file server arrangement with the data files located on the file server itself, and the user interface and the search engine residing on the client workstation.

(ii) a centralised approach, where both data and search engine and interface reside on a multi-user machine, with the workstation acting as a terminal.

(iii) a client-server approach, where the data file and the

search engine reside on the server machine, and the user interface with the client woskstation. This arrangement reduces the communications lead by keeping the processing close to the data storage, and enables the full power of the workstation to be available to the client.

In order to acquire knowledge about CD-ROM technology and its impact on library, NISSAT have established National Information Centre for CD-ROM (NICCD ROM) at National Aerospace Laboratory, Banglore in 1988. This centre provides information on CD-ROM products, details of suppliers, reference tools and databases on CD-ROM technology by publishing a bimonthly newsletter entitled CD-Focus. It helps Indian users to adopt CD-ROM technology by organsing workshops on CD-ROM technology with practical training.

14
Microform Technology

14.1. INTRODUCTION

Library and information centres are a growing organism. Books and other reading material are continuously added. The increasing growth of information sources has become a challenge in efficient management and service. The explosion of literature has further added to the problems of acquisition, storage and retrieval. How to meet these challenges and problems has always engaged the attention of library and information managers. In dealing with books and other conventional sources, problems of rising prices, procurement time lags, postage, storage and binding, dusting, preserving, etc., upkeepment costs are being increasingly faced. Financial crunches add to these problems. However, the need to reproduce and permanently preserve documents of research value is on steady increase.

Microforms are the best answer. Document supply centres, book distribution centres and suppliers of information products have resorted to this technology and hence more and more information sources are now available in microform. Users not apathetic to microforms espouse the cause of microform technology and enthusiastically welcome microforms when hard copy is unavailable. Libraries and information centres necessarily must switch over to microform technology in order facilitate larger access and keep costs, space and other problems under control to any extent. It is a common practice all over, that libraries have converted their rich and useful retrospective collections to microform.

Microform, right from the stage of its inception has undergone considerable change. The wide variety of user needs have given rise to a number of different forms in which microphotograph is made, stored and used. Some of the microforms are described here.

14.2. MICROGRAPHY

Microforms are those where the images are reduced considerably and require magnification devices for viewing and reading. Microform is an information carrier which can be used as a storage and communication medium. There are in different forms. Important ones are given below:

14.2.1. Microfilm

Microfilm on reels was one of the earliest microforms. It is still a popular choice because large quantities of information can be stored in a very little space at very low cost. Microfilm which provides a high measure of file integrity, is desirable where information is added continuously in sequence with less frequent updation. Microfilms are normally in two sizes: 16 mm and 35 mm (width). Depending on the original documents from which microfilms are made, the size of the film is selected. 16 mm films are housed in cartridges and 35 mm in spools. 16 mm films are used to store large quantities of information when the information is in text form. 35 mm films are used for graphics, drawings, maps and newspapers. Cartridges function as conveninet packaging for rolls of microfilms. Microfilms in cartridge are well protected and are not subject to finger prints and other possible kinds of damage which is normally the case with microfilms in spools. Data is filmed in a sequential form on microfilm to be viewed consecutively.

14.2.2. Microfiche

A microfiche or fiche is a sheet of film containing multiple micro images in a grid pattern. The size of a microfiche usually is 14.5 cm x 10 cm. A standard microfiche can accommodate 98 pages in X-Y direction, X–14 and Y–7. It usually contains identification information that can be read with the naked eye. Information can be viewed at random on microfiche when compared to a microfilm where it is in a sequential order. Microfiche can be easily duplicated for mailing, security or reference purposes. The reduction range is 18X to 48X. Enlargement/reduction is normally interpreted in terms of X in photographic jargon. 18X means reduction of the size of the original to 1/18 and 48X to 1/48.

14.2.3. Ultrafiche

Ultrafiche is the same as microfiche but with a higher reduction ratio of more than 90X, thus permitting thousands of images per fiche. Ultrafiche offers the advantage of storing more information in less space than a standard microfiche.

14.2.4. Aperture Card

These cards are available in many sizes, an aperture card is an opaque tab card with a rectangular opening or openings (apertures) designed for mounting on inserting microfilms. It combines key punched data and access information with microfilm. It can contain a single image or upto eight page-size images on one frame. When accessed information is punched into aperture cards, they can be sorted at high speeds in an electric accounting machine (EAM).

14.2.5. Jacket

Closest microfom to fiche in terms of format is jacket microfilm. The jacket is a plastic carrier with single or multiple sleeves or channels designed to accept strips of 16 mm or 36 mm films. Jackets protect the microfilm and facilitate organization of materials. Images may be copied or read directly from the jacket without removing the film. Jacket can be visibly titled for quick, easy file reference.

14.2.6. Micro Opaque

Similar to microfiche in configuration, micro opaques are, as their name implies, images on opaque stock. Therefore, images may be stored on both sides. Unlike microfiche, where transmitted light is used for blow back, opaques use reflected light. This is primarily used for reading because this cannot be easily duplicated.

Advantages

The advantages of microforms need not be overemphasized. Besides being a space saving meduim they have additioal merits. They are easy to handle, easy to maintain, easy to mail and transport and are not subject to quick wear and tear. Data integrity and maintainability, savings in acquisition costs, preservation for archival purpose, easy retrieval of information (by manual as well as automatic reader/printer devices), easy duplication (easier and cheaper than reproduction on paper copies), labour saving (less time for sorting and filing than paper records), convenient and standard format and ready availability in the library (for consultation and reference because reading/copying facilities exist in libraries) are other major advantages of micro forms.

A major advantage of microform collection is that we can have more information at relatively reduced cost. This advantage has led many a distribution agency to bring out more and more microform publications.

These advantages will greatly help libraries to turn to microforms in future. Libraries can also consider converting the existing hardcopy collection into microforms in view of the advantages they have. However, the following decisions/factors have to be considered before venturing on conversion of existing hard copy collection into microform:

(i) the collection has to be converted so that the microform is more advantageous than original hard copy.

(ii) availability of facilities to read the micros and reproduce hard copy if required.

(iii) coverage of period (i.e., literature belonging to particular periods).

(iv) economic aspects (conversion or acquisition if available).

(v) dispensation/disposal of hard copy collection after the conversion.

Libraries in India have been operating on tight budgets with no space for collection building. Almost 60-70% of the library budgets are being spent on periodicals in special libraries. The rise in subscription costs of journals takes a heavy toll on the library finances. Under these circumstances, microform technology is a viable proposition.

14.3. MICROFORM APPLICATIONS

Microform finds various applications. Book trade uses microform for producing catalogues, lists of out of print books, indexes to books and non-book materials. Universities in USA and UK publish their prospectus and admission material for graduate and post-graduate studies in micform to distribute them free of cost to the students. Engineering design, drawings, etc. are invariably stored in microform as the originals are unwieldy to use. Storage of such drawings in their original form is a difficult task too. Organisations that collaborate on research projects make available materials mutually in microform so as to ensure their integrity and reliability. Newspaper offices and archives use microform technology for preserving their records. Oriental manuscripts, literature on palm leaves and pre-historic materials can be preserved permanently using microform technology. There applications are outside the purview of libraries and information centres.

Microform technology application in libraries and information centres is an established fact. There is no record or documents which cannot be microfilmed. The major beneficiary is journal publishing. Jorunal publishers world over have been bringing out journals both in microform and paper copy editions. A discount of 50% is offered on subscription to both versions. While the current subscription to microform is the same as its paper copy counterpart, the microform of back volumes are cheaper than their paper copies. By subscribing to both versions of current journals, we can eliminate binding of journals completely as we can retain microform version. This saves expenditure on binding and preservation, storage space and maintenance. Cumulative indexes ranging from 5 to 20 years can be easily stored in a microfiche. A library which cannot afford to acquire complete back sets of journals can get cumulative indexes in microfiche. The cumulative index provides access to information for the complete journal (all volumes from its inception). To cite an example IEEE (Institute of Electrical and Electronic Engineers) microfilm system provides the most cost effective way to access the burgeoning literature, totalling over 5000 pages annually. Complete back sets of IEEE transactions, continuation of AIEE transactions from 1884-1964 are available in microfilm format at a cost of about $7000. In addition, a cumulative index covering the years 1884 through 1959 in microfilm format is also available. Major advantage of this microfilm according to the publishers (IEEE) is that the searching time for information is reduced by 80%. Such a back volume collection in paper copy form would have taken enormous shelf space in a library. But for microform technology, the cumulative index of such magnitude dated back to 1884 would not have been made available for easy reference. This means access to more information at less cost and at minimum time. Dissertation abstracts published by University Microfilms International, Ann Arbor, Chemical Abstracts by American Chemical Society, Biological Abstracts, Engineering Index, Electrical and Electronic Abstracts and many more abstracting journals are simultaneously available in microfilm along with print forms. In all cases, back files dating back to 19 th century are available in microfilm.

Next to journals, these are available in microfilm. American University theses are converted to microfilms and these microfilms are distributed by University Microfilms International (UMI), Ann Arbor. M.S. and Ph.D thesis of any American University can be obtained on microfilm from the UMI. Of late, the UMI is also accepting thesis from a few other countries including India for publication and distribution in microfilm format. UK University thesis are available with British Library Reference Division. Likewise, many countries bring out University thesis in microform which is a standard format for thesis world over. In addition to University thesis, some out of print books are brought out in microfilm by UMI and other publishers.

The impact of microform on what are called micro documents like technical reports, standard specifications, patents, etc., is also equally great. National Technical Information Services (NTIS), Virginia, USA is a clearing house for US federal Government reports. NTIS converts all reports, that are deposited with them into microfiche and make available the same on subscription. It has a fortnightly supply service of select research in microfiche (SRIM). Under the service, reports in microfiche are mailed every fortnight on a standing order. While each report costs around $5, a specific order costs $13.50 and hard copy costs a minimum of $50. Research reports published by various research and development institutions are also published in microfilms and are available from the respective institutions.

International standards and some national standards are marketed in microfiche and microfilm formats. These are much cheapter in subscription when compared to their paper copy counterpart. Updataion of the standards in microfilm is much easier than paper copy. International Electro Technical Commission (IEC) and International Standards Organisatin (ISO) publish standards at the international level. These standards are brought out by Information Handling Service, a private agency engaged in microform. This agency distributes and sells world standards in microform by accepting subscriptions to the same.

Complete collection of patents of the United States is available on microfilm reels for the period 1790-1984 and patents in the areas of mechanical engineering and electrical engineering are available for the period 1952-1987. The cost of subscription to patent abstract journals published by Derwent Publications Ltd., UK is about £ 1200 and in microform it is about £ 600. Cumulative index to patent abstracts of 7 years is available for the period 1975-90.

14.4. READERS AND PRINTERS

Microimages on the microform are too small to be read with the naked eye. We need viewers and readers to magnify these images to readable size. Some, coupled with computers select the information quickly and automatically so that users can view immediately from a file. Whether operated manually or connected to computers, readers can be coupled with mechanisms that make paper copies. Microform readers, like slide projectors can project and enlarge an image from the front to an opaque reflecting screen or work like a television set by doing the same thing from the reader of a translucent screen. Front project screens are normally placed near at table top height. They are usually angled much like hand held reading material and are comfortable to look at even with bifocals. From edge to edge their illumination is quite even. They reflect an image from a matt screen that is easy for the eyes and can be viewed from almost any angle enabling a user to move around freely and continue reading conveniently for long.

Readers are available in various sizes. Depending on the size reduction of images of microform, the reader lens is to be selected. For example, when the micro image is in 24X size, the reader should have a lens of 24X magnification. Most of the readers will have provision to accept varying lenses. A reader will have primarily a lens mechanism, a screen, an attachment to hold a microform, a rotating mechanism to view the required page in a microform and a bulb. Some microform readers are built for light duty, others are made for heavy use. Readers may be portable or stationary, depending on the intended use. Portable readers may be so small and light that they can be held on the lap or in the palm of the hand. Stationary readers are desktops or floor models. Floor model readers can be exceptionally rugged.

The large variety of applications for microform has led to the development of many microform readers. With the advent of microprocessors, many readers have attached microprocessor devices which help in scanning and locating the required images automatically on the screen without manually turning the film to that page. There are semi-automatic and fully-automatic readers. The entire microfilm can be loaded to a reader and with the help of an automatic retrieval device the image frames can be programmed and the desired page can be mounted for viewing within seconds. Computer-aided retrieval systems (CAR) aim at using computer technology in microform technology for information retrieval.

CONCLUSION

Information technology has influenced microform technology to a very great extent. From paper copy, microform took over. From microform, magnetic and optical storage has taken over. Optical scanners have arrived. Previously microimages were produced from the print form through photographic technique. Now optical scanners are used to scan the microimages and the are then entered into an optical memory like CD-ROMs. Once they are converted into computer memory, the retrieval of information has become an easy proposition. Hence it is not far away that optical disks will take over from microforms. Microfom technology will exist because the archieval literature can be preserved only on microform.

15
Information Systems and Services

15.1. INTRODUCITON

After independence in 1947, the national government gave due recognition to the vital role well-organised library and information services would play in the programmes of national development and reconstruction. The need for developing an effective system for information transfer became all the more essential because of factors such as (i) vast proliferations in the universe of knowledge and the resultant phenomenon of 'document explosion' in the world as a whole, and (ii) the varied and complex needs of users for information in R & D activities and in research programmes for socio-economic development of the country.

As a result, a fairly good infrastructure of library and information services has been developed in the country during the past five decades or so. To highlight some of the achievements, it may be mentioned that the country now has (i) four national libraries, viz., the National Library at Kolkata, the National Science Library and National Medical Library at Delhi and the Indian Agricultural Research Institute Library at Delhi which can also be considered as the national agricultural library, (ii) an infastructure of public library services in almost all the States and Union Territories with public library legislation, (iii) libraries of varying sizes and services in colleges, universities, institutions of higher learning, research laboratories and institutions, as well as government ministries/departments, (iv) bibliographhic control of Indian publications with the publishing of the Indian National Bibliography since 1958, (v) documentation services at the national level provided by the Indian National Scientific Documentation Centre (INSDOC), (Now NISCAIR), the Defence Science Information and Documentation Centre (DESIDOC) and National Social Sciences Documentation Centre (NASSDOC), (vi) information systems in sceince and technology, medical and health science, environmental services, etc., and (vii) educational and research facilities in library and information science in about 75 library schools.

Several institutions such as Bhabha Atomic Research Centre (BARC) at Mumbai and the Indian Council of Agricultural Research (ICAR) are already functioning as input centres for the international databases, INIS and AGRIS, respectively. Collaboration with several other global information programmes and databases, such as UNISIST, ASTINFO, APPINESS, DIALOG has been developed so as to have an access to the information resources at the international level. Several special libraries and information centres provides such services as SDI, CAS, repacking of information and referral services. Computerized information services are already extended by several special libraries in the country. Science Information Centre at Bangalore, developed by the University Grants Commission, aims at providing computerized bibiliographic information to teachers and other researchers in the country.

Further developments are envisaged during the period of the 8th Five year Plan. A Working Group to make recommendations for this period has already been appointed by the Planning Commission, Government of India. The two reports: one by the Planning Commission Working Group on the Modernization of Library Services and Informatics for the Seventh Five Year Plan (1985-90) submitted in 1984, and the other called National Policy on Library and Information Systems: A Presentation submitted in May 1986 by the Committee on National Policy and Information Systems appointed by the Government of India, Department of Culture are some of the noteworthy developments in this direction.

15.2. EMERGENCE OF INFORMATION SYSTEMS AND SERVICES

Like in other countries, in India also libraries, documentation centres and information centres got established as independent units. Some of the institutions which have played a singificant role in building up information resources and services in the country are: NISCAIR (formerly INSDOC), Bhabha Atomic Research Centre, Indian Council of Agricultural Research, Indian Council of Social Science Research, Council of Scientific and Industrial Research, Electronics Commission, Indian Space Research Organisation, Indian Council of Medical Research and the University Grants Commission. Some of the R & D units in industries and private institutions have also been playing active role in this direction.

Scattered resources, inadequate communication linkages, lack of proper co-operation and co-ordination have, however, been some of the weak points of these libraries, documentation centres and information centres. Though the need for developing systems of co-operation and co-ordination between them had always been emphasised, yet it was only during the mid-1970s that concrete steps were taken in this direction. The underlying need for developing inter-linkage between them has been emphasised in order to: (i) develop programmes of sharing of resources and services so as to minimise duplication and maximise the utilization of financial resources and other facilities, and (ii) provide access to their resources so that any user, living anywhere, may have the required information at a time when he needs it and in a form that would best suit his purpose. Some of the developments in the country during the past few years in telecommunication and information technology which provide optimism for vast activities in this direction are: (i) use of satellite communication technology, and (ii) increasing availability of micro-processors, P.C.s and growth of indigenous computer industry.

15.3. NATIONAL INFORMATION SYSTEM IN SCIENCE & TECHNOLOGY (NISSAT)

In the overall context of UNESCO's programmes viz. UNISIST and NATIS, the Government of India in 1971 made a request to UNESCO for a short-term mission of consultant for advising the Government about the establishment of an information network in Science and Technology in the country. Dr. Peter Lazar, who worked as a consultant, submitted a report on NISSAT in 1972. At the Government level, the proposal for establishing NISSAT under the Department of Science and Technology (DST), was duly recommended by the Panel Group for the information sector of the high-powered apex body called the National Committee on Science and Technology (NCST) for the Five Year Plan 1974-79 and its impementation was finally authorised in early 1977. With the reorganisation of the Government of India in 1985, NISSAT was put under the charge of the Department of Scientific and Industrial Research (DSIR) in the Ministry of Science and Technolgy. NISSAT, which is rather a programme than an information system as such, was formally launched in September, 1977. It is being implemented as a decentralized network involving standardized and mutually compatible systems for collection, storage and dissemination of information. The NISSAT headquarter at present functions as the national focal point in the field of S & T information.

Objectives

The NISSAT aims are fulfilling the following objectives:

(i) Provision of national information service relevant to present needs and capable development to meet the future needs of the generators, processors, disseminators and users of information.

(ii) Optimum utilisation of existing information services and systems and the development of new ones.

(iii) Promotion of national and international co-operation and liaison for exchange of information.

(vi) Support and active encouragement for the development of facilities for education and training in information science and technology and in communication to provide qualified manpower for the implementation of the national science information policy.

(v) Support and active participation in research development and innovation in information sciences and communication to enhance both the efficiency of information services and the quality of the information provided by these services.

(vii) Support and promotion of research, development and innovation in information technology.

Structure

National Focal Point: The DST has been designated as the National Focal Point (NFP) of NISSAT. The NISSAT is advised and guided by :

(a) Advisory Committee

(b) Executive Committee

(c) Adhoc Working Group and Expert Groups.

It is serviced by a small secretariat.

NISSAT Network

The NISSAT Network comprises the following:

(i) Sectoral Information Centres (SIC)

(ii) Regional Information Centres (RIS)

(iii) Other specialized services.

One of the guiding principles of NISSAT has been to achieve maximum exploitation of the existing resources and facilities, particularly in view of the visual financial constraints for the programme. The system has already taken steps to integrate and coordinate the existing sources and facilities and to fill up the gaps rather than to duplicate them or to build up new ones. Some of the existing information centres and services were upgraded, whenever reqired, by providing additional inputs from NISSAT so that services at the national level could be offered by these centres.

Role of the Sectoral Information Centres (SICs)

The SICs are expected to meet the information need concerning a particular discipline, mission or product. A SIC should coordinate its activities with the other relevant information centres called Local Information Units (LIUS) in that particular field.

An SIC has, therefore, to be a part of a national level research laboratory engaged in R & D work in the particular discipline, mission or product so that services of subject specialists would also be available for various jobs such as abstracting information analysis, etc. This would also help in a better utilization of the information facilities and products created by the Centre.

The main functions of these SICs include all those areas concerned with the planning, co-ordination and co-operation of their activities as well as acquisition, organisation and dissemination of information to the clientele.

The following Sectoral Centres have been established till now.

NISSAT's Sectoral Centres

S. No. 1	*Sectoral Centre* 2	*Institution* 3	*Info. System* 4
1.	Leather Technology	Central Leather Research Institute (CLRI), Chennai	National Information Centre for Leather and Allied Industries (NICLAI)
2.	Food Technology	Central Food National Technological Research Institute (CFRTI) Mysore	Information Centre for Food Science and Technology (FOSTIS)
3.	Machine Tool	Central Machine Tools Institute (CMTI) Bangalore	National Information Centre for Medicine Tools and Allied Product (NICMAP)
4.	Drugs and Pharmaceuticals	Central Drugs Research Institute (CDRI), Lucknow	National Information Centre for Drugs and Pharmaceutical (NICDAP)
5.	Textiles	Ahmedabad Textile Industry Research Association (ATIRA) Ahmedabad	National Information Centre for Textile and Allied Subjects (NICTAS)
6.	Chemicals	National Chemical Laboratory INCL), Pune	National Information Centre for (NICHEM)
7.	Glass and Ceramic	Central Glass and Ceramics Res. Instt. (CGCRI), Kolkata	National Information Centre for Advanced Ceramics (NICAS)
8.	Crystallography	Deptt. of Crystallography and Bibophysics Univ. of Madras, Chennai	National Information Centre for Crystallography (NICRYS)
9.	Bibliometrics	NISCAIR (INSDOC)	National Centre for Bibliometrics (NCB)
10.	CD-ROM	National Aerospace Laboratory, Banglore	National Information Centre for CD-ROM (NICDROM)

Development of Infrastructure and Services in the SICs

During the past ten years these SICs have been provided financial support by the NISSAT so as to augment their equipment facilities, information resources and publication activities. Each of these centres has consequently built-up large document colllections and has acquired a wide range of equipments, items such as plain-paper copier, microfiche reader-printer and processing system, off-set printing system, etc. In addition, some of them have acquired their own computer systems (e.g. NICFOS AND NICDAP) or use the computer facilities of their parent organisation (e.g. NICMAP) or make use of the one available in some other institution locally (e.g. NICLAI uses the facility at the Indian Institute of Technology, Chennai).

Each of the first four SICs provides a wide range of information services such as Current Awareness Service (CAS), Selective Dissemination of Information (SDI), translation, reprographic and micrographic services. It prepares state-of the-art report, subject bibliographies, directory of the ongoing projects, and does repackaging of information on a regular basis to meet the varied interests and demands of the clientale. In addition, these centres organize seminars, lectures, etc., on the basis of their interest and activity.

NICRYS which is the youngest among the centres, differs from others in the sense that it provides both hard and soft data in a limited area, namely organic chemical crystallography. These data are compiled on global basis in Cambridge (U.K.) by the Cambridge Crytallographic Data Centre. These are computerized there and the data tapes are made available to NICRYS for dissemination in India. The current database includes information on: (i) compounds: organic and organometallic, excluding polymers and proteins, (ii) Techniques: crystal structures determined by X-ray or neutron diffraction, and (iii) Structures: for each structure three dimensional coordinates are determined for the atoms.

NICRYS also publishes a quarterly newsletter of its

activities and various items of interest to crystallographers in chemical science in India.

Regional Information Centres (RICs)

In view of the large size of the country, it was agreed in the original plan that a system of Regional Information Centers (RICs) to act as contact points be created in the NISSAT network. However, because of various reasons, including financial constraints, these centres are yet to be created.

Other Activities under NISSAT

Among the several specialized services provided or experiments carried out under the NISSAT, a few may be mentioned as follows:

(a) Computerized SDI service using commercial databases: With assistance of UNESCO, this service was started in January 1976 using the IBM 370/150 computer of the Indian Institute of Technology, Madras with the Chemical Abstracts Condensates. A few users from Asian countries also participated in this experiment. From January 1977, INSPEC A & B and COMPENDEX databases were added to the SDI service and the number of profiles was increased to about 300. Expenses for the SDI, which was initially free of charge, were met from the NISSAT budget. After the initial free service, a pricing mechanism was introduced later on. The project, however, could not continue because the experience was not quite encouraging.

(b) On-Line Access to Foreign Database: Few demonstrations, to have online access to foreign detabases such as ESRIN/RECON Database system at Frasceti (Italy) and European Space Agency (ESA) database, were held in 1976 and 1981, respectively. However, a system to have online access to international databases, such as DIALOG and others, on regular basis is yet to be made operational in the country.

(c) Creation of Databases: NISSAT has by now promoted the development of several databases notable among them being:

(i) Current Research Projects on S & T

(ii) Directory of Testing Facilities

(iii) National Union Catalogues

These have been developed by NISCAIR (INSDOC).

Besides these, NISSAT has sponsored special studies and projects on different areas of information processing and dissemination, micrographic, manpower development, etc.

Internationl Collaboration

NISSAT has also been playing an active role in bilateral co-operation programmes in S & T Information with several countries such as USA, Russia, France, FRG and GDR within the overall framework of India's agreements in the field of Sceince and Technology. The NISSAT Advisory Committee functions as National Committee on UNISIST in India as well as for collaboration with UNESCO including ASTINFO. It also collaborates with several other programmes such as International Referral System for sources of Environmental Information (INFOTERRA), Commonwealth Regional Renewable Energy Resources Information System (CRRERIS) and others.

15.4. INTITUTIONAL INFORMATION SYSTEMS

15.4.1. National Institute of Science Communication and Information Resources (NISCAIR)

National Institute of Science Communication and Information Resources (NISCAIR) was formed on 30th September, 2002 with the merger of National Institute of Science Communication (NISCOM) and Indian National Scientific Documentation Centre (INSDOC). Both NISCOM and INSDOC, the two premier institutes of the Council of

Scientific and Industrial Research (CSIR), were devoted to dissemination and documentation of S & T information.

NISCOM had been in existence for the last six decades. Over the years, NISCOM diversified its activities, and through a host of its information products, comprising search journals, encyclopaedic publications, mongraphs, popular science journals, books and information services. It had been reaching out to researchers, students, enterpreneurs, industrialists, agriculturists, policy planners and also the common man.

INSDOC came into being in 1952 and was engaged in providing S & T information and documentation services through myriad activities such as abstracting and indexig, design and development of indigenous databases, translation, library automation, providing access to international information sources, human resource development, consultancy services in setting up modern library cum-information centres and so on. INSDOC was also host to the National Science Library and the SAARC documentation centre.

Now, with the formation of NISCAIR, all of the above mentioned multifaceted acitivities have been amalgamated, making NISCAIR and institute capable of serving the society using modern IT infrastructure, in a more effective manner and taking up new ventures in the field of science and communication, dissemination and S & T information management systems and services. Broadly, the core activity of NISCAIR will be to collect/store, publish and disseminate S & T information through a mix of traditional and modern means, which will benefit different segments of the society.

Main Functions of NISCAIR

(i) To provide formal linkages of communication among the socientific community in the form of research journals in different areas of Science and Technolgoy.

(ii) To disseminate science and technology information to public, particularly students, to inclucate their interest in science.

(iii) To collect, collate and disseminate information on plant and mineral wealth and industrial infrastructure of the country.

(iv) To harness information technology application in information management with particular reference to science communication and modernizing libraries.

(v) To act as a facilitator in furthering the economic, social, industrial, scientific and commercial development by providing timely access to relevant and accurate information.

(vi) To develop human resource in the fields of science communication, library documentation, information science, science and technology, information management systems and services.

(vii) To collaborate with international institutions and organisations having objectives and goals similar to those of NISCAIR.

(viii) Any other activity in consonance with the mission statement of NISCAIR.

Major Programmes of NISCAIR

To provide communication links among members of the research community, NISCAIR publishes 19 research journals (including one in hindi) and two abstracting journals of international repute, covering all the major disciplines of science and technology. Publication in all the research journals is subject to proper reviewing, and the journals are covered in most of the major abstracting/indexing/current awareness services.

The journals published by NISCAIR are as follows:

(i) Journal of Scieneitific and Industiral Research (JSIR) (Monthly).

(ii) Indian Journal of Chemistry, Section A (IJC-A) (Monthly).

(iii) Indian Journal of Chemistry, Section B (IJC-B) (Monthly).

(iv) Indian Journal of Experimental Biology (IJEB) (Monthly).

(v) Indian Journal of Pure and Applied Physics (IJPAP) (Monthly).

(vi) Indian Journal of Chemical Technology (IJCT) (Bi-monthly).

(vii) Indian Journal of Engineering and Materials Science (IJEMS) (Bi-monthly).

(viii) Indian Journal of Biochemistry and Biophysics (IJBB) (Bi-monthly).

(ix) Indian Journal of Radio and Space Physics (IJRSP) (Bi-monthly).

(x) Journal of Intellectural Property Rights (JIPR) (Bimonthly).

(xi) Natural Product Rediance (NPR) (Bi-monthly).

(xii) Indian Journal of Marine Science (IJMS) (Quarterly).

(xiii) Indian Journal of Fibre and Textile Research (IJFTR) (Quarterly).

(xiv) Indian Journal of Biotechnology (IJBT) (Quarterly).

(xv) Indian Journal of Traditional Knowledge (IJTK) (Quarterly).

(xvi) Annals of Library and Information Studies (ALIS) (Quarterly).

(xvii) Bharatiya Vaigyanik Evam Audyogik Anusanthan Patrika (BVAAP) (Half-yearly).

(xviii) Medicinal & Aromatic Plants Abstracts (MAPA) (Bimonthly).

(xix) Indian Science Abstracts (ISA) (Fortnightly).

Other Publicitions of NISCAIR

1. The institute publishes three well circulated popular science magazines: Science Reporter (English, monthly), Vigyan Pragati (Hindi, monthly) and Science Ki Duniya (Urdu, quarterly).
2. NISCAIR has also brought out as many as 60 popular science books in English under different series. Also, 28 books have been brought out in Hindi.
3. NISCAIR has also launched a new series of books on 'IT for kids'.
4. NISCAIR brings out the encyclopaedic publication, 'The wealth of India' on Indian raw materials, and monographs on specified topics. The Hindi version of 'The wealth of India, Bharat Ki Sampada' is also being published.
5. R & D Newsletters: To provide a useful link between various CSIR labs/institutes and also to disseminate infor mation regarding the activities of CSIR to other R & D organisations, academia, industry, etc., in India and abroad, NISCAIR brings out CSIR News (Fortnightly) and its Hindi version, CSIR Samachar (monthly).

Other Activities:

1. **Raw Materials Herbarium & Museum:** NISCAIR has a Raw Materials Herbarium and Museum, which acts as a respository of raw materials. The Herbarium houses over 4000 species of economic and medicinal plants of India and the museum comprises over 2500 samples of crude drug, animal and mineral specimens.
2. **Database Design and Development:** NISCAIR has developed expertise in the design and development of databases. Some indigenously developed databases include Indian Science Abstracts Database, National Union Catalogue of Scientific Serials in India Database,

Indian Patents Database and Medicinal and Aromatic Plants Abstracts Database. All these databases are available online.

3. **National Science Library (NSL):** National Science Library (NSL) is a comprehensive collection of science & technology publications in the country offering services on a national scale. It subscribes to almost all Indian S & T periodicals and has over 1,80,000 bound volumes of books and periodicals.

NSL also has an Electronic Library Division with a rich collection of more then 5,000 foreign journals, conference proceedings, etc., and a large number of databases including CA, CAB, SCI, Current contents, Indian Standards and US patents. It is planning to eventually digitise the NSL holding and to facilities storing of digitized information in the emerging electronic library environment, eventually converting NSL into a National Science Digital Library (NSDL), which would serve as a model for other libraries throughout the country.

4. **Consortium for Accessing E-Journals:** NISCAIR is the model organisation for developing a 'Consortium for CSIR Laboratories for Accessing E-Journals. The activity shall range from creation to monitoring of the access facility of scientific periodicals published by leading international institutions. To start with, an agreement has been signed with M/s. Elsevier for a period of four years for all their E-Journals. Under the scheme, CSIR scientists shall be able to access these journals and download material for their personal use.

5. **Information Services:** NISCAIR offers a host of information services based on indigenous and international information resources.

   (i) Medicinal and Aromatic plants information service.

(ii) Contents, abstracts and photocopy service.
(iii) Literature search service.
(iv) Assign ISSN numbers to serials published in India.
(v) S & T translation services.
(vi) Bibliometrics services.
(vii) Consultancy services.

6. **Human Resource Development :** NISCAIR organises Human Resources Development (HRD) Programmes to train and prepare library information, documentation and science communication professionals in meeting the challenges of the changing IT scenario. The courses / programmes offered are as follows:

6.1. **Associateship in Information Science (AIS):** Two year advanced Master's degree level academic course in documentation and reprography.

6.2. **Training Programmes:** (i) Short-Term Training Courses on contemporary areas of information science technology & computer applications such as Library Automation, Database design, Desk Top Publishing, Bibliometrics, Internet and Online Information Retrieval, E-commerce etc. Training courses are also held in technical writing and herberium techniques.

(ii) **Attachment Training Programmes:** For persons requiring specialised training in the field of information science, information management, information technology and related other activities.

(iii) **On-site Training Programmes:** For customers at their own premises subject to a minimum of ten participants.

(iv) **Academic Counselling:** NISCAIR has been

designated as a programme study centre for some programmes of Indira Gandhi National Open University (IGNOU), such as Masters in Computer Applications (MCA), Bachelors in Computer Applications (BCA), Master of Library and Information Science (MLISc), and Bachelor of Library and Information Science (BLISc.)

7. **SAARC Documentation Centre:** The SAARC Documentation centre (SDC) has been setup at NISCAIR for exchanging science and technology (S & T) information among SAARC nations, and has been functioning since January 1994. Out of a number of programmes planned by SCD for execution during next 2-3 years, human resource development in the SAARC region has been accorded top priority. Consequently, SDC has initiated several training progammes in the field of Information Science and Technology.

15.4.2. National Social Science Documentation Centre (NASSDOC)

The National Social Science Documentation Centre (NASSDOC) was set up in 1970 by the Indian Council of Social Science Research (ICSSR) with the objective of providing information support to social science research activities in the country.

Activities of NASSDOC

The main activities of NASSDOC are:

(i) Building up a collection of reference materials and works on research methodology, collecting (a) unpublished doctoral thesis approved by Indian universities and foreign thesis on India, (b) research reports of the projects undertaken by ICSSR and other social science research institutions assisted by ICSSR, (c) working papers presented at ICSSR funded seminars and conferences, and (d) periodicals of research standard in social sciences.

(ii) Providing bibliographical information about Indian publications in social science disciplines to international documentation agencies.

Striving for bibliographic control over social science materials by bringing out various documents under Research Information Series. (About one hundred titles have so far been brought out. A list of these is available on request).

(iii) Providing selected bibliographies on request.

(iv) Providing duplicating and reprographic services.

(v) Providing document supply services to scholars from outside Delhi.

(vi) Awarding study grants to scholars for working at libraries of their interest in India.

(vii) Providing consultancy to social science institutions in setting up documentation and information centres.

(viii) Providing facilities for staff participation in professional seminars and conferences through contributing papers and taking active part in their deliberations, deputing staff to attend short refresher courses.

(ix) Conducting professional training courses under Continuing Education Programme.

(x) Processing project proposal involving financial assistance to documentation and bibliographical projects for consideration under ICSSR Committee on Documentation Services and Research Information.

(xi) Entering into agreement with national and international organisations or mutual exchange of publications (At present 2000 institutions are on exchange list).

Collection Development of NASSDOC

(i) More than 100,000 backup volumes of social science periodicals.
(ii) Comprehensive collection of books on the field of social sciences.
(iii) A good collection of reference material on social sciences.
(iv) A very rich collection of theses and research reports on social sciences procured from universities and research institutions in India.
(v) Microform copies of old social science research journals from India, etc.

Documentation Activiies

(i) Union List of Social Science Periodicals;
(ii) Union Catalogue of Social Science Serials;
(iii) Union Catelogue of Newspapers in Delhi Libraries;
(iv) Inventory of Social Science Institutions and Organisation in India;
(v) Mahatma Gandhi Bibliography;
(vi) Retrospective Cumulative Index of Indian Social Science Periodcials;
(vii) Area Studies Bibliographies;
(viii) Language Bibliographics, etc.

Financial Assistance

NASSDOC provides financial assistance for:

(i) Assistance for documentation projects;
(ii) Publication assistance for a number of social science periodicals and indexing journals;
(iii) Financial assistance to libraries, and documentation centres for documentation activities, subscription of journals, etc.

Cooperation and Collaboration

NASSDOC has collaboration with several national, regional and international organisations, like- international committee for Social Science Information and Documentation (Paris) : International Bulletin of Bibliography on Education (Madrid); International Geographical Bibliography (Paris) : UNESCO (Paris) : Asia-Pacific International Network in Social Science (APINESS) (Bangkok); etc.

Human Resource Development

NASSDOC conducts short-term training programmes in library and documentation services, especially in the application of information technology.

Documentation

Its documentation programmes include compilation of Union lists/catalgoues, directories. (Indian research organisation, associations, periodicals, etc.), area study bibliographies (states and union territories in India), bibliographies of macro research material in the regional languages and bibliographical documents under Research Information Series (over 150 titles till now).

Some of the selected publications brought out by NASSDOC are:

(i) Current Contents of Indian Social Science Periodicals.

(ii) Acquisition Update.

(iii) Conference Newsletter.

(iv) Apiness Newsletter.

Services

NASSDOC provides reading room facilities, information/literature search service, referral, consultancy, reprographic and photocopying services and compiles short bibliographies for researchers on request.

The services of the NASSDOC are based on its rich resource collection consisting of:

1. Specifically discipline-oriented reference sources like

dictionaries, encyclopaedias, directories, bibliographies.

2. NASSDOC priced and non-priced publications brought out with financial support of ICSSR. viz.
   - (i) Indian Dissertation Abstracts (Q) : 1973.
   - (ii) ICSSR Research Abstract Quarterly : 1971.
   - (iii) ICSSR Journal of Abstracts and Reviews : Economics (Q) 1971.
   - (iv) ICSSR Journal of Abstracts and Reviews Geography (Biannual); 1977.
   - (v) ICSSR Journal of Abstracts and Reviews : Political Science (Biannual); 1977.
   - (vi) Indian Psychological Abstracts (Q) : 1972.
   - (vii) Indian Journal of Social Science (Q) : 1988.
   - (viii) ICSSR Newsletter (Q) : 1969.

There are number of Surveys of Research (e.g., Accounting Theory, Demography, Economics, Geography, Management, Political Sceince, Psychology, Public Administration, Sociology and Social Anthropology) and other publications (viz., Youths in India, Index to periodicals-Sociology & Psychology 1886-1970); Religion, Society and State; Social Information of India : Trends and Structures; Law : The Crisis of the Indian Legal System : National Register of Social Scientists in India; Gandhi Bibliography.

3. Indian Doctoral Dissertations, research reports, working papers and back files of social science periodicals; and
4. Documents on microfilm/fiche.

Database Services

Information Technology input has faciliated creation of machine readable databases, periodicals in libraries, doctoral dissertations in NASSDOC, research reports in NASSDOC.

UNESCO CD-ROM prototype installed by NASSDOC contains six databases, viz.,

1.	UNESCO BIB	:	46,000 bibliographic references to documents and publications issued by UNESCO.
2.	IBE DOCs	:	12,700 references to world-wide literature in education.
3.	ICOMMOS	:	25,000 references to world-wide literature on museums, monuments and sites.
4.	DARE	:	4,650 research institutes and information services, 4,500 periodicals in social sciences.
5.	ENERGY	:	4,200 research institutes and information centres concerning renewable energy sources.
6.	UNESDATA	:	Directory of UNESCO data-bases (66 databases).

15.4.3. Defence Scientific Information And Documentation Centre (DESIDOC)

Realising the value of scientific information in defence research, the Defence Research and Development Organisation (DRDO) of the Government of India created a Scientific Information Bureau (SIB) in 1958 to collect and process S & T information of defence interest and disseminate it to the concerned R & D scientists and other agencies of the Minstry of Defence. In 1967, SIB was reorganized and renamed as DESIDOC with wider scope and responsibilities. Since 1970 it has been functioning in the DRDO as a central agency to collect scientific and technical information from various published and unpublished sources, process it in different usable forms and disseminate the same to about 40 DRDO laboratoreis and several other establishments of the

Ministry of Defence. It is responsible for developing a database and an information system in Defence Science and Technology and coordinate the library and information activities of the DRDO as a whole. It is also expected to carry out R & D work in information science relevant to defence needs. Today DESIDOC has become one of the India's premier national information centres. Over the years, it has grown in terms of competence and services.

Objectives of DESIDOC

(i) Function as a central resource for providing scientific information/documentation/library/ reprographic/ translation service to the Defence Research and Development Organisation headquarters, laboratories, establishments and to coordinate DRDO scientific information programmes.

(ii) Develop a data bank on scientific information system for defence science and technology and to cooperate with other national and international agencies in the field of scientific information.

(iii) Provide training and user education programmes for Defence Research and Development Organisation and carry out research and development work in the field of scientific information.

(iv) Provide consultancy and referral services to Technical Information Centres.

(v) Publish scientific and technical journals including books and monographs of the Defence Research and Development Organisation.

Functions of DESIDOC

(i) maintaining an up-to-date research and reference library capable of catering the needs of the scientists enageged in defence research and development work;

(ii) sifting through current literature indexing and subject classification of scientific and technical information of interest to defence research and development;

(iii) providing bibliographical service to scientists in all defence establishments/laboratories on demand as well as in anticipation of demand;

(iv) abstracting information under specific topics of interest to defence research and development;

(v) translating into English language scientific and technical documents appearing in other languages;

(vi) disseminating information to the scientists in defence research and development establishment and laboratories through:

 (a) List of latest arrivals in the library;

 (b) Abstracts of selected papers from current scientific periodicals and technical reports;

 (c) Microfilms/photocopies of articles/documents when required by the defence research and development scientists;

(vii) maintaining liaision with universities, research institutins in India and abroad, and

(viii) editing and publishing science journals, and other defence research and development publications.

Divisions of DESIDOC

To perform above functions, DESIDOC has the following primary functional divisions:

1. Library;
2. Documentation;
3. Polygraphy;
4. Publications;
5. Reprography;
6. Translation;

7. Technical Coordination and
8. Administration.

Defence Science Library (DSL)

The Defence Science Library acquires books, journals, reports, patents, etc., for the use of scientists and research scholars of DRDO. In addition, the library has built-up a comprehensive collection of microforms, CDs, etc. in the recent past.

Dissemination of Information

The library and information scientist of DESIDOC provide information in anticipation as well as against specific requests from the users. As anticipatory information service provider, DESIDOC brings out abstracts/indexes bulletins, state-of-the art reports, technical digests, etc. Literature searches are regularly conducted for providing information to the Scientific Advisor to the Union Defence Minister, Chief Controller of R & D, and other users in DRDO headquarters and its laboratories. Modern information technologies have been inducted into the system for quick and effective communication of the processed information.

DESIDOC's information service includes online searching of information from various international databases.

Computerization of Information Services

To meet the enormous information needs of the scientists working in DRDO laboraties, establishments and other institutions such as CSIR, universities, etc. DESIDOC has already developed the software for creating a database of scientific information and for online searching and information retrieval on the Prime-750 system available in the DRDO at Delhi. Computer-based SDI and retrospective information services are being provided and online access to international database is being developed.

A computer based information network called DRDO Information Retrieval System (DRDO-IRS) covering libraries and Technical Information Centres (TICs) of the DRDO laboratories and establishments is being planned. Under this plan, details of the documents received by them will be sent to DESIDOC for inputing into the central database and the printouts will be sent to concerned laboratories/ establishments. This sytem will ensure that scientists of DRDO are intimated as and when documents of their interest will be received in these libraries and TICs. The system would provide project-oriented and mission-oriented information as well.

DESIDOC collaborates with DRDO in the publishing of its quarterly journals, viz. Defence Science Journal and R & D Bulletin. It also organizes short-term courses in areas such as information science, computer-based information service, indexing and abstracting.

Publications of DESIDOC

1. Bibliographies/literature searches on demand.
2. SDI Bulletins : DESIDOC issues from time to time SDI Bulletins on various subjects like military warfare, documents, missiles and rockets, nuclear weapons, etc.
3. Current Abstracts on Electronics.
4. Patents Information Alert (bi-monthly).
5. DESIDOC List. (bi-monthly).
6. State-of-the-Art Repors.

The following are worthy of mentioning:

(1) Thermal Imaging System. (2) Defence R & D in Coming Decades. (3) Remotely Piloted Vehicles. (4) Reconnaisance Sensor System. (5) Chinese Space Programme. (6) Falkland Wars : A Literature Survey Report.

Others

(i) Popular Science & Technology;

(ii) Defence Science Journal;

(iii) Defence Reports Abstracts;

(iv) DESIDOC Bulletin of Information Technology;

(v) DESIDOC List of Current Scientific Literature;

(vi) Patent Information Alert;

(vii) R & D Bulletin;

(viii) R & D Digest.

Other Activities

DESIDOC provides translation services and also maintains a 'translation bank'. It has a potential unit for software development, designing of networks, management, training and also organised several seminars and conferences on key areas and issues of information management. DESIDOC has been establishing an information network of DRDO laboratories spread all over India. DESIDOC has also computerised its various house-keeping operations.

Bibliography

1 Agarwal, J. C., Development of Education System in India, Shipra, New Delhi.

2 Agarwal, S. P., National Information System in Social Science; A Study in Perspective (in Gupta B. M and others eds. Handbook of Libraries & Information Centres in India) New Delhi : Information Industries Publication, Vol. 3, 1986, 179-195.

3 Agrawal, S. N., ed. Perspective in Library and Information Science, 1, 1983.

4 Aptagiri (Devika). Optical Character Recognisation: A Solution for the data entry bottleneck. Lib. Sc. 32, 1995, Paper-C, p. 26-27.

5 Arun Kumar, S. and Khanna, Vivek. Re-engineering with IT Times of India : Oct. 1994.

6 Ashok Babu, T. Internet Service for Libraries. Kumar, P. S. G and Vashisth, C. P., Ed. CALIBER-99 Papers, Ahmedabad. INFLIBNET Centre, 1999.

7 Baker, K., The Impact of Information Technology, Amsterdam : North Holland, 1982, pp. 77-80.

8 Balakrishnan, M. R., Magnetic and Optical Storage of Information. NISSAT Newsletter. 10(1), 1991.

9 Barak, Erik, The Context of National Information Systems in Developing Countries : India and China in a comparative perspective fund : Sweden Research Policy Institute, 1937, p.-212.

10 Battin, Patricia. "The Electronic Library : A Vision for the future". Educom Bull. Vol. 9, summer, 1984, pp.12-17.

11 Bawden, D. and Blakeman, K., Going Automated : Implementing and Using Information Technology in Libraries and Information Units. London : ASLIb. 1990.

12 Bawden, D. and Blakeman, K., Going Automated, London : ASLIB, 1990.

13 Bawden, D. and Blakeman, K. H., IT Strategies for Information Management, London : Butter worths.

14 Bawden, David, Software for Information Management : Perspectives in Information Management. London : Butterworths. Vol. 1, 1989, pp. 25-62.

15 Bedi, D. S., Information professional and the new technology, DESIDOC Bulletin of Information Technology. 11(3), 1991, Vol. 4.

16 Belkin, N. J. and Robinson, S. E., Letters to the editor. JASIS. 28, 1978, p. 212.

17 Bell, D., Social frame work of information theory. Detrouzps, M. L. Mosses, J. Ed. The Computer Age : A twenty years view, 1979. MIT press, Cambridge. p. 163-211.

18 Bhargava, J. K., Srivastava, R. K. and Murthy, S. S., Sanjay-An Indian Library Automation Package Based on CDS/ISIS Programme, 1993, 27(1), 51-66.

19 Bhasker Raj, A. S., CD-ROM A storage gaint, Telematics India. 6(5), 1993.

20 Bhattacharya (Avra). "How is it possible to Protocol a File from Unauthorised Users?". The Telegraph, May 1995, p. 4.

21 Bhol, Marilyan, Information processing. Ed. 3. Chicago : Science Research Associates, Inc., 1980.

22 Biddiscombe, R. and Others, Developing a Web Library

Guide for an Academic Library : Problem, Solutions and Future Possibilities, Programme, 1997, 31(1), 59-74.

23 Bills, Linda G. and Helgerson (Linda W). CD-ROM Public Access Catalgues : Database creation and maintenance. Lib. Hi Tech, Vol. 6, n 1, pp. 67-88 In Panda (K. C.) and Karisiddappa (CR), eds. New Dimensions on Information Science and Technology, 1993. Parimal Pub. 1988, p. 89-90.

24 Blackmore, P., The Development of Internet within a college of Further and Higher Education. Aslib Proceedings, 49(3), 67-72.

25 Blissmer, R. H., Introduction to Computer Concepts. New Delhi, York . John Wiley, 1993.

26 Borgman (Christine L.), Automation is the answer, but what is the question? Progress and Prospects for Central and Eastern European Libraries. Journal of Documentation, 1996, 52(3), 252-295.

27 Bourne, C. P., "Methods of Information Handling", N. York, Wiley, 1963.

28 Bradley, P. and Smith, A., World Wide Web : How to Design and Construct Home Pages. London : Aslib, 1995.

29 Burton, P. F. and Petric, J. H., Information Management Technology, London : Chapman and Hau.

30 Bush (Vanne Var). "As we May Think". Atlantic Monthly, V. 176, July, 1945, pp. 101-108.

31 Butler (Mark). "How to Use the Internet : Join the Internet Revolution Today's, 1994. Ziff-Davis Press, Emery Ville.

32 Cairs Library System. http/ INTERNT www.cairs.co-uk/Library htm. 20th March, 1999.

33 Chamberlain (Carol E.), The Impact of Library

Automation and Electronic Publishing : Towards Distributed Acquisitions. The Acquisitions Librarians, nl, 1989, p. 3-8.

34 Chaube, A. and Prasad, H. M. : Disaster Management of CDS/ISIS : A Study of Stability and Integrity of the Database. Annals of Lib. Sci. Doc. 1997, 44(3), p. 93-97.

35 Chopra, M. G. and Kumar, R. Fortran-VI. Programing New Delhi, Vikas Pub. 1980, p. 1.

36 Chouwdhury, G. G. and Chowdhury, Sidatta. : Text Retrieval and Library Management Software in India. Programme, 1994, 28(3), 253-261.

37 Chowdhury, S. and Chowdhury, G. G. CIRC: A prototype Circulation System Using Micro CDS/ISIS. IASLIC Bull, 37(2): 1992, p. 73-81.

38 Cochrane (Paul inne A), Information Technology in Libraries and Ranganathan's Five Laws of Library Science, Libri, Vol. 42, 3, p. 235.

39 Cogliano, Besty F., Techlib and Techlib plus in a special Library, Library Software Review. Jan-Feb. 1992.

40 Crumlish (Christian), The Internet Dictionary, San Francisco (U.S.A), Sybex : 1995, p. 213.

41 Datta, V. K. , Use of Cairs at the Tropical Development and Research Institute. Programme, 21(4), 360-375.

42 Davis, Charles H. and Rush, James Ed., Guide to Information Science, London : The Library Assn, 1979.

43 Dawson, Andy, The Internet for Library and Information Service Professionals, 2nd ed. London : Aslib.

44 Dawson, Andy. : The Internet for Library and Information Services. Ed. 2 London : Aslib, 1997.

45 Dayananda, P. A. I. and Bhat, K. Shivananda, Modern Technology and Health Science Libraries (In Gupta, S. P. and others, Ed. Information technology and health

science libraries, Papers presented at the national convention and workshop), Medical Library Association, New Delhi, 1993, p. 235-241.

46 DESIDOC, A Central resource for scientific information Delhi : DESIDOC, p 12.

47 Desikan, R. S. and Muthusamy, R. "Local Area Networks : A System for TIC". In Jain. H. C. and Gupta, B. M. ed. S. & T. Information Management in India, Aditya Prakashan, New Delhi, 1993, p. 132-143.

48 Dhaliwal, R. S., Gupta S. K. and Kumar S. Programming with Fortran-77 (A Structural Approach), New Delhi, Wiley Eastern, 1989, p. 4.

49 Excellence in information technology. Raj Publishing Jaipur, 2000, p. 12-18.

50 Eyre, J. : A review of some significant development in microcomputer hardware and software : Their implications for selection. Programme, 23(2) : p. 27-39.

51 Finnegan, R. : Communication and Technology, Linguistics and Communication, 9(3), p. 107-127.

52 Fishenden, R. M. : Methods by which research workers find information in proceedings of the International Conference, 1958, Washington. National Academy of Science, Washington, p. 163-179.

53 F. J. ALIBRANT (NANCY). : Why User Education and How can Information Technology help? IFLA JI. 16(4), 1990, p. 405.

54 Floren (Paul). "The World Wide Web will expand into Phone Sector", The Asian Age, Vol. 3, n 17. 4.3.96, p. 17, (reprinted from International Herald Tribune).

55 Fosdick, Howard. : Computer Basic for Librarians and Information Scientists, Arlington Information Resources.

56 Garlok, K. L. and Piontek, S. : Building the Service-

based Library Website : A step by step to design and option : Chicago : ALA, 1996.

57 Gates, H. : Directory of Library and Information Retrieval Software for Micro-computers, Brook-field: Gower Pub. Co., 1985.

58 Ghan, Annat. : Impact of information technology on library and information service. Recent trends in Vyas and other, Ed.

59 Govindarajan, M. "Global Marketing Possibilities via world wide web", The Hindu, Madras, 16.3.96 p. 23.

60 Gowda, (S. Rame), Foreword, Panda, K. C. and Karisiddappa, C. R. Eds., New Dimensions in Inforormation Science and Technology, Parimal Pub., Delhi 1993. p. IX.

61 Guha, B. : Documentation and information services, techniques and systems, World Press, Calcutta, 1978, p. 55.

62 Harries, Steve. : Networking and Telecommunications for Information Systems : An Introduction to Information Networking, London : Library Association Publishing, 1993.

63 Hasan, S. K. and Salgav, S. M. : Internet protocol addressing scheme for INFLIBNET, In. Kumar and Vasishth, Ed. CALIBER-99 papers. Ahmedabad: INFLIBNET, 1999.

64 Heiliger, (Edward M.) and Henderson Jr. (Paul B.). : Library Automation : Experience, Methodology and Technology of the Library as an Information System, 1971, NY : McGraw Hill Book Co., Chapter-1, p. 25-35.

65 Husain Nargis, CD-ROM : An appropriate technology for developing countries, Herald of Library Science. 27(1-2), 1988.

66 INFLIBNET Memorandum of Association and Rules, New Delhi, UGC, 1996.

67 INFLIBNET Review Committee Report, New Delhi : UGC.

68 INSDOC in the service of the nation, New Delhi : INSDOC, p. 16.

69 Internet : Global Curriculum, New Delhi : NIIT, 1997.

70 Jain, R. K. and Jain A. K. : Questions and Answers on Computer Science, Delhi, Khanna Pub., 1995, p. 93.

71 Jain, R. K. and Jain, A. K. : Conventional and Objective Type Questions and Answers on Computer Science, Khanna Pub., Delhi, 1995, p. 252-255.

72 Jain, V. K. "Videotex and Teletext". In Gupta, B. M. et. al. Handbook of Libraries and Information Centres in India, New Delhi, Information Industry Pub., 1987, p. 129-135.

73 Jain, V. K. and Hazarika, S. : Dictionary of Computers, Academic (India) Pub., New Delhi, 1994, p. 245-246.

74 Jain, V. K. and Hazarika, Sanjay, Dictionary of Computers, New Delhi, Academic Pub., 1994, p. 222.

75 Jain, V. K., Computers for Beginners, 4th revised, 1990, Delhi, Pustak Mahal, pp. 19-24.

76 Jalaya, V. and Koovakkai, Dineshan. : Library services to career in the electronic era (In Sardana, J. L., Ed. Libraries and information services in electronic information era : Seminar papers, 44th All Library Conference, ILA, Delhi. 1999. p. 488-492.

77 John, Jessi. Information Needs: Use pattern and use behaviour of social science researchers. Indian Journal of Information Library and Society. 1997; 10 (1-2); 78-86.

78 Karch, (Linda S.). "Serials Information on CD-ROM : A Reference Perspective", RSR; v 8; n2; 1990; pp. 81-86.

79 Kashyap, M. M., Database System : Design and

Development. Delhi : 1993, Sterling Pub. P. 129-136.

80 Kashyap, M. M. Database System; Design and Development, New Delhi, Sterling Pub. 1993, p. 47-49.

81 Kashyap, M. M., Database System : Design and Development, Sterling Pub. New Delhi, 1993, p. 5.

82 Kasi Rao, V., CD-ROM technology in the field of library and information science management environment (LISME) - An overview/by V. Kasi Rao and A. I. Shahjahan. BILISAR Bulletin. 6(3), 1990.

83 Kaul, H. K. Library Networks : An Indian Experience,New Delhi : Virgo Publications, 1992.

84 Kaul, H. K., Library Resource Sharing and Networ- ks, New Delhi : Virgo Publication.

85 Kawatra, P.S., Library user studies. A manual of librarians and information scientists. Jaico Publishlis-hing, Bombay, 1992. p. 130.

86 Kent, A. and Galvin, T., The Structure and Governance of Library Networks, New York : Marcel Dekker, 1979.

87 Kent, Allen. Network Anatomy and Network Objective. In: Kent, Allen and Galvin, Thamas J. Eds. The Structure and Governance of Library Networks. Marcel Dekker; 1979; NY. P. 6-9.

88 Kent, Allen. The Goals of Resource sharing in Libraries. In Kent, Allen and Golvin, Thomas J. Eds. Library Resource sharing. C. 1977. Marcell Dekker; NY; p. 16.

89 Khan, M.T.M., Information organization and communication, New Delhi, Ess Ess Publication, 1999.

90 Kimberly, R. ed., Text Retrival : Directory of Software. Aldershot : Gower, Marrable. Disintergrating Library House Keeping Systems. As library information, 1990, 1989, 17(9), 207-209.

91 Kochen, Manufred, Technology and Communication in Future. JASIS. 1981, 148-157.

92 Krishna, K. M. Intenet/Internet Technology : Its scope of library services. In Kumar Vashisth, Ed. CALIBER-99 papers. Ahmedabad : INFLIBNET, 1999.

93 Kumar P. S. G., Fundamentals of information science. Delhi : S. Chand, 1998.

94 Kumar, K., "Library Organisation", New Delhi, Vikas, 1987.

95 Kumar, Pramod and Arora, O. P., Information and Library Network (INFLIBNET) Programme. DESIDOC Bulletin of Information Technology, 16(2), 35-45

96 Kumar, R. P., An overview of modern technologies : Applications in Indian Libraries. International Information and Library Review, 26, 327-339.

97 Lakshmana Moorthy (A). Impact of Electronic Media on Library and Information Centres with a specific referenceto India. Ph. D. Thesis. Karnataka Univer- sity, Dharwad. 2000.

98 Levert, V. M., Library Specific Microcomputer Software Library Software Review. 4 (May-June), 1985, 33-38.

99 Lynch (Baverly P.) Application of Technology in Libraries. ILA Bul., xxix; 3-4; Oct. 93 March '94; p. 111.

100 Lynch (Clifford A.) and Preston Cecilia M. "Internet Access to Information Resource". Annual Review of Information Science and Technology, V. 25; 1990; p. 264.

101 Mahajan, S. G. Resource Sharing and Networking of University Libraries in India. University News. 38 (35); 1992; p. 79-85.

102 Mangla, P. B., and other, 50 years Library and Information Services in India, 1998, Shipra, New Delhi.

103 Mangla, P. B., National Information System in Scoience & Technology (NISSAT) in India : A decennial review, 1976-85, Outlook on Research Libs. 9(8), 1937, p. 6-10.

104 Martin, Susns K. Library Networks. Knowledge Industry Pub. 1981. N.Y.; p. 1.

105 McGraw-Hill Encyclopaedia of Science and Technology : An International Reference Volume Including Index 7th ed. New York : McGraw-Hill, 1992, Vol. 18, p. 151.

106 Meera, B. M. Advances in Library Networking Technology for Resource sharing Activities for LAN. To WAN. Lib. Sc. 31(2); June, 1994; p. 59.

107 Miller (Frank W.) and Leading (Deborah Viogt). 'The Market Place : An Internal View of Future of CD-ROM. The Perspective of the H. W. Wilson Company." RSR; Vol. 17 n;1, 1989; pp. 21-32.

108 Molhott, P., The Influence of Technology on Library Networking. Special Libraries, 80(8), 1989, 82-89.

109 Moorthy, A. L. and Mangla, P. B. Information Technology applications in academic libraries (Papers presented at the Fourth National Convention for Automation of libraries in Education and Research

110 Muller, Nathan, J., Desktop encyclopedia of the Internet. Boston : Artech House.

111 Murthy, C. S. V., and others. Networks topologies and Communication standards (In fundamentals of Information Technology), Himalaya Publishing House, Mumbai, 1999.

112 Murthy, S. S. : (ed), Bibliography Databases and Networks. New Delhi : Tata MacGraw-Hill, 1989.

113 Narayanan Kutty, CDS/ISISI Program for record duplication. In : Information Studies, 1999, 5(2), 99-108.

114 Narayanan Kutty, N. Preparing Copy of CDS/ISIS Database. In : Information Studies. 5(2) 95-98.

115 Neelameghan, A. and Tocatalian J. International Cooperation in information system and services, JASIS 33,1985, (3), 153-163.

116 Nissley, Meta. Taking License : Librarians, Publishers and the New Media. In. Strauch (Ketina) and Strauch (Bruce), Eds. Legal and Ethical Issues in Acquisition, NY : The Hwroth Press; 1990; p.-71.

117 Nolan, J. M., Micro Software Evaluation. Torrance CA : Nolan Information Services, 1984.

118 Paisely, W. J., Information needs and users, Annual Review of Information Science and Technology. 3; 1968 (In Devarjan, C. T. Library Information users and users studies. Beacon Books, New Delhi, 1995, p. –88.

119 Panda, K. C. "CD-ROM : The Modern Papyarus." Some Miens of Modern Librarianship. Ajanta Pub. Delhi. 1994, p. 1-11.

120 Panda, K. C. and Karisiddappa, C.R. Eds. New Dimensions in Information Science and Technology, Delhi; Parimal pub. 1993, p. 90-91.

121 Panda, K.C. "CD-ROM is LIS : Superb or Sombore". In Panda, K. C. and Karisiddappa, C. R. ed. New Dimensions in Information Science and Technology. Parimal Pub. Delhi. 1993, p. 1994.

122 Patel, D. R. and Bhargava, Rachna. Comparative Study of Software Available in the Indian Market for Library Automation. DESIDOC Bulletin of Information Technology. 1995, 15(3), 3-12.

123 Pathak, Nityanand. Necessity of Internet to University Library and Information Services in North-East (NE) Region. In Kumar and Vashisth, Ed. CALIBER-99 papers Ahmedabad : INFLIBNET, 1999.

124 Pawar, S. S Impact of new information technology in development of library services (In vashishth, C. P. and others. Ed. Library and Information Technology; in pursuit of excellence : Seminar papers of 38th all India Library Conference. 1992. ILA, New Delhi; p. 27-31.

125 Peltu. Information Technology : An Over View. In :

Taylor, H. (ed.). Information Management and Organisational Change. London : ASLIB, pp. 81-86.

126 Perrow, David, Implementing CAIRS-LMS in a small Academic Library. Programm, 1991, 25(3), 207-221.

127 Poole, B. J. : Education for an Information Age : Teaching the Computerised Class Room, Madison : WCB Brown and Benchmark, 1995.

128 Poole, B. J., Education for an Information Age. Wisconsin : WCB Brown & Benchmark, 1995.

129 Poole, B. J. : Essential Miscrosoft Works : Tutorial for Teacher. Madison : Brown and benchmark, 1994.

130 Potdar, S. P. and Joshi, D. K. Library networking A proposal for Amravati University region. Caliber 97. INFLIBNET Centre, Ahmedabad.

131 Poulfer, Alan, Hiom, Debra, and Tseng, Gwyneth. The Library and Information Professional's Guide to the Internet. Ed. 3 London : The Library Assn. 2000.

132 Prem Singh and Khanna,J. K, Information Technolgy in Libraries, Delhi : Pragati Publications.

133 Raitt, D. New Information Technology social aspects, usage and trends (in Tedd, L. et. al. Proceedings of the Fifth International Online Information Meeting, 1982. Learned Information, Oxford.

134 Raiz, M., Modern Techniques of Documentation and Information Work. Atlantic Publishers; New Delhi, 1989, p. 183-84, 207.

135 Rajan, T. N. and Satyanarayana, R. : Application of Information Technologies in India. In : Handbook of Libraries and Information Centres in India. New Delhi : Information Industry Publication. 1987.

136 Raju (GVSLN), IATLIS Communication; Vol. 13; no. 4/5; Sept.-Dec.' 1993; p.2.

137 Rama Reddy, Ed. and Varatharajan, N. Search engines

: Need, selection and use. (in Kumar and Vashisth. Ed. CALIBER-99 papers. Ahmedabad : INFLIBNET, 1999.

138 Ramaiah C. K. "Is Hypertext a more flexible Teaching tool for Education?". Annals of Lib. Sc. and Doc. 39(1); 1992; p. 1-8.

139 Rao (M. K. Raghavendra) and Kamath, V.A. OCR-A Revolutionary Technique for Information Processing. Jl of Lib. & Inf. Asc. (Delhi University) 1(2) ; Dec. 1976; p. 233.

140 Rao, S. S. Janardana and others. Networking solutions for academic libraries. Experience of Andhra University Library (In Moorthy, A. L. and Mangala, P. B.), Ed. Information technology applications and academic libraries : Papers presented at the 4th National convention for Automation of Libraries in Education and Research (CALIBER-97), Information and Library Network Centre, Ahmedabad, p.-97-100.

141 Reddy, K. C. Generations of computers (in University of Hyderabad. PGDLAN course materials).

142 Reynold, M. M., Library cooperation. Coll. & Res. Libraries, 57, 1995.

143 Rouse, William, B. and Rouse (Sandra H.) Management of Library Networks : Policy Analysis, Implement Implementation and Control. C 1980. John Wiley : NY: p. 84.

144 Rowely, Jennifer. The Electronic Library, 4th Edition of Computers for Libraries London : Library Association Publishing, 1998.

145 Rowley (Jennier E.), The Basics of information technology. London, Cline Bingley, 1988.

146 Rowley, Jennifer, The Electronic Library, London : Library Association Publishing, 1998.

147 Rowley, Jennifer. The Electronic Library, Fourth

Edition of Computer for Libraries, London : Library Association Publishing, 1998.

148 Rowley. Electronic Library : 4th Edition of Computers for Libraries. London, 1997.

149 Russon, David. "Libraries and Electronic Document Delivery". In New Information Technologies and Libraries. Ed. By H. Liebaers; W. J. Haas; and W. E. Blervilet, Dordrecht; D. Riedel Pub. 1984, p. 219-35.

150 Saffady (William). "Library Automation : An : Overview :. In Panda, K. C., New Dimension in Information Science and Technology. Parimal Pub. Delh. 1993. p. 16.

151 Saffady (William). Introduction to Automation for Librarians. 2nd ed., 1989. Chicago; ALA : P. 327-350.

152 Saffady (William). Introduction to Automation for Librarians. 3rd ed. Chicago; ALA; p. 52.

153 Saffady, William. Introduction to Automation for Librarians. 2nd ed. 1989. ALA; Chicago; pp. 189, 212.

154 Saffady, William. Micrographic Systems. 3rd ed. 1990. MD U.S.A; AIIM, Pub. p. 13-14.

155 Saffady, William. Optical Storage Technology, A State of the Art Review, Meckler, U.S.A; 1989, p.Vol. viii-3

156 Sajaraman, V. Fundamentals of Computer, Delhi; Prentice Hall Pub. 1991, pp. 198-201.

157 Satyanarayana, R. : Information Technology and Its Facets. New Delhi : Namak Publications, 1996.

158 Satyanarayana, R. : Information Technology and University Libraries in India. In : Prasher, R. G. ed. University Libraries in India : 1980s and Beyond. New Delhi : Medallion. pp. 19-50.

159 Satyanarayana, R. and Rajan, T. Information Networks : Structure and Operation with Reference to India. INCAE. 4(2), 155-167.

160 Savio, Roberto, "Communications for Development.' Development J, 1990; 2; p. 7-8.

161 Saxena, S. C. and Srivastava, R. K. Software Packet for Library Automation and Networking. In : Kaul, (ed.). Library and Information Networking. Delhi : DELNET, 1998, pp. 300-319.

162 Seva Singh. Reference Service in Academic Libraries in India. Ess Ess Pub. New Delhi, 1986, p. 10-17.

163 Sharma, Ajay Kumar, Modern Information technology technology and library and information services. S.R. Scientific publication, 2002.

164 Sharma, Hemant and Jain, Yogesh Kumar, Freeflow of information and its constraints. Library Herald. 39(1-2); 2001; 56-64.

165 Sharma, P. L. Information technology and libraries. (In Vyas, S. D. and others, Ed. Excellence in information technology, Raj Publishing, Jaipur, 2000, p.-76-82.

166 Sheshagiri, N.,l Government data network : A case study of National Informatics Centre (in Gupta, B. M. and others Handbook of Libraries, Archieves and Information Centre in India (1986), New Delhi : Information Industry Publications, Vol.-3, p.-37-57.

167 Smith, R. L and Cambell, B. : Information Technology Revolution, New York : Longman, 1992.

168 Smith., John W. T., Networking and the Future of Libraries. Westport : Meckler. 1993.

169 Sreenivasulu, V. and Nandwana, Dr. H. B. Web browsers and search engines : The Knowledge mining tools for academic libraries. (in Kumar and Vashisth) ed. CALIBER-99 papers. Ahmedabad : INFLIBNET, 1999.)

170 Stevens, Richard. Understanding Computers, Oxford; OUP; 1986. p. 18.

171 Stokes, A. V. Concise Encyclopaedia of Information Technology. 2nd ed. London : Cower, 1985, pp-114-115.

172 Suebsonthi, Prapavapao. Application of information technology in Thai libraries. International Information Communication and Education. 5(2); 1986; 143-151.

173 Teague S. John, Microform, Video and Electronic Media Librarianship. 1985. Butterworths Pubs; London. Pp. 96-111.

174 Teng, G., Poulter, A. and Sargnet, G. The Library and Information Professional's Guide to the World Wide Web. London : Library Association Publishing.

175 Tenopir, Identification and Evaluation of Software for Micro-computer based in-house Database. Information Technology and Libraries. March 1984, 21-34.

176 Tseng, G. : Poulfer, Alan and Hiom, Debra. The Library and Information Professional's Guide to the Internet, London : The Library Assn., 1997.

177 University Grant Commission (India). Development of an information and library network : Report of the Inter Agency Working Group. (1988), xxx, p-473.

178 University Grant Commission, Development of an Information and Library Network (INFLIBNET). Report of the Inter-Agency Working Group. New Delhi : UGC, 1988.

179 Upadhyay Padma, V. Information technology and academic libraries. In : Moorthy, A. L. and Mangla, P. B. Ed. Information technology application in academic libraries. Papers presented at the 4th National Convention for Automation of Libraries in Education and Research (CALIBER-97). Information and Library Network Centre, Ahmedabad, 1997, p.-43-45.

180 Vasantha, R. Patri. Education in India Programmes and Policies. New Delhi, Authors' press, 2000.

181 Veeranjaneyulu. K. Information technology in academic libraries (Library and Information studies in cyber age), Authors press. 2004; 297-300.

182 Venkata Ramana, P., Information Technology Application in Libraries, New Delhi, Ess-Ess Publication, 2004.

183 Verma, G.C., Modern Education, Its Growth and Development, Jaipur, Publication Scheme, 1984, p.-208-238.

184 Vinayak, Kamlesh. Networking of college libraries in Delhi : A Plan (Library and Information Studies in cyber age), Authorspress, 2004; 281-287.

185 Viswanathan, C.G. Elements of Information Science and Technology. 1986. Lucknow; Print House Pub.; 93-94.

186 Wiberley, Stephan E. and Jones William, G. Pattern of information seeking in Humanities. College and Research Libraries. 50(6); 1989; 638-645.

187 Williams, M. R. : History of Computing Technology, New Jersey : Prentice Hall.

188 Wilson, T.D., On user studies and information needs. Journals of Documentation. 37(1); 1981;3.

189 Woords, Lawrence, A. and Notan, F.P., Guide to Microcomputer Technology and Applications, White Plains : Knowledge Industry Publications, 1989.

190 Wright, Patrica. "Interface Alternatives for Hypertext". Hypermedia; 1(2), 1989; pp. 146-66.

191 Yip, K. F., Selecting Internet Resources. The Electronic Library, IS (2), 1997, 91-98.

List of Library Science & Technology Journals

Sl. No.	*Name of the Journal*
1.	Alis Bulletin.
2.	American Libraries.
3.	Annals of Library Science and Documentation.
4.	Aslib Proceedings.
5.	Australian Library Journal.
6.	Biblio Tech Review.
7.	British Journal of Academic Librarianship.
8.	Bulletin of Information Technology.
9.	Bulletin of the American Society for Information Science & Technology.
10.	College and Research Libraries.
11.	Computers in Libraries.
12.	DESIDOC Bulletin of Information Technology.
13.	D-lib Magazine.
14.	Electronic Information Report.
15.	Electronic Library.
16.	EMedia.
17.	IFLA Journal.
18.	Information and Software Technology.

19. Information Processing and Management.
20. Information Research.
21. Information Society.
22. Information Systems.
23. Information Technology and Disabilities.
24. Information Technology and Libraries.
25. Information Today.
26. Information Today and Tomorrow.
27. Information World Review.
28. International Cataloguing and Bibliographic Control.
29. International Information & Library Review.
30. International Journal of Information management.
31. International Journal of Special Libraries.
32. International Journal on Digital Libraries.
33. International Library Movement.
34. Internet on a Disk.
35. Internet Research.
36. Issues in Science and Technology Librarianship.
37. Journal of Academic Librarianship.
38. Journal of Digital Information.
39. Journal of Documentation.
40. Journal of Education for Library and Information Science.
41. Journal of Electronic Publishing.
42. Journal of information management and scientometrics.
43. Journal of Information Science.
44. Journal of Information, Communication, and Library Science.
45. Journal of Librarianship and Information Science.

46. Journal of the American Society for Information Science & Technology.
47. Knowledge Organization.
48. Library & Information Science Research.
49. Library and Information Science Abstracts.
50. Library and Information Update.
51. Library Association Record.
52. Library Computer Systems and Equipment Review.
53. Library Herald.
54. Library Hi Tech.
55. Library Journal.
56. Library Journal Net Connect.
57. Library Literature and Information Science.
58. Library Management.
59. Library of Congress Information Bulletin.
60. Library Quarterly.
61. Library Resources and Technical Services.
62. Library Review.
63. Library Science with a Slant to Documentation.
64. Library Technology Reports.
65. Library Trends.
66. Libri.
67. Link-up.
68. Managing Information.
69. Marketing Library Services.
70. Microcomputers for Information Management.
71. NISSAT Newsletter.
72. OCLC Systems and Services.
73. Online and CD Notes.
74. Portal: Libraries and the Academy.

75. Program.
76. Progressive Librarian.
77. Reference and User Services Quarterly.
78. Reference Librarian.
79. Resource Sharing & Information Networks.
80. School Library Media.
81. Science and technology Libraries.
82. Searcher: The Magazine for Database Professionals.
83. Serial Librarian.
84. Special Libraries.
85. SRELS Journal of Information Management.
86. The Journal of Academic Librarianship.
87. The Library Journal.
88. Vine.
89. Wilson Library Bulletin.
90. Year's Work in Librarianship.

Useful Websites for Librarians

* Gabrel: Gateway to Europe's National Libraries.
  URL: http://portico.bl.uk/gabriel/
* Argentina: Biblioteca Nacional de la Republica Argentina.
  URL: http://www.bibnal.edu.ar/
* Australia: National Library of Australia.
  URL: http://www. nla.gov.au/
* Austria: Osterreichische Nationalbibliothek (Austrian National Library).
  URL: http://www.onb.ac.at/
* Belarus: National Library of Belarus.
  URL://www.beltelecom.by/~nacbibl/
* Belgium: Bibliotheqwue Royale Albert ler (Royal Library Albert).
  URL: http://www.kbr.be/
* Brazil: Bibliotheque Royale Albert ler (Royal Library Albert I).
  URL: http:info.lnfo.incc.br/dimas/bibl nac.htm
* Canada: National Library of Canada.
  URL: http://www.nlc-bnc.ca/
* Chile: Biblioteca Nacional Chile.
  URL: http://www.dibam.renib.cl/ISC137.
* China: National Library of China.
  Chinese *URL: htp://nlc.nlc.gov.cn/ (requires GB-compatible Chinese software)*

* Croatia: Nacional Seveucilisna Knjiznica u Zagrebu (National and university Library Zagreb).
  URL: htp//www.nsk.hr/
* Cuba: Biblioteca National de Ciencia y Technologia.
  URL:http//www2.cuba.cu/ciencia/sitiobnct/kindex.html
* Czech Republic: Narodni knihovna Ceske republiky (NK) (The National Library of the Czech Republic).
  URL: http://www.nkp.cz/
* Denmark: Det kongelige Bibliotek (The Royal Library).
  URL: http://www.kb.dk/
* Estonia: Easti Rahvusraamatukogu (National Library of Estonia).
  URL: http://www.nlib.ee/i.index.html
* Finland: The Helsinki University Library - The National Library of Finland.
  URL: http://linnea.helsinki.fi/hyk/
* France: French National Library.
  URL: http://www.bnf.fr/
* Germany: The National Library of Germany.
  URL: http://www.ddb.de/
* Hungary: National Szechenyi Library.
  URL: http://www.oszk.hu/
* Iceland: The National and University Library of Iceland.
  URL: http://www.bok.hi.is/
* India: National Library of India
  URL: http://nlindia.org/index2.html.
* Ireland: National Library of Ireland.
  URL: http://sites.huji.ac.il/jnul/
* Italy: The Central National Library of Florence.
  URL: http//www.nlj.org.jm
* Jamaica: National Library of Jamaica.
  URL: http://www.nlj.org.jm

* Japan: National Diet Library.
  URL: http//www.ndo.go.jp/index-e.html
* Korea (South-The Republic of): National Library of Korea.
  URL: http://www.nl.go.kr/
* Latvia: National Library of Latvia.
  URL: http://vip.latnet.lv/lnb/
* Lithuania: National Library of Lithuania.
  URL: http//www.lnb.lt/
* Luxembourg: Bibliotheque Nationale.
  URL: http://www.nubsk.edu.mk/
* Malaysia: National Library of Malaysia.
  URL: http://www.pnm.my/
* Namibia: National Library of Namibia.
  URL: http://yaotto.natlib.mec.gov.na/
* Netherlands: National Library of the Netherlands.
  URL: http://www.konbib.nl/
* Alexicon Library Information Service.
  URL: http://vyww.konbib.nl/kb/sbo/bdi-en.html
* New Zeland: National Library of New Zealand.
  URL: http://www.natlib.govt.nz/
* Norway: Norwegian National Library
  URL: http://www.nb.no/
* Pakistan: Pakistan Library Network.
  URL: http://www.planwel.edu/Research/libraries.html
* Poland: National Library of Poland.
  URL: http://www. bn.org.pl/
* Portugal: National library of Portugal.
  URL: http://www.bn.pt/
* Russia: Russian State Library.
  URL: http://www.rsl.lru/
* Scotland; National Library of Scotland.
  URL: http://www.nis.UK/

* Serbia: National Library of Serbia.
  URL: http://www.nbs.bg.ac.yu/indexe.htm
* Singapore: National Library Board of Singapore.
  URL : http://www.lib.gov.sg/nlb.html
* Slovak Republic: The Slovak National Library.
  URL: http://www.matica.sk/
* Slovenia: Narodna in univerzitetna Knjiznica v Ljubljani (National and University Library Ljublijana).
  URL: http://www.nuk.uni-lj.si/
* South Africa: South Africa Library.
  URL: http://wwwaleph.salib.ac.za/
* Spain: Bibklioteca Nacional (National Library of Spain).
  URL: http://www.bne.es
* Sweden: The Royal Library.
  URL: http://www.kb.se
* Switzerland: National Library of Switzerland.
  URL: http://www.snl.ch/
* Taiwan: National Central Library.
  URL: http://www.ncl.edu.tw/
* Turkey: National Library of Turkey.
  URL: http://portico.bl.uk/
* United States: Library of Congress.
  URL: http://lcweb.loc.gov/
* United States: National Library of Medicine.
  URL: http://www.nlm.nih.gov
* Venezuela:(Bibloteca Nacional de Venezuela)
  URL: http://www.bnv.bib.ve/
* Wales: National Library of Wales.
  URL: http://www.llgc.org.uk
* Adinet: Ahmedabad Library Network
  URL: http://www.alibnit.org
* Bonet: Bombay Library Network.
  URL: http://www.bonet.ernet in

* Callibnet: Calcutta Library Network.
  URL: http://www.calibnet.org
* Delenet: Developing Library Network.
  URL: http://www. delnet.nic.in
  URL: http://Inflibnet
* Information and Library Network Centre.
  URL: http://www.inflibnet.ac.in
* Mylibnet: Mysore Library Network.
  *URL: http://www.mylibnet.*org
* PuneNet: Pune Library Network.
  URL: http://202.41.70.20:6588/ punenet/index.asp
* ILA: Indian Library Association.
  URL: http://www.ilaindia.org
* SIS: Society for Information Science.
  URL: http://sis-india.netfirms.com
* IASLIC: Indian Association of Special Libraries and Information Centres.
  URL: http://www.iaslic.org
* MLAI: Medical Library Association of India.
  URL: http://www.medlibassindia.org
* Infolibrarian.
  URL: http://www.infolibrarian.com
* NISCAIR: National Institute of Science communication & Information Resources.
  URL: http://www.niscair.res.in
* NASSDOC.
  URL: http://www.icssr.org/final.htm
* IFLA.
  URL: http://www.ifla.org

Index